Early Anglican Church Records *of* Cecil County Maryland

Henry C. Peden, Jr.

HERITAGE BOOKS
2007

HERITAGE BOOKS
AN IMPRINT OF HERITAGE BOOKS, INC.

Books, CDs, and more—Worldwide

For our listing of thousands of titles see our website at
www.HeritageBooks.com

Published 2007 by
HERITAGE BOOKS, INC.
Publishing Division
65 East Main Street
Westminster, Maryland 21157-5026

Copyright © 1990 Henry C. Peden, Jr.

All rights reserved. No part of this book may be reproduced or transmitted in any form or by any means, electronic or mechanical, including photocopying, recording or by any information storage and retrieval system without written permission from the author, except for the inclusion of brief quotations in a review.

International Standard Book Number: 978-1-58549-183-4

Table of Contents

Introduction vii
Records of St. Stephens' Parish (North Sassafras Parish) ... 1
Records of St. Mary Anne's Parish (North Elk Parish) 57
Index 83

Dedicated
to the memory of my good friend and genealogist

RAYMOND B. CLARK, JR.
1927 - 1990

A GENERAL MAP OF CECIL COUNTY, MARYLAND
(ST. MARY ANNE'S AND ST. STEPHEN'S PARISHES)
by
Henry C. Peden, Jr., 1990

KEY:
1 CONOWINGO CREEK
2 OCTORARO CREEK
3 ROCK RUN
4 PRINCIPIO CREEK
5 NORTHEAST RIVER
6 ELK RIVER
7 BACK CREEK
8 BOHEMIA RIVER
9 JOHNS CREEK
10 PEARCE CREEK
11 SASSAFRAS RIVER
12 CHESAPEAKE BAY
13 SUSQUEHANNAH RIVER

INTRODUCTION

When the Established Church of England, or Anglican Church, [predecessor of the Protestant Episcopal Church of America] was established as the Church of Maryland in 1692, Cecil County was laid out as North Sassafras Parish. When founded North Sassafras Parish covered North Sassafras Hundred, Bohemia Hundred and Elk Hundred. The first vestrymen of North Sassafras Parish were Casparus Hermen, William Ward, John Thompson, Edward Jones, Henry Rigg and Matthias Vanderhuyden. There were about 1284 persons living in the parish at the time of its establishment. Rev. Lawrence Vanderbush became the first Parish minister of North Sassafras Parish. The Parish Church was dedicated in 1705 as St. Stephen's which name was eventually used in reference to both the church and the parish.

In 1706 North Elk Parish was established for the inhabitants of Cecil County north of the Elk River. Thus Cecil County was delineated into two parishes. With the erection of the Parish Church of St. Mary Anne's at North East the parish became known as St. Mary Anne's Parish. The first regular minister, Revd. Walter Hackett, was assigned in 1722. According to George Johnston in his *History of Cecil County Maryland* the records previous to 1743 were destroyed by fire. However one will note that a great number of births, deaths, and marriages, predate this.

This compilation was taken from the copies of the registers done by Lucy H. Harrison. Original records of St. Stephen's Parish records, 1693-1913 are held by the Manuscript Division of the Maryland Historical Society. An original of the St. Mary Anne's Parish records is held by the church itself in a local bank vault.

Other books of interest dealing with church records in this area follow:

1. George Johnston, *History of Cecil County*. Repr. Baltimore, Genealogical Publishing Co., with new index, 1989.
2. Edna A. Kanely, *Directory of Maryland Church Records*. Family Line Publications, 1987.
3. Alice L. Beard, *Nottingham Quakers, 1680-1889*. Family Line Publications, 1989. Records of meetings in Cecil County, Maryland and Lancaster and Chester Counties, Pennsylvania.
4. Bill and Martha Reamy, *St. George's Parish Registers, 1689-1793*. Family Line Publications, 1988.
5. F. Edward Wright, *Maryland Eastern Shore Vital Records*. Family Line Publications, 1982. A series of 5 volumes covering the period, 1648-1825, covering church records of Kent County and southward.
6. F. Edward Wright, *Vital Records of the Jesuit Missions of the Eastern Shore 1760-1800*. Family Line Publications, 1986. Includes Catholic records of Old Bohemia Mission at Warwick, Cecil County.

Henry C. Peden, Jr.

ST. STEPHENS' PARISH (NORTH SASSAFRAS PARISH)

Marriages Registered by Thomas Powell, Clerk of North Sassafras Parish - Cecil County, Md.

Jno. Jones & Mary Machahay married Aug 13 1695
William Savin & Sarah Hill dau of Samuel & Elisabeth Hill married Oct 6 1695
Henry Eades & Elizabeth --- married Sep 17 1696 by Robert Crook
Mr. Jno. Hynson & Mary Stoop dau of Mr. Jno. Stoop married Jun 1 1695 by Mr. Laurance Vanderbush
Mr. Thomas Robinson Esq. & Miss Sarah Frisby dau of James Frisby Esq. married 1 Jul 1697 by Mr. Lehiton
Mr. John Pearce and Margarett Blake widow married 17 Jun 1697 by Mr. Wm. Dare
Jno. Midford & Jaine Hyland widow married ---
George Cozine & Ann Johnson married 30 Jan 1696
Ahip Robinson & Margarett Pryer dau. of Thomas Pryer & Margarett married 28 Aug 1697 by Mr. Richard Sewell
James Gray & Alice Wood married 21 Mar 1696 by Coll. Casparus Augt. Herman
Jno. Veeres & Ann Winn widow married 30 Jul 1687 by Mr. Richard Sewell
John Linckhorne & Elizabeth Browning married 3 Sep 1697 by Mr. Richard Sewell
William Boyer & Phillis Holeoger married 26 Dec 1688
James Bowers & Margaret Cock married 9 Nov 1697 by Mr. Richard Sewell
Aron Degroate & Mary Collens married 10 Nov 1697 by Mr. Richard Sewell
William Broxson & Elizabeth Nicholson widow married 18 Nov 1697 by Mr. Richard Sewell
Jno. Broxson & Briggett Moor widow married 15 Nov 1697 by Mr. Richard Sewell
Henry Lankaster & Anne Satchell widow married Jan. 15, 1697 by Mr. Richard Sewell
Richard Sewell & Jane Ellis married by license by Rev Mr. Stephen Bordly Minister of St. Pauls Parish in Kent Co 13 Jun 1699
James Grey & Hono Kannington married by banns May 27 1701 by Richard Sewell Minister of N. & S. Sassafras Parishes
George Browning & Mary Kennard widow married by banns 19 Jun 1701 by Richard Sewell
William Direkson & Marack Care married by licence by R. Sewell 26 Aug 1701
Otho Ottorson & Mary Matthiason widow married by license 25 Dec 1704 by Mr. Richard Sewell
Walter Scott & Grace Rumsey married by licence 17 April 1707 by Rev. Dr. Richard Sewell
John Copping & Angelico Atkey dau of Jno. Atkey of Cecil Co married by Licence 13 May 1703
George Veasey & Alice Ward dau of William Ward & Elizabeth his late wife married by banns 18 Nov 1708 by Rev Dr. R. Sewell
Matthias Van Bebber & Haramonica dau of Adam Peterson of New Castle Co in the Territories of Pennsylvania married by licence 17 Nov 1705

Rogber Laramore & Margaret Dare Junr. married by License 17 Feb 1707
Jonas Mattox & Ann Bentley married by banns 22 April 1711
Peter Numbers & Ann Pennington widow married by banns 9 Oct 1711
John Ward & Mary his wife were married 17 Jul 1701
Thomas Pope & Elizabeth Partridge married 23 Feb 1711
Casparus Smith & Ann Robinson widow married by banns 11 Oct 1703
Robert Money & Margaret Dorrell spinster married by banns 4 Oct 1706
Capt. James Frisby & Ariana Vanderhyden spinster married by licence by Mr. Richard Sewell 9 Feb 1713/14
John Hamm & Holinor Hollins married 16 Nov 1703
John Hackett & Anne Evins spinster married 13 Feb 1711 by Mr. Richard Sewell minister by banns
Henry Peninton & Elizabeth Drake spinster married -- Dec 1708 by banns by Richard Sewell
Phillip Barrat and Kathrin Werrey spinster married 3 May 1713 by Richard Sewell
Daniell Nowland & Mary Hill widow married 6 Jan 1713 by banns
Jacob Archer & Mary Freeman spinster married 4 Oct 1713 by License by Richard Sewell
John Rye & Mary Clements widow married 9 Feb 1710 by banns by Rich. Sewell
William Peninton & Mary Atkey spinster married 14 Sep 1713 by banns by Rich. Sewell
Michael Clements & Elizabeth Jonson spinster married 1 Nov 1713
John Chamberlin & Jane Ashford spinster married 6 Feb 1713 by banns by Rich. Sewell
William Beeston & Sarah Chisups spinster married 19 Dec 1706 by banns by Rich. Sewell
Francis Steele & Rebecca Peirce spinster married 26 Feb 1705 by banns by Mr. Sewell
Jacob Young & Mary Price spinster married 31 Dec 1713 by banns by Mr. Vanderhyden
Mr. Stephen Knight & Sarah Robinson married 24 Feb 1708 by license by Rich. Sewell
Cornelius Tobias & Eleanor Shutten spinster married 24 Feb 1712 by license by Rich. Sewell
Nathaniell Sapington & Margaret Huntly spinster married 27 Dec 1713 by banns by Mr. Sewell
Richard Peninton & Mary Wheelar married 4 Sep 1711 by Mr. Sewell
William Price Junr. & Kathrin MacCandrick widow married 7 Jul 1707 by banns by Mr Sewell
John White & Mary Griffin spinster married 4 Dec 1711
William Sinclar & Rachel Denbo spinster married 8 Apr 1714 by banns by Mr. Sewell
Jacob Williams & Mary Cox spinster married 8 Jun 1714 by banns by Mr. Sewell
John Price & Mary Davis spinster married --- Nov 1714 by banns by Mr. Sewell
John Jobson & Hester Holyday widdow married 23 Jul 1711 by Mr. Sewell

ST. STEPHENS' PARISH (NORTH SASSAFRAS PARISH)

Thomas Brooks & Mary Currey widdow married 4 Apr 1713 by banns by Mr. Sewell
Alexander Ffrazzer & Mary Stoops widow married 20 Aug 1713
John Crow & Martha Newman spinster married 19 Oct 1713 by banns by Mr. Sewell
John Newman & Elizabeth Malone spinster married 9 Apr 1713
David Young & Margaret Porter spinster married 7 Nov 1714 by banns by Mr. Sewell
Nicholas Pooley & Sarah Rynolds spinster married 9 Jan 1709 by banns by Mr. Sewell
Richard Foster & Sarah Kare spinster married 12 May 1715 by Mr. Sewell
Ffrancis Scott & Elizabeth Single spinster married 7 Jun 1715 by banns by Mr. Sewell
John Peninton & Sarah Beadle spinster married 3 Apr 1716 by licence by Mr. Sewell
George Veasey & Kathrin Beard spinster married 3 Apr 1716 by banns by Mr. Sewell
Joshua Latham & Mary Kare widow married 30 Aug 1716 by banns by Matt. Vanderhyden
Hugh Watson & Mary ----- married 10 Jan 1716 by banns by Mr. Sewell
Richard Parsley & Sarah Brace spinster married 5 Aug 1716 by banns by Mr. Sewell
Joshua Lathan & Anne Laurance spinster married 16 Feb 1714/5 by bans by Mr. Sewell
John Ward & Susana Veasey spinster married 2 Mar 1717 by licence by Mr. Sewell
John Cox & Rose Davis spinster married 20 Apr 1717 by banns by Mr. Sewell
James Glann & Mary Newman widow married 23 May 1717 by banns by Mr. Sewell
William Price & Sarah Wallis widow married 1 Aug 1717 by banns by Mr. Sewell
John Hollins & Abigale Bateman widow married --- Nov 1709 by banns by Mr. Sewell
Jacob Garrat & Margaret Wisecarvor spinster married 22 Sep 1717 by banns by Mr. Sewell
Robert Veasey & Lucie Dermote spin. married 1 Jan 1716 by banns by Mr. Sewell
Richard Taylor & Anne Perrey spin. married --- Jun 1716 by banns by Mr. Sewell
Abram Alman & Margaret Deane spin. married 13 Jan 1717 by banns by Mr. Sewell
Thomas Beadle & Elizabeth Boulding spin. married 1 Jan 1717 by banns
Richard Bell & Jane Denhoe spin. married 28 Aug 1704
John Hutchison & Mary Pirkens married 27 Jun 1716 by banns by Mr. Sewell
John Comes & Sarah Newman spin. married 31 Dec 1715 by banns by Mr. Sewell
David Price & Kathrin Flinn spin. married 31 Dec 1715 by banns by Mr. Sewell
Walter Newman Junr & ---- spin. married 31 Oct 1716 by Mr. Sewell

Phillip Barrat & Mary Burnham spin. married 8 Jun 1719 by banns by Mr. Sewell

James Husband & Alice Parr wid. married 1 Jan 1717 by licence by Mr. Sewell

James Gallaway Junr & Mary Beck wid. married 22 Feb 1718 by banns by Mr. Sewell

Henry Hendrickson & Elizabeth Etherinton married 5 Jun 1717 by banns by Mr. Sewell

James Veazey & Mary Mercer spin. married 20 Nov 1716 by banns by Mr. Sewell

Daniell Allin & Rebecca Newman spin. married 9 Feb 1719 by banns by Mr. Sewell

Richard Bouldin & Mary Hews spin. married 17 Jan 1716 by banns by Mr. Sewell

Rogar Larramore & Augustin Ffrisby wid. married 22 Dec 1719 by licence by Mr. Sewell

James Wallis & Sarah McKnight spin. married 2 Feb 1719/20 by banns by Mr. Sewell

John Wallas & Elizabeth Ross spin. married 2 Feb 1718/20 by banns by Mr. Sewell

Andrew Clements & Kathrin Sefferson wid. married 20 Nov 1718 by banns by Mr. Sewell

John Collins & Juliana Peninton spin. married 17 Feb 1719 by banns by Mr. Sewell

John Kimball Junr & Rebecca Atkins spin. married 6 Nov 1717 by Mr. Sewell

John Bedle Junr & Mary Mounce married 2 Feb 1715 by banns by Mr. Sewell

James Collins & Ellinor Ozey wid. married 1 Aug 1717 by banns by Mr. Sewell

Phillip Barrat & Jane Merrut married 20 Feb 1710 by banns by Mr. Sewell

John Simons & Rebecca Smith spin. married 1 Dec 1721 by banns by Mr. Sewell

Wm. Husband & Mary Kinkey spin. married 20 May 1720 by banns by Mr. Sewell

Thomas Watts & Mary Dorrell wid. married 16 Jul 1721 by banns by Mr. Sewell

Henry Rippin & Augustine Larramore wid. married 30 Nov 1723 by license by Mr. Sewell

William Foster & Mary Smith spin. married 15 Apr 1724 by banns by Mr. Henry Ward

John Sefferson & Sarah Sapinton spin. married 11 May 1725 by banns by Mr. John Vrmston

William Wittam & Elizabeth Smith spin. married 31 Jan 1722 by Mr. Sewell

Robert Peninton & Mary Ryland spin. married 13 Oct 1716 by banns by Mr. Sewell

William Crow and ---- Wm Price Junr & Anne Browning spin. married ---- 1723 by banns by Mr. Sewell

John Cockrell & Mary Newman spin. married 4 Mar 1728 by banns by Mr John Umston

Andrew Price & Elizabeth Perrey married --- Jun 1725 by banns by Mr. John Umston

ST. STEPHENS' PARISH (NORTH SASSAFRAS PARISH)

Nicholas Vandergrift & Susana Perrey spin. married 3 Aug 1727 by banns by Mr. Urmston
Richard Price & Sarah Clark spin. married 27 Jul 1726 by banns by Mr. Urmston
Michell Ruly & Anne Winterbery spin. married 21 Jun 1728 by banns by Mr. Urmston
Phillip Stoop & Mary Price spin. married 12 Oct 1721 by banns by Mr. Sewell
George Holton & Mary Money spin. married 19 May 1726 by banns by Mr. Urmston
Thomas Beker & Mary Cox spin. married 10 Aug 1723 by banns by Mr. Sewell
Robert Roberts & Sarah Morgan spin. married 16 Feb 1728 by banns by Mr. John Urmston
David Young & Margaret Porter spin. married 7 Nov 1714 by banns by Mr. Sewell
James Latamus & Diana Severson spin. married 22 Oct 1727 by banns by Mr. Urmston
Henry Whiter & Sarah Newman spin. married 29 Jan 1727 by banns
Jonathan Hine & Sarah Roberts married 20 Feb 1730 by Mr. Urmston
Thomas Burnham & Mary Numers spin. married 21 Aut 1729 by Mr. Urmston
James Wroth & Anne Walmsly spin. married 18 Feb 1723 by banns
Abell Vanburkeloo & Cathrin Herman spin. married 7 Jun 1715
Peter Bouchelle & Mary Hayatt spin. married 28 Mar 1716
Thomas Davis & Rachell Oyzer spin. married 1 Jun 1732 by Rev. Mr. Hugh Jones
Henry Rippon & Mary Sewell spin. married 26 Oct 1727
William Ward & Anne Douglas spin. married 14 May 1718
Hugh Terry & Sarah Christian spin. married 28 Sep 1727
Charles Scott & Elizabeth Terry wid. married 17 Aug 1732
John Simpson & Elizabeth Dehoff married 19 Apr 1733
Michael Robinson & Margaret McGumerry married 24 May 1733
Walter Scott & Cathrin Burninham married 4 Jul 1733
Thomas Ward & Mary Caulk wid. of Jacob Cault married 24 Jun 1729
Robert Mercer & Ann Mounce married 1 Aug 1727
Edward Rumsey & Margaret Ramsey married 10 Jul 1727
Peter Hendrickson & Catherine Boushell married 9 Oct 1728
John Morgan & Dorothy Newbanks married 16 Jan 1725
Henry Childs & Hannah Clark married 14 Jul 1732
Thomas Mercer & Jane Oliver married 13 Dec 1732
Thomas Ederington & Ann Oliver married 30 Jan 1732/3
Robert Redick & Catherine Dliason married --- Aug 1730
Evard Everson & Elizabeth Harper married 29 July 1731
William Smith & Catherine Everson married Oct 7 1732
Thomas Merrit & Martha ---- married May 6 1725
David Rice & Elizabeth Watts married Oct 16 1729
John Wright & Hannah Darling married Oct 15 1707
Robert Wethers & Mary Hollingsworth married Jun 5 1726
Everd Everdson & Annacart Clow (or Plow) married -- --- 1731
Richard Bentham & Elizabeth Severson married 24 Feb 1730
Matthias Fellows & Honner Price married -- --- 1720
Jeremiah Larkins & Rachel Sincklar wid. married 11 Jun 1733

John Carrin & Margaret Rumsey wid. of Charles Rumsey married 7 Sep 1727
William Husbands & Margaret Kenedey married 26 Jul 1733
John Morris & Anne Condon married 18 Aug 1733
John Hukill & Mary Husbands married 18 Jun 1733
John Cole & Margaret Wright married 17 Dec 1728
Thomas Fanhake & Sarah Adams married 26 Aug 1733
William Rumsey, son of Charles Rumsey & Catherine his wife decd of Bohemia & Sabina Blaidenburgh dau. of Benjamin Blaidenburgh & Margaret his wife married on Wed 15 May 1728 by John Urmston
Dominick Carroll & Marry Frisby wid. of William Frisby married 3 Dec 1725
John Kimber & Mary Etherinton married 17 Jun 1731
John Penington & Margaret Penington married 4 Jun 1733
James Hughes & Alice Davis married 15 Aug 1733
Richard Smith & Margaret Williams married 10 Jun 1733
James VanBebber son of Hendrick VanBebber of the City of Utrecht of Holland & Anna Laroun married -- --- 1720
Jacob Probal & Elizabeth Phillips married 2 Jan 1733/4
Humphrey Wells Stokes of Baltimore Co son of Capt. John Stokes of said Co & Mary Knight dau of Stephen Knight of Cecil Co married 31 Dec 1730 by Mr. Sewell of Kent Co
Thomas Eltharp & Elizabeth Numbers married 18 Nov 1733
Benjamin Childs & Martha Bellows married 26 Dec 1733
Thomas Murroin & Mary Hadaway married 25 Dec 1733
William Abbott & Mary Freeman married 7 May 1731
Cornelius Cook & Ann Jacobs married 16 Oct 1729
Cornelius Wolostain & Mary Hapton married 26 Dec 1733
Robert Money Junr. & Ruth Machdolwle wid. married 2 Feb 1733/4
Henry Huckil & Eliener Butcher married 16 Feb 1729
Thomas Boulding & Ann Clark married 29 Jan 1733/4
Thomas Minar & Margaret Wallace married 25 Jan 1733/4
Thomas Stratton & Hannah Mannering married 13 Sep 1733
Henry McCay & Rebecca Noble married 3 Feb 1726
Edward Reynolds & Mary Altham married 18 May 1722
William Parsons & Gerturett Laurux married 6 Jan 1734
Benjamin Pearce & Margarett Ward dau of Mr. Henry Ward married 31 Jul 1734
Edward Morgan & Elienor Parsley married 14 Nov 1733
Patrick Matthews & Mary Strough married 23 Jan 1734/5 by Rev. Mr. Hugh Jones
Thomas Davis & Rebeeka Gregory married 9 Jan 1734/5
George Hampton & Mary Hooten married 8 Nov 1733
Samuel Bayard & Fransinah Malding dau of Mr. Francis Malding married 3 Jul 1729
John Fillengam & Margaret Money married 12 Mar 1733/4
Joseph Wood Junr. & Sarah Hodgson dau of Robert Hodgson married 17 Feb 1734/5
Jessey Holton & Sarah Porter dau of James Porter married 16 Nov 1734
This is to certifie that on 16 Sep 1735 by virtue of a License from His Excellency the Governor Mr. Simon Wilmer Junr of Kent Co MD was married at St. Stephens Church North Sassafrass to Mary dau of Mr. John Pryce dec. of Comb in the parish of Prosteigne

ST. STEPHENS' PARISH (NORTH SASSAFRAS PARISH)

in the Counties of Hereford and Radnor Great Britian by me her father-in-law Hugh Jones Rector of N. Sas. Parish
William Hamman & Mary Bayley married 27 Oct 1735
Henry Pennington Junr & Ann Clements wid. of Cornelius Clements married 14 Dec 1735
Manaseh Loge & Sarah Derrel married 27 Feb 1734/5
Francis Ozier & Mary Wood dau of Catherine Wood married 7 Feb 1736/7
Robert Wamsley & Elizabeth Vanhorn married 20 Feb 1734/5
Barnett Vanhorn & Elizabeth Ozier married 1 Nov 1734
John Beedles Junr son of John Beedles & Rachel Pennington dau of John Pennington Senr married 6 Nov 1737
Abraham Cox & Ann Maclan married 15 Nov 1735
Joshua Meakins & Elizabeth Browning married 29 Sep 1728
John Pennington son of John Pennington & Alice Ward dau of John Ward married 19 Oct 1735
John Wallace & Mary Hollins married Feb 24 1736
James Rob & Jane Gordon married 16 Jul 1737
John McManus & Elizabeth Campbell married 12 Jan 1734/5
Robert Othoson & Rebecca Numbers spin. married 28 Feb 1737/8
John Thompson & Mary Julian seemstress married 19 Aug 1734
John Money & Rachel Ashley married 26 Oct 1738
Nathaniel Childs & Mary Hungarford married 23 Aug 1737
Fredrick Tylar & Mary Dugall married 23 Feb 1733/4
Matthew Cole & Mary Collins dau of James Collins married 12 Nov 1738
William Price Junr & Mary Roberts dau of John Roberts married 12 Feb 1737/8
Robert Wood & Ann Numbers dau of James Numbers married 23 Jul 1739
John Thompson of Cecil Co & Mary Griffith of Annapolis married 12 Mar 1738/9 by Mr. Hugh Jones
William Walmsley & Sarah Ward dau of John Ward married --- Nov 1740
John Pennington Senr & Mary Othoson dau of Garriet Othoson married -- --- 1740
James Price & Sarah Rickets dau of John Thomas Rickets married 18 Dec 1740
Richard Thompson Junr & Mary Alman dau of Abraham Alman married 12 Nov 1739
John Harper & Mary Weithers married Nov 1740
James Lattymus & Mary Hugg married 21 Sep 1740
John Wood & Frances Flinton married Dec 26, 1736
John Kimber & Catherine Money dau of Robert Money Senr. married 23 Jan 1740
John Roberts & Dorety Morgain wid. of John Morgain married 15 Jul 1740
Thomas Skurrey & Mary Price married 28 Feb 1738
Peregrine Ward & Mary Chew married 11 Oct 1736
by Rev. Mr. Wilkinson in Baltimore Co Thomas Cox & Sarah Rumsey dau of Charles Rumsey & Mary his wife married 15 Jan 1740
Edward John Wright & Alice Hood wid. of William Hood married 20 Jun 1742

EARLY ANGLICAN CHURCH RECORDS OF CECIL COUNTY

Thomas Fowler & Mary Hunter dau of William Hunter married 30 Mar 1738
James Readus & Catherine Parsons dau of William Parsons married 15 Dec 1741
Anthoney Repose & Elizabeth Armstrong married 24 Dec 1739
John Wood & Rebecca Eliason dau of Cornelius Eliason married 19 Dec 1737
James Taylor Junr. & Catherine Smith married 26 Feb 1741
Bartholemew Parsley & Judith Roberts dau of John Roberts dec married 17 Dec 1741
John Cann & Rachel Dormatt dau of Charles Dormett married 2 Jan 1740
Thomas Rose & Jean Bell dau of Richard Bell married 17 Jan 1736
Peter Bouchell & Catherine Herman dau of Coll. Epha. Augt. Herman dec married 28 Dec 1737
Jacob Everdson & Hester Vanhorn dau of Nicholas Vanhorn married 30 Dec 1742
Richard Beedle & Augustina Bavinton dau of John Bavington married 6 Aug 1741
Edward John Wight & Elizabeth Hood wid. of William Hood married 20 Jun 1742
John Carnan & Rachel Alman dau of Abraham Alman married 19 Oct 1742
Nathaniel Bohaning & Eleanor Vansandt dau of Garrict Vansandt married 6 Dec 1742
James Penington & Elizabeth Beastin dau of William Beastin married 11 Dec 1742
Sluyter Bouchell & Mary Bayard dau of Samuel Bayard married 25 May 1738
by Rev. Mr. Hugh Jones Samuel McCleary & Magdelem Bassett dau of Arnold Bassett married 20 May 1740
George Lewis & Eliza Hamn wid. of Ephraim Hamn married 2 Mar 1742
Edward Ryan & Susannah Symmonds married 22 May 1743
Evan Ricketts & Rachel Ward dau of John Ward married 2 Mar 1742
Thomas Cox Junr. & Margarett Hendrickson dau of Henry Hendrickson married 19 Jan 1743
John Knight of Cecil Co Chyurgeon son of Stephen Knight married Mary Thompson dau of Coll. John Thompson 15 May 1740
?????? of Cecil Co & Jane Houston married 17 Apr 1748 by Mr. Jones by licence of the Gov.
Joseph Price & Jane Barratt wid. of Philip Barrat married 19 Nov 1734
Dr. John Knight son of Stephen & Sarah Knight of Cecil Co married Mary Thompson dau of John & Mary Thompson 15 May 1740 by licence by Mr. Hugh Jones Rector of Saint Stephens Parish.
George Milligan & Catherine Baldwin dau of Coll. John Baldwin married 23 Mar 1750/1 by license by Mr. Hugh Jones Rector of Saint Stephens Parish
Daniel Pearce son of Coll. Benjamin Pearce of Cecil Co & Sarah Alman dau of Abraham Alman of said Co married 4 May 1752 by Mr. Jones

ST. STEPHENS' PARISH (NORTH SASSAFRAS PARISH)

Captain John Brown & Mrs. Jane Thompson wid. of Mr. John Thompson married 23 Jan 1752 by licence by Mr Jones Rector of St Stephens Parish in Cecil Co Md
Benjamin Terry & Alifere Cosdon dau of Alphonsi Cosdon married 26 Jan 1743 OS [Old style]
Thomas Wroth & Mary Penington wid. of John Penington married 12 Jan 1747
William Bordley son of Thomas Bordley Esq. of Annapolis & Sara Pearce dau of Col. Benjamin Pearce of Cecil Co married 14 Nov 1755 by licence in St Stephens Parish Md
George Hold & Catherine Price dau of William Price married 26 Jun 1763 by Rev. William Barroll
William Ward & Rebecca his wife dau of Thomas Davis married 11 March 1757
John Thompson son of John Thompson of Cecil Co & Mary Haly of Philadelphia married 4 May 1765 by licence
Jonathan Woodbury Junr eldest son of Samuel Woodbury brother to Jonathan Woodbury late of Bristol New England & Ly---- Lyndsey of Bristol married 4 Dec 1750
William Lyndsey Junr. son of William Lyndsey of Bristol and Catherine Woodbury dau of Jonathan Woodbury late of Bristol dec married 26 Apr 1772
Peregrine Howland and Rebecca his wife dau of William Savin married 1 Feb 1787
Dr. John E. Veazey son of Dr. Thomas B. & Mary Veazey & Sarah Ward dau of William & Ann Ward
26 Jan 1815 Thomas Severson & Sarah Mercer married 21 Sept 1790
Thomas B. Veazey son of Dr. Thomas B. & Mary Veazey & Ann Ward dau of William & Ann Ward married 12 Jun 1817

Burialls of Men, Women & Children-Registered by Thomas Powell of North Sassfras Parish
Annica Price wife of Jno. d in Bohemia 28 Nov 1695
Mr. Daniell Smith of Bohemia was buryed 30 Nov 1695
Mr. George Stevens was buryed 30 Dec 1695
Ann Hill wife of William was buryed 23 Nov 1695
Mr. Jno Hyland dyed 17 Jan 1695
Elizabeth Ward wife of Mr. Wm. was buryed 14 Nov 1696
Mary Morgan wife of James, taylor was buryed 13 Jan 1696/7
Ann Severson dau of Thomas & Katherine was buryed 31 Feb 1696/7
Mr. Robert Cooke was buryed 23 May 1697
Thomas Nicholson of Bohemia was buryed 30 Jul 1697
Mary Boyer dau Ephraim Thompson son of Coll John & Judith was buryed 1 Oct 1697
Edward Johnson was buryed 29 Oct 1697
Elizabeth Lapage dau of Edward & Joan was buryed 12 Dec 1697
Peter Severson was buryed 10 Jan 1697/8
Mary Worgan wife of Joseph was buryed 24 Apr 1698
Matthias Matthiason of Sassafrass River was buryed 7 May 1702
Esther Scott wife of Walter of Bohemia River was buryed 17 Dec 1706
Thomas Watts of Sassafras River was buryed 11 Apr 1711
Jacob VanBebber Senr of Bohemia River was buryed -- Sep 1705

EARLY ANGLICAN CHURCH RECORDS OF CECIL COUNTY

Christiana VanBebber wife of Jacob Senr was buryed 4 Sep 1711
Elizabeth Cox wife of Benjamin of Sassafras River was buryed 28 May 1711
Edwd Laramore was buryed 1 Feb 1710
John Robinson son of Capt. Thos. & Sarah was buryed 30 Nov 1by Mr. Richard Sewell
Frisby Knight son of Stephen & Sarah was buryed 26 Apr 1712
Anne McKey dau of Alexander & Susana was buryed 14 Jun 1711
Christopher Mounce of the ponds was buryed Anno Dom-------
Charles Mounce son of Christopher was buryed 12 Sep 1713
Casparus Mounce son of Christopher was buryed 16 Dec 1713
Peter King of Bohemia River was buried -- Dec 1713
---- King wife of Peter was buryed -- Dec 1713
Elias Marques of Bohemia river was buryed 25 Nov 1713
Thomas Currey of Bohemia River was buryed 7 Dec 1713
Richard Smith of Sassafras River was buryed 7 Nov 1713
Thomas Price son of Wm. Jr. & Kathrin was buryed -- Jan 1712
Martha Barrat wife of Phillip of Bohemia River was buryed 28 Mar 1713
Elizabeth Griffeth wife of John was buryed 12 Oct 1713
Thomas Cox son of Thomas Senr of Sassafras River was buryed 7 Oct 1712
Elizabeth Cox dau of Thomas Senr & Kathrin of Sassafrass River was buryed 28 Oct 1712
Thomas Cox Senr of Sassafras River was buryed 21 Mar 1712/13
Sarah Smart dau of John & Sarah was buryed 23 Oct 1713
Cornelius Clements of the ponds was buryed 7 Nov 1713
Mary Price wife of John of the ponds was buryed 11 Aug 1713
Sarah Price dau of John & Mary was buryed 20 Oct 1713
Anne Allin wife of Paul of Sassafrass River was buryed 24 Nov 1713
Richard Morgan son of James & Elizabeth was buryed 2 Nov 1712
Rebecca Peninton dau of Robert & Anne of Sassafrass River was buryed 3 Jan 1712
Alice Veazey wife of George of Bohemia was buryed 28 Nov 1712
John Wollinger of Sassafras River was buryed 13 Jul 1713
Jellian Crow wife of Charles of Bohemaia Manor was buryed 18 Dec 1713
Aron Degrote of Bohemia river was buryed 23 Feb 1713
William Hill of Sasafrass River was buryed 10 Feb 1712
Rebecca Griffeth dau of John & Elizabeth was buryed 4 Sep 1712
Thomas Steele son of Francis & Rebecca was buryed 17 Nov 1708
George Thompson of Sasafrass River was buryed 25 Apr 1713
James Gray of Bohemia River was buryed 24 Apr 1713
Nathaniel Child of Sasafrax River was buryed 25 Sep 1712
Mary Sapington wife of Nathaniel of Sassafras River was buryed 2 May
Nathaniel Sapington of Sassafras River was buryed 2 May
James Sapington son of Nathaniel of Sasafras River was buryed 12 Jul 1713
Samuel Holyday of Sasafrass River was buryed 2 Mar 1710
Samuel Hows of Bohemia River was buryed 11 Jul 1713
Sarah Davis dau of Morris & Sarah was buryed -- --- 1712
Sarah & James Davis twins of Mauris & Sarah was buryed -- --- 1712

ST. STEPHENS' PARISH (NORTH SASSAFRAS PARISH)

Elizabeth White (son) of John & Mary was buryed 12 Nov 1713
Mary White dau of John & Mary of Bohemia River was buried 14 May 1714
Mary Hollins spinster of Bohemia River was buried 1 May 1714
Mary Hollins dau of John & Abigall was buryed 20 Oct 1713
Gilder Huckin son of Danll & Elizabeth was buryed 2 Aug 1713
William Huckin son of Daniel & Elizabeth was buried 20 Jan 1712
Susana Foster wife of Richard of Elk River was buried 15 Jul 1714
William Davis of the ponds was buryed 3 Oct 1714
Walter Newman son of John was buryed 20 Nov 1714
Jonathan Newman son of Walter & Mary was buryed 20 Oct 1714
Walter Crow son of John & Elizabeth was buryed the last of Nov 1714
George Bristow son of Wm. & Milfred was buryed 26 Feb 1714
Sophia Child dau of Nathaniel & Helinere was buryed 7 Jan 1713/14
Francis Ozey of Sasafras River was buryed 6 Jan 1714
Samuel Boulding son of William & Thomasin was buryed 27 Feb 1714
Daniel Wells of Bohemia River was buryed 6 Mar 1714
John Rye of the ponds was buryed Mar 15 1714
Susana Pooley dau of Nicholas & Sarah was buried ---- John Burgis son of Francis & Mary was buryed 12 Feb 1710
Robert Morgan son of James & Elizabeth d 11 May 1715
Samuel White son of John & Mary was buried 24 Jul 1716
Mary Larramor dau of Roger & Margarett was buried 28 Apr 1715
Sarah Larramore dau of Roger & Margaret was buried 27 Aug 1716
Elizabeth Price dau of Thomas & Mary was buried 16 Sep 1716
Mary Price dau of Thomas & Mary was buryed 16 Sep 1716
Thomas Foster son of Richard & Sarah was buryed last of Aug 1715
Thomas Pearce Senr of Bohemia River was buryed 20 Feb 1716
Anne Latham wife of Joshua of Bohemy River was buryed 7 Mar 1715/16
Thomas Kare of Bohemia River was buryed 13 Mar 1715/16
John Stanly of Bohemia River was buryed 9 Jun 1716
Mary Stanly dau of John & Jane was buried 16 Jan 1716/7
Thomas Parsley son of Thomas & Elizabeth was buried 23 Jan 1716/7
Anne Broxon wife of Thomas of Bohemia River was buryed 23 Jan 1716/7
John Brace son of John & Elizabeth was buryed 28 Jan 1716/7
Mary Watts dau of Thomas & Elizabeth was buryed 13 Feb 1716/7
James Etherington son of Thomas & Elizabeth was buryed 12 Feb 1716/7
Bartholemew & Elizabeth Etherinton son & dau of Thomas & Elizabeth were buryed 17 Feb 1716/7
John Price son of Wm & Mary was buryed 7 Mar 1716/7
Sarah Clements dau of Henry & Sarah was b 22 Oct 1707
(Eror) Edward Robinson son of James and ----- was buryed 27 Feb 1716/7
John Sedberrey was buryed 11 Mar 1716/7
Susanna Makey wife of Alexander was buryed 11 Mar 1716/7
Mary Cox dau of Thomas & Kathrin was buryed 11 Mar 1716/7
Kathrin Cox of Sasafras River was buryed 2- Mar 1716/7

EARLY ANGLICAN CHURCH RECORDS OF CECIL COUNTY

Rebecca Price dau of Wm. & Mary was buryed 18 Mar 1716/7
John McKandrick son of ---- McKandrick & Kathrin was buryed 23 Mar 1716/7
Kathrin Price wife of Wm. Junr. was buryed 23 Mar 1716/7
John & James Gibbons sons of James & Elizabeth was buryed 28 Feb 1716/7
James Gibbons of Bohemia River was buryed 5 Jul 1717
Sarah Beeston dau of William & Sarah was buryed 28 Apr 1716
    Elizabeth Huckin wife of Daniell was buryed 2 May 1718
    Elizabeth Beck dau of Jonathan & Mary was buryed 5 Apr 1714
Jonathan Beck son of ditto was buryed 23 Sep 1716
Jonathan Beck of Bohemia River was buryed 23 Sep 1718
Margaret Larramor wife of Rogar was buryed 16 Sep 1718
Capt. James Ffrisby of St. Stephens Paris was buryed 6 Jan 1719/20
Samuel Bedle son of John was buryed -- --- ----
Natthaniel Ward son of William Senr of Sasafras River was buryed 29 Apr 1718
William Ward of Sasafras River was buryed 17 Apr 1720
Rebecca Sinclar dau of William & Rachell was buryed 19 Jul 1720
    Kathrin Barrat dau of Phillip & Kathrin was buryed 11 Feb 1720

Mary Pope dau of Thomas Pope & Elizabeth was buryed 26 Aug 1719
    Rogar Larramore of St. Stephens Parish was buryed 24 Feb 1720
    William Boston of Bohemia River was buryed 2 Feb 1722
John Collins son of John & Julian was born 13 Nov 1722 [error?]
    Rebecca Watts dau of Thomas & Mary was buryed 31 Oct 1723
Thomas Wamsly Cordwainer was buryed 23 Aug 1722
Denis Seeney was buryed 28 Jun 1725
John Peirce son of Thos. & Mary was buryed 16 Nov 1722
Mary Veazey dau of James & Mary was born 13 Jan 1728
Richard Ffoster Senr of Bohemia hundred was buryed 6 Apr 1732
    Rachel Burnham dau of Thos. & Mary was buryed 8 Sep 1731
John Oats shoemaker was buryed 14 Apr 1732
Ephraim Vanburkeloo son of Abell & Cathrine was buryed 9 Oct 1725
    Thomas Boushall son of Peter & Mary was buryed 8 Sep 1732
Mary Boushall dau of Peter & Mary was buryed 11 Sep 1732 Registered by Col. Benjamin Pearce Reg. Elected and duly qualified on this day 1 May 1733
Elizabeth Key wid. was buryed 25 Apr 1733
William Veazey d 15 Apr 1733
Esabella Herman wife of Ephraim Augt. was buried 29 Mar 1732
    Casparus Herman son of Ephraim Augt. & Isabella was buried 24 Sep 1732
Rachel Huchison wife of Alexander d 22 Jan 1732/3
Joseph Sealey d 16 Sep 1732 & was buried 19 Sep
Augustine Terry d 29 Jan 1731/2 buried 1 Feb
Jacob Caulk d 11 Feb 1724/5
Eleoner Everdson wife of Everd d 26 Apr 1730
Charles Rumsey d 1726 Charles Carnan son of John & Margaret d 12 Aug 1728
Charles Rumsey son of Wm. & Sabina d 16 May 1729
Mary Kimber dau of John & Rebecka d 24 Dec 1727
Rebecka Kimber wife of Jno. d 1 Mar 1727/8
Rebecka Kimber dau of John & Rebecka d 27 Jun 1729

ST. STEPHENS' PARISH (NORTH SASSAFRAS PARISH)   13

Mary Beedle Senr d 20 Sep 1733
Martha Beedle wife of William d 3 Oct 1733
Ann Sayer wife of Stephen d 14 Apr 1733
Thomas Merret son of ---- & Elizabeth d 12 Nov 1733
Thomas Husband son of Jno. & Sarah d 9 Jan 1733/4
Rachell Davis wife of Thomas d 14 Jan 1733/4
Benja. Merrit d 20 Dec 1733
Thomas Brouch d -- Dec 1733
Elizabeth Campbell wife of John d 12 Dec 1732
Rachael Campbell dau of John d 7 Mar 1732/3
William Bryan d 4 Aug 1732
Coll. Benjamin Pearce of Cecil Co son of Coll. William Pearce &
    Isabella of Kent Co d 4 Apr 1734 about 12 o'clock at night
John Beedle Senr. d 16 May 1734
Henry Ward d 9 May 1734
Mary Matthews wife of Patrick d 17 Feb 1734/5
Elizabeth Sluyter wife of Benjamin d 2 Jan 1734/5
Garriot Othoson d 8 Feb 1735
Fouch Davis d 19 May 1738
Peter Numbers d -- May 1737
John Thompson d 7 Feb 1735
John McManus d 2 Feb 1737/8
James Young son of Joseph d 20 Jan 1738/9
Christofore Beedle son of John Senr d 20 Jan 1738/9
Augustine Beedle son of John d 9 Sep 1735
Benjamin Pearce second son of Benjamin & Margaret d 30 Nov 1739
Sarah Penington wife of John d 3 Sep 1739
Robert Weithers d & was buryed 20 Mar 1739
by Rev. Hugh Jones Dianna Lattymus wife of James d 29 Aug 1739
Mary Harper, wife of John, blacksmith, d 22 Jul 1741
Margaret Parsons dau of William d 25 Jan 1739
Mary Parsons wid. of William d 13 Feb 1739
William Parsons son of William d 1 Dec 1741
Gartrick Parsons wid. of William Junr d 26 Dec 1741
Rachel Money dau of John & Rachel d 25 Jan 1743
William Pearce fourth son of Benjamin & Margaret d 14 Sep 1743
Benjamin Ward Pearce third son of ditto d 30 Sep 1743
John Knight of Cecil Co Chyurgeon otherwise called Dr. John Knight
    son of Mr. Stephen Knight of Cecil Co d -- --- ----
Mary Pearce wid. of Coll Benjamin Pearce of Cecil Co d 14 Nov 1753
    age 61 yrs & was buryed 17 Nov
Benjamin Pearce son of Coll. Benjamin of Cecil Co d 10 Apr 1756 at
    Phila. age 45
Mary Ann Wroth dau of Thomas & Mary d 11 Nov 1756
Julian Wroth dau of Thomas & Mary d 26 Nov 1756
Sarah Beadle wife of William d -- Oct ----
Catherine Milligan wife of George Milligan Esq. d Christmas Eve 24
    Dec 1760
William Bordley son of Thomas Bordley Esq. d 17 Feb 1762 age 47
    Sarah Beadle wife of William Jr. d 28 Aug 1764
Rebecca Veazey wife of Coll. John d with the small pox 24 Apr 1761
Coll. John Veazey d with small pox age 77 4 May 1777
Edward Veazey son of Coll. John & Rebeka d 24 Apr 1784

14   EARLY ANGLICAN CHURCH RECORDS OF CECIL COUNTY

Robert Porter Senr. son of James & Inibar d 28 Sep 1775 age 77 yrs wanting 15 days

BIRTHS
Matthias Peninton son of ------- and ---- b 9 Oct ---- Thomas Peninton son of Thomas & A--- b 2 Nov 1694
Mary Bolden dau of Wm & Thomaston b 2 Jan 1689
Richard Bolden son of Wm & Thomason b 5 Dec 169-
Elizabeth Bolden dau of Wm & Thomason b 3 Jul 169-
Judah Branklin dau of Wm Branklin & Anne b 23 Nov 1688
Susanna Vasey dau of Wm Vasey & Rosemond b 20 Jun 1696/7
Mary Porter dau of James & Junibar b 15 Apr 1689
Rosemond Porter dau of James & Junibar b 1 Mar 1690
James Porter son of James & Junibar b 22 Jan 1692/3
Elizabeth Porter dau of James & Junibar b 22 Jan 1692/3
Margaret Porter dau of James & Junibar b 1 Apr 1694/5
---- Porter son of James & Junibar b 10 Oct 1698
Mary Archer dau of Jacob & Mary b 10 Nov 1687
Elizabeth Severson dau of Thomas & Elizabeth b 2 Dec ----
Elizabeth Barker dau of Richard & Mary b 26 Aug 1692
Jno Barker son of Richard & Mary b 28 Oct 1688
Mary Barker dau of Richard & Mary b 24 Jul 1691
Richard Barker son of Richard & Rebeccah b 16 Sep 1697
Ephraim Herman son of Casparus Augt. & Catherine b -- --- ----
Catherine Herman dau of Coll. Casparus Augustine & Catherine b 20 Oct 1697 Augustina Herman dau of Coll. Casparus & Catherine b 16 Sep 169-
Rynerius Vangazely son of Jacob & Gertruy b 16 Dec 1696
Mary Lapage dau of Edward & Joan b 18 Dec 1695
Edward Lapage son of Edward & Joan b 25 Jun 1692
Isaac Penninton son of Thomas & Alie b 16 Oct 1692
Sarah Brace dau of Jno Brace & Elizabeth b 4 May 1695
Robert Merser son of Thomas & Elizabeth b 19 Dec 1691
Mary Usher b 2 Feb 169-
Ephraim Thompson son of Co. Jno. & ---- (his wife) b 24 Sep 169-
William Horne son of Darby & Sarah b 26 Dec 1696
Thomas Watts son of Thomas & Elizabeth b 23 Mar 1696
Sarah Mounce dau of Christopher & Sarah b -- --- ----
Andrew Clements son of Andrew & Elizabeth b 22 Dec 1692
William Crow son of Charles & Jillian b 12 Sep 1696
Rosemond Terry dau of Thomas & Rosemond b 4 Oct 1693
Owen Hews son of Owen & Mary b 16 Aug being Thursday ye sunn being one half an hour hight in ye morning 1689
Mary Hewes dau of Owen & Mary b 27 Mar being fryday between nine & tenn a clock in ye morning 1691
Gabriell Hewes son of Owen & Mary b 3 Nov ye sunn about 2 hours high in ye morning 1694
Jno Crew son of Jno & Katherine b 6 Mar 1695
Thomas Cock son of Thos & Katherine b 26 Jan 1695
Jno Cock son of Thos & Katherine b 12 Jan 1697
Anne Terry dau of Thomas & Rosemond b 12 Oct 1696
Elizabeth Brace dau of Jno & Elizabeth b 21 Nov 169-
Daniell Macary dau of Richard & Ester b 22 Nov 168-
Mary Macary dau of Richard & Ester b Feb 16 1688

ST. STEPHENS' PARISH (NORTH SASSAFRAS PARISH)

Mary Sherwood dau of Wm & Mary b 23 Sep 1696
Ann Watkins dau of James & Mary b 8 Mar 169-
Mary Severson dau of Peter & Mary b 15 Aug 169-
Rebecka Penninton dau of Robert & ---- b 5 May 169-
Esther Browning dau of Thomas & ---- b 13 Apr 1697
Abraham Clemenson son of Cornelius & Juniber b 20 Aug ----
Mary Boyer dau of Wm. Boyer & ----- b 13 Sep ----
Augustine Boyer son of Wm. Boyer & Phillis b 15 Dec 1691
William Boyer son of Wm. Boyer & Phillis b 23 Aug 1695
Jno. Stoop son of Jno & Mary b 15 Oct 1692
Phillip Stoop son of Jno & Mary b 15 Feb 1695/6
Ellinor Rice dau of Hugh & Sarah b 3 Dec 1696
Rebecca Ward dau of John & Mary b 22 Nov 1705
Thomas Ward son of John & Mary b 17 Dec 1707
Peregrine Ward son of John & Mary b 23 Feb 1709
Rachel Laramore dau of Roger Laramore & Margarett b 18 1708
Edward Laramore son of Roger & Margarett b 27 Dec 1710
John Ryland son of John & Alice b 28 Apr 1699
Mary Ryland dau of John Ryland & Alice b 10 Aug 1701
Thomas Ryland son of John & Alice b 10 Mar 1705
Rigg Cox son of Benjamin & Elizabeth b 15 Nov 1699
Mary Cox dau of Benjamin & Elizabeth b 8 Oct 1701
Elizabeth Cox dau of Benjamin & Elizabeth b -- Spt 1703
Margaret Cox dau of Benjamin & Elizabeth b 5 Jan 1706
Charles Scott son of Walter & Grace b 12 Jan 1708
Jacobus King son of Peter King & --- b 8 Mar 1699
Isaac King son of Peter & ---- b 18 Sep 1702
Susanna King dau of Peter & ---- b 26 Jun 1709
Sophia Child dau of Nathaniel & Eleanor b 25 Dec 1711
Jane Pope dua of Thos & Elizabeth b 2 Feb 1711
Thomas Walmsley son of Thomas & Katherine b 10 Jul 1704
Ann Walmsley dau of Thomas & Katherine 6 Jan 1706
John Walmsley son of Thomas & Katherine b 21 Nov 1709
Daniell Smith son of Casparus & Ann b 20 Jan 1705
Mary Smith dau of Casparus & Ann b 27 Jan 1707
Sarah Smith dau of Casparus & Ann b 2 Apr 1709
Mary Money dau of Robert & Margaret b 18 Jul 1708
Robert Money son of Robert & Margaret b 27 Feb 1709
Martha Macahee dau of Alexander Junr & Susanna b 26 Mar 1708
John Morgan son of James & Elizabeth b 6 Oct 1702
Richard Morgan son of James & Elizabeth b -- Mar 1705
Sarah Morgan dau of James & Elizabeth b 15 May 1706
Robert Morgan son of James & Elizabeth b 14 Jan 1708
Azarias Copping son of John & Angelica b 13 Apr 1712
Mary Numbers dau of Peter & Anne b 4 Jul 1712
Mary Etherington dau of Thomas & Elizabeth b 1 Aug 1712
Rebecca Pierce dau of Thos. Pierce Junr. & Mary b 20 Dec ----
    Ffrisby Knight son of Stephen & Sarah b 15 Apr 1712
David Perrey son of David & Susana b 9 Sep 1705
Thomas McKeye son of Alexander McKeye & Susana b 3 Jun 1712
Darnel McCullah dau of William & Kathrin b 1 Oct 1711
Josias Gibbons son of James & Elizabeth b 17 Dec 1704
Mary Gibbons dau of James Gibbons & Elizabeth b 17 Mar 1706/7
John Gibbons son of James Gibbons & Elizabeth b 28 Mar 1709

James Gibbons son of James & Elizabeth b 31 Oct 1711
Robert Roberts son of John & Debra b 1 Dec 1704
John Roberts son of John & Debra b 13 Nov 1707
Sarah Roberts dau of John & Jul--th b 14 Dec 1712
John Numbers son John Junr. & Elizabeth b 20 Dec 1711
Wm. Foster son of Richard & Susana b 27 Nov 1701 or 1703
Richard Foster son of Richard & Susana b 11 Jun 1704
James Foster son of Richard & Susana b 1 Jun 1707
John Foster son of Richard Foster & Susana b 11 Jan 1710
Frederick Williams son of Jacob Williams & Jane b 7 Aug 1703
Ephraim Hamm son of John & Helinor b 21 Sep 1704
John Hamm son of John & Helinor b 28 Mar 1706
Abraham Hamm son of John & Helinor b 20 Aug 1708
Isaac Hamm son of John & Helinor b 10 Jan 1710
John Bell son of Richard & Jane b 18 Feb 1710
Thomas Bell son of Richard & Jane b 8 Mar 1712
Sarah Mounce dau of Christopher & Martha b 7 Apr 1696
Mary Mounce of same b 6 Sep 1698
Anne Mounce of same b 9 Jan 1702
Martha Mounce of same b 16 Mar 1704
Christopher Mounce Anderson son of same b 18 Oct 1708
Margaret Larramore dau of Roger & Margaret b 10 Jan 1712
Anne Smith dau of Casparus & Ann b 10 Aug 1713
Wm Peninton son of Henry & Elizabeth b 7 Feb 1709
Henry Peninton son of Henry & Elizabeth b 10 Aug 1712
Emme Currey dau of Thomas & Marey b 11 Nov 1713
Thomas Price son of Wm Junr. & Kathrin b 20 Jan 1710
William Price son of William Junr. & Kathrine b 4 Feb 1713
Thomas Cox son of Thomas & Kathrin b 14 Feb 1708
Elizabeth Cox dau of Thomas & Kathrin b 7 Feb 1711
Elizabeth Veazey dau of George Veazey & Alice b 5 May 1710
William Veazey son of George & Alice b 16 Sep 1712
Samuel Beadle son of John Beadle & Mary b 6 Mar 1699
Sarah Beadle dau of same b 11 Apr 1702
Benjamin Beadle of same b 13 Nov 1707
William Beadle of same b 27 Dec 1709
Martha Hazelhurst dau of Benjamin & Diana b 13 Mar 1710
Mary Crouch dau of Thomas & Mary b 25 Jan 1700
Thomas Crouch son of same b 25 Apr 1704
Susanna dau of same b 27 Feb 1707
Rachall Crouch dau of same b 3 Apr 1712
Robert Mercer son of Thomas & Elizabeth b 17 Oct 1703
William Mercer son of same b 29 Apr 1709
John Mercer son of same b 6 Aug 1711
Alice Davis dau of William & Angell b 30 Jul 1710
Rebecca Peirce dau of Thomas Junr. & Mary b 20 Dec 1707
William son of same b 1 Sep 1710
Thomisson dau of same b 21 Nov 1712
Walter Evitt son of John & Rachell b 11 Jul 1712
Anna Marya Bayard dau of Samuel & Susana b 19 Jul 1700
Samuel Bayard son of same b 27 Apr 1705
Petrus Bayard son of same b 10 Jul 1702
Jacobus Bayard son of Samuell & Susana b 1 Apr 1708
Benjamin Sluyter son of Henry & Rachell b 25 Nov 1700
Isaac Sluyter son of same b 30 May 1706

ST. STEPHENS' PARISH (NORTH SASSAFRAS PARISH)

Elizabeth Sluyter dau of same b 7 Apr 1708
Mary Bavinton dau of John & Mary b 4 Dec 1701
Hugh Bavinton son of same b 4 Mar 1703
Jonathan Bavinton son of same b 1 Jan 1707
Rose Bavinton dau of same b 25 Mar 1710
Robert Walmsley son of Thomas & Kathrin b 2 Feb 1712
Sarah Price dau of John & Mary b 2 Aug 1713
Benjamin Beck son of Jonathan & Mary b 18 May 1707
Jane Beck dau of same b 13 Mar 1710
Elizabeth Beck dau of same b 1 Apr 1711
Rebecca Atkins dau of John & Mary b 15 Jan 1701
Margarett Money dau of Robert Money & Margaret b 15 Dec 1712
Edward Morgan son of James & Elizabeth b 21 Oct 1712
Sarah Clements dau of Henry & Sarah b 22 Oct 1707
Robert Othoson son of Garratt & Sarah b 22 Sep 1712
Anne Clements dau of John & Mary b 27 Apr 1707
William Rye son of John & Mary b 10 August 1713
Sarah Newman dau of Daniell & Mary b 6 Nov 1710
Solomon Newman son of Daniell & Mary b 17 Oct 1713
Jane Merrit dau of Thomas & Elizabeth b 10 Apr 1701
Thomas Merrit son of Thomas & Elizabeth b 24 Nov 1703
William Merrit son of Thomas & Elizabeth b 30 Nov 1706
Mary Merrit dau of same b 10 May 1709
George Merrit son of same b 31 Aug 1710
John Merritt son of same b 24 May 1716
Henry Simons son of John & Mary b 13 Jan 1713
Thomas Parsley son of Thos. & Elizabeth b 25 Aug 1701 (1707?)
Israel Parsley son of same b 10 Oct 1709
Eleinor Parsley dau of same b 14 Feb 1710
Bartholamew Parsley son of same b 18 Oct 1713
Thomas Griffeth son of John & Elizabeth b 9 Jan 1711
Elizabeth Griffeth dau of same b 23 Sep 1713
Kathrin Parsons dau of Thomas & Mary b 13 Apr 1713
Thomas Sefferson son of Thomas & Kathrin b 24 Mar 1701/2
Tabitha Sefferson dau of same b 24 Jul 1704
Peter Sefferson son of same b 9 apr 1706
Jeffrey Sefferson son of same b 6 Oct 1708
Mary Sefferson dau of same b 16 Mar 1710/11
Margaret Sefferson dau of same b 14 Jul 1713
John Veazey son of Edward & Susanna b 12 Feb 1700/1
Margaret Price dau of Thomas & Mary b 2 Sep 1704
Martha Price dau of same b 6 Jun 1705
Wm. Price son of same b 25 Oct 1708
Thomas Price son of same b 29 Mar 1711
Mary Price dau of same b 7 Jan 1713
William Husband son of John & Sarah b 2 Feb 1708
Mary Husband dau of same b 13 Nov 1710
John Husband son of same b 3 May 1712
William Price son of William Senr. & Mary b 18 Sep 1699
Richard Price son of same b 10 Jan 1701
Andrew Price son of same b 16 Nov 1704
Hyland Price son of same b 13 Jan 1709
Susanna Morrison dau of Morris & Mary b 1 Jan 1700
William Beeston son of Wm. & Sarah b 3 Oct 1707
Benjamin Beeston son of same b 8 Mar 1709

Mary Beeston dau of same b 7 Nov 1712
Thomas Steele son of Francis & Rebecca b 1 May 1707
Rachel Steele dau of same b 28 Jan 1708
Mary Steele dau of same b 11 Mar 1710
Susanna Child dau of Nathaniel & Helinor b 1 Apr 1706
Francis Child son of same b 7 Oct 1710
Thomas Tobias son of Cornelius & Helinor b 5 Dec 1713
William Knight son of Stephen & Sarah b 9 Feb 1709
James Etherington son of Thomas & Elizabeth b 13 Jan 1712
Mary Rose dau of Thos. & Sarah b 9 Aug 1704
William Rose son of same b 10 May 1710
Thomas Rose son of same b 10 Sep 1713
Samuel Boulding son of William & Thomasin b 7 Jan 1709
James Boulding son of same b 4 Sep 1712
Rebecca Morgan dau of Richard & Mary b 10 Apr 1706
Richard Morgan son of same b 11 Jun 1709
William Stoops son of John & Mary b 18 Feb 1707
Benjamin Stoops son of same b 11 May 1710
Mary Stoops dau of same b 20 Jul 1712
Prudence Roaden dau of Robert & Margaret b 25 Dec (?) 1705
Susana Dyer dau of Cornelius & Margarett b 5 Mar 1709/10
William & Alexander Boulding (twins) sons of William & Thomasin b 29 Jun 1704
Thomas Boulding son of same b 15 Jan 1706
Mary Chicken (son) of John & Anne b 5 Mar 1703
John Chicken son of same b 8 Jan 1705
Edward Chicken son of same b 11 Aug 1708
John Broxon son of Thomas Broxon & Ann b 31 Mar 1710
Anne Broxon dau of same b 3 Dec 1712
Otho Peninton son of Richard & Mary b 27 Oct 1712
Hester Hendrickson dau of Chri. & Mary b 23 Feb 1708
Sarah Hendrickson dau of Christopher & Mary b 6 May 1711
Rebecca Hendrickson dau of same b 13 Oct 1712
Killon Holyday son of Samuel & Hester b 25 Nov 1702
Mary Holyday dau of same b 23 Feb 1709
John Jobson son of John & Hester b 6 May 1712
Mary Stanly dau of John & Jane b 16 Apr 1706
Sarah Stanly dau of same b 14 Sep 1708
Elizabeth Stanly dau of same b 14 Jun 1711
Rachell Stanly dau of same b 16 Nov 1713
John White son of John & Mary b 11 Aug 1708
Elizabeth White dau of same b 12 Aug 1712
Mauldin Johnson dau of Garrat & Hester b 28 Mar 1706
Susanna Johnson dau of same b 26 Jan 1708
Garrat Johnson son of same b 15 Jan 1710
Kathrin Johnson dau of same b 24 Jan 1712
Mary Henning dau of John & Ann b 2 Feb 1704
Susanna Henning dau of same b 22 Oct 1706
Jediah Henning son of same b 7 Jan 1709
Sarah Henning dau of same b 29 Sep 1713
Mary White dau of John & Mary b 8 May 1714
Elizabeth & Mary Hollins twins daus of John & Abigall b 16 Jan 1712
Abraham Hollins son of same b 28 Sep 1710
Frances Clark dau of John & Hannah b 4 Mar 17--

ST. STEPHENS' PARISH (NORTH SASSAFRAS PARISH)

Sarah Clark dau of same b 18 Apr 170-
Mary Clark dau of same b 10 May 1709
Hannah Clark dau of same b 7 Aug 1711
Rubbey Clark dau of same b 5 Sep 1713
Richard Huckin son of Daniell & Elizabeth b 28 Jul 1699
Daniell Huckin son of same b 13 Nov 1701
Henry Huckin son of same b 18 Jul 1704
John Huckin son of same b 14 Mar 1707
Bartholamew Huckin son of same b 16 Feb 1713/14
Gilder Huckin son of same b 8 Dec 1709
William Huckin son of same b 2 Jan 1712
Mary Christian dau of Andrew Christian b 4 Dec 170-
Elizabeth Eliason dau of Cornelius b 21 Feb 1704
Elias Eliason son of same b 25 Jul 1706
John Eliason son of same b 10 Dec 1708
Cathrin Eliason dau of same b 14 Jun 1711
Susannah Eliason dau of same b 9 May 1714
John Brock son of Barnet b 14 Feb 1705
---- & Thomas McCullah twins sons of Wm. & ---- b 25 Mar 1714
Thomas Husbands son of John & Sarah b 6 Jun 1714
Richard Peninton son of Wm. & Mary b 22 Jun 1714
Martha Barrat dau of Phillip & Kathrin b 27 Apr 1714
James Hatrey son of Henry & Christian b 16 Dec 1709
Nathaniel Chick son of John & Christian b 20 Jan 1708
John Chick son of same b 25 Mar 1711
William Chick son of same b 10 Nov 1713
Mary Chick dau of William & Margaret b 29 Jan 1703
Thomas Bavington son of John & Mary b 27 May 1714
Mary Bowin dau of Charles & Jane b 30 Aug 1702
Elizabeth Bowin dau of same b 7 Dec 1704
Richard Bowin son of same b 14 May 1707
Solamon Bowin son of same b 27 Aug 1709
Charles Bowin son of same b 15 Jun 1712
Susana Care dau of Thomas & Mary b 15 Aug 1713
Jacob Bowers son of James & Margaret b 11 Jun 1708
Wm. More son of Thomas & Liddey b 31 Aug ----
Elias More son of same b 15 Sep 1705
Thomas More son of same b 23 Jun 1707
Elizabeth More dau of same b 23 Jan 1709
Judith Thompson dau of Richard & Magdalen b 11 Mar 1707
John Thompson son of same b 12 Mar 1710
Richard Thompson son of same b 5 Nov 1713
William Newman son of Danniel & Mary b 6 Jun 1708
Marey Newman dau of same b 6 Jun 1705
Edward Ford son of Richard & Elenor b 1 Sep 1707
Richard Ford son of same b 28 Aug 1712
Francis Ozey son of Francis & Elinor b 8 May 1714
John Worgin son of Joseph Worgin & Mary b 31 Jul 1699
Mary dau of same b 7 Jun 1703
Joseph Worgin son of same b 16 Oct 1705
James Conyer son of Thomas & Mary b 13 Sep 1701
Patrick Conyer son of same b 15 Mar 1708/9
Thomas Conyer son of same b 15 Mar 1711
Mary Oliver dau of John & Margery b 27 Aug 1706
Anne Oliver dau of same b 25 Sep 1708

Jane Oliver dau of same b 7 May 1711
Thomas Oliver son of same b 2 Nov 1713
John Tippin son of ----- b 15 May 1706
Fredick Tippin son of ----- b 30 Apr 1708
Kathrin Stitson dau of Yargin Stitson & ----- b 9 Aug 1712
William Broxon illegitimate son of Wm. Broxon & Mary Burnham spinster b 22 Aug 1712
Rebeca Price dau of Wm. & Mary b 18 Oct 1714
Sarah Ffrisby dau of Capt. James & Ariana b 7 Dec 1714
Mary Currey dau of Thos. & Mary b 6 Feb 1706
Thomas Currey son of same b 26 Dec 1708
Robert Currey son of same b 10 Apr 1711
Nathaniel Sapinton son of Nathaniel & Margaret b 15 Jul 1714
Walter Newman son of John & Elizabeth b 18 Aug 1714
Elizabeth Buckworth dau of Charles & Ruth b 7 Feb 1708
Charles Buckworth son of same b 28 Oct 1712
Elizabeth Newman dau of Walter & Mary b 2 Feb 1707
Kathrin Newman dau of same b 28 Aug 1709
Jonathan Newman son of same b 4 Feb 1711
Samuel Newman son of same b 15 Mar 1713
Walter Crow son of John & Martha b 20 Oct 1714
Jane Dillafroe dau of Joseph & Jane(?) b 26 Oct 1709
Andrew Dillafroe son of same b 21 June 1705
George Beeston son of George Beeston & Jane b 31 Oct 1702
Mary Archer dau of Jacob & Mary b 25 Dec 1714
John Bristow son of Wm. & Mildred b 13 Feb 1708
George Bristow son of same b 4 Jun 1711
Mildred Bristow dau of same b 18 Jan 1714
John Gullet son of John & Sarah b 30 Apr 1711
John Ford son of Richard & Helinor b 29 Aug 1714
Rachall Hill dau of Wm. & Mary b 3 Jun 1707
William Hill son of same b --- 1709
Mary Hill dau of same b 3 Jun 1712
Henry Graham son of George & Elizabeth b 6 Apr 1712
Mary Graham dau of same b 25 Jan 1713
Margaret Mahaney dau of Denis & Sarah b 6 Sep 1704
Charles Mahaney son of same b 26 Apr 1710
Denis Mahaney son of same b 19 Apr 1714
John Burk son of John & Honor b 21 Apr 1708
Mary Burk dau of same b 8 Jun 1711
Patrick Burk son of same b 31 Oct 1714
Robert Simons son of John & Mary b 6 Feb 1714
Susana Pooly dau of Nicholas & Sarah b 28 Jan 1710
Wm. Peninton son of Richard & Mary b 22 Jan 1714/15
Anne Lawson dau of David & Elizabeth b 10 Feb 1700
Peter Lawson son of same b 2 Dec 1713
Jacob Hamm son of John & Elinor b 9 Feb 1714
William Starling son of John Sterling & Mary b 22 May 1711
Sarah Starling dau of same b 30 Nov 1714
Isabela Campbell dau of John & Elizabeth b 4 Oct 1711
Charles Campbell son of same b 10 Nov 1712
Elizabeth Campbell dau of same b 11 Apr 1715
Charles Melane son of Elexander & Sarah b 15 Feb 1700
Johnathan Melane son of Elexander & Sarah b 15 Sep 1709

ST. STEPHENS' PARISH (NORTH SASSAFRAS PARISH)

Mary Hattrey dau of Thomas & Sarah b 10 Dec 1714
Francis Burgis son of Francis & Mary b 7 Mar 1708/9
William Burgis son of same b 12 Oct 1710 Anne Burgis dau of same b 1 Dec 1712
Anne Jonson dau of Bartholmew & Mary b 30 Apr 1709
Margaret dau of same b 18 Jan 1711
Mary Jonson dau of same b 31 Aug 1714 Aron More son of Thos. & Liddey b 29 Sep 1714
Thomas Collins son of Robert & Abigall b 28 Dec 1714
William Owlfield son of Jerimiah & Elinor b 13 Apr 1711
John Owlfield son of same b 12 Jan 1713
Urina Cashner dau of John & Margery b 26 Jan 1703
John Cashner son of same b 16 Aug 1706
Mary Cashner dau of same b 1 Sep 1709
Augustin Ungle son of Elizabeth Ungle b 5 Jan 1713/4
Samuel Lumm son of Samuel & Anne b 28 Aug 1706
Jonas Lumm son of same b 16 Jun 1710
Sarah Lumm dau of Samuel & Anne b 24 Oct 1714
Hanah Nowell dau of Evan & Hanan b 29 Nov 1714
Elizabeth Powell dau of Richard Powell & Margaret Ferrell b 10 Jan 1704
Marey English dau of Thos. & Frances b 10 Mar 1703
Richard English son of same b 23 Nov 1707
Robert English son of Thos. & Margaret b 23 Nov 1710
William English son of same b 5 Nov 1714
Nicholas Harper son of Thomas & Elizabeth b 5 Jun 1705
Thomas Harper son of same b 24 Mar 1707/8
Jacob Harper son of same b 23 Feb 1711/12
Elizabeth Harper dau of same b 9 Aug 1715
John Wood son of Robert & Kathrin b 11 Mar 1713
Kathrin Wood dau of same b 11 Mar 1715/6
Margarett Ward dau of Mr. Henry & Elizabeth b 27 Dec 1715/16
Nathaniell Child son of George & Elizabeth b 28 Nov 1714
Tabitha Chick dau of John & Christian b 8 Oct 1714
Sarah Clements dau of Henry & Sarah b 22 Oct 1707
John Oliver son of John & Margery b 28 Dec 1716
Elizabeth Bavinton dau of John & Mary b 27 Feb 1717
Sarah Hooper dau of Edward & Elizabeth b 8 Feb 1716/17
John Merrit son of Thos. & Elizabeth b 21 May 1716
Sarah Beeston dau of Wm. & Sarah b 14 Nov 1715
Sarah Beeston dau of Wm. & Sarah b 20 Apr 1717
James Numbers son of Peter & Anne b 30 Nov 1717
John Peninton son of John of Bohemia River & Sarah b 20 Oct 1717
George Child son of George & Elizabeth b 6 Nov 1717
Richard Simons son of John & Mary b 22 May 1718
Rachell Hozer dau of John & Elizabeth b 5 Sep 1710
Jacob Hozer son of same b 24 Jul 1717
Elizabeth Hozer dau of same b 20 Nov 1714
Sarah Hozer dau of same b 12 Nov 1716
Nicholas Wood son of Robert & Kathrin b 31 Aug 1718
Bartholemus Etherinton son of Thomas & Elizabeth b 12 Feb 1712
John Price son of Wm. & Mary b 9 Aug 1718
James Taylor son of Richard & Anne b 27 Jan 1717
Joseph Alman son of Abraham & Margaret b 26 Nov 1718
William Bedle son of Thomas & Elizabeth b 3 Mar 1718/9

Thomas Hamm son of John & Elinor b 19 Sep 1718
Jane Bell dau of Richard & Jane b 9 Nov 1715
Rachel Bell dau of same b 9 Mar 1716/7
Esther Mash dau of Cornelius Mash b 18 Apr 1715
John Beaumont son of John & ---- b 18 Feb 1714
Anne Beaumont dau of same b 31 Jan 1719
John Gallaway son of James & Margaret b 28 Aug 1711
Francis Gallaway son of same b 28 Feb 1714
Mary Gallaway dau of same b 3 Jul 1717
Margaret Gallaway dau of same b 20 Aug 1718
Edward Condon son of John & Diana b 31 Aug 1718
Jonathan Newman son of Walter & Mary b 5 Aug 1716
Walter Newman son of John & Elizabeth b 10 Mar 1718
Walter Crow son of John & Martha b 23 Aug 1717
Mary Crow dau of same b 24 Dec 1715
Mary Comes dau of John & Sarah b 19 Oct 1717
Henry Price son of David & Kathrin b 29 Oct 1718
Martha Fflin day of Kathrin Fflin b 1 Feb 1713
John Huchison son of John & Mary b 15 Oct 171-
James Fford son of Richard & Elinor b 4 Apr 1716
George Fford son of same b 19 Dec 1717/8
Chas. Fford son of same b 3 Feb 1718/9
James More son of Thomas & Lidey b 4 Dec 1718/9
Peter Newman son of Walter Junr. & Elizabeth b 18 Nov 1718
Kathrin Franklin illegitimate dau of Jane Franklin b 28 Feb 1718/19
Richard Ellwood son of Richard & Mary b 31 Oct 1717
Rebeca Bowen dau of Solomon & Anne b 20 Dec 1713/4
Ezacariah Bowen son of Solomon & anne b 19 Sept 1717
Samuel Bowen son of Chas. & Jane b 8 Apr 1717/18
Jane Bowen dau of same b 10 Jun 1719
Marey dau of Anne Taylor b 27 Feb 1718/9
Joseph Fisher son of Wm & Marey b 11 May 1706
Mary Evett dau of John & --- b 27 Jan 1715/6
John Evett son of same b 17 Apr 1719
Macklen Lytner dau of Adam & Macklen b 19 Mar 1716
Christopher Noaser son of John & Kathrin b 14 Jan 1707
Godfrit Woolbark son of Christopher & Lydey b 29 Aug 1715
Christopher Woolbard son of same b 13 Mar 1718/9
Henry Hendrickson son of Henry & Elizabeth b 3 May 1717
John Harper son of Thomas & Elizabeth b 24 Mar 1717/8
Anne Hopkins dau of Elexander & Sarah b 12 Feb 1718/9
Alice Husband dau of James & Alice b 11 Jun 1718
Mary Bouldin dau of Richard & Mary b 19 Nov 1717
Sarah Cox dau of John & Rosamond b 26 Oct 1719
Ffrisby Knight son of Stephen & Sarah b 15 Apr 1712
Mary Knight dau of same b 11 Oct 1714
John Knight son of same b 18 Oct 1716
Sarah Knight dau of same b 1 Apr 1719
Arianna Margarett Ffrisby dau of Capt. James & Arianna b at noon 8 Sep 1717
Ffrancina Augustina Ffrisby dau of same b Sunday 16 Aug 1719
Martha Veazey dau of James & Mary b 20 Jul 1717
Thomas(?) Veazey son of same b 2 Jul 1719
Mary Veazey dau of Robert & Lucie b 13 Oct 1719

ST. STEPHENS' PARISH (NORTH SASSAFRAS PARISH)

Elizabeth Whitle dau of Nicholas & Kathrin b 14 Feb 1716
Anna Schiels dau of John & ----- b 28 Sep 1713
John Schiels son of same b 29 May 1716
Ephraim Schiels son of same b 2 Mar 1719
Elinor Campbell dau of John & Eliz. b 2 Apr 1716
John Campbell son of same b 28 Mar 1718
Mary Campbell dau of same b 25 Apr ----
Aron Latham son of Joshua & Mary b 28 Dec 1719
John Bedle son of John Junr. & Mary b 4 Apr 1717
Christopher Bedle son of John Junr. & Mary b -- Feb 1715/6
Alice Ward dau of John & Susana b 22 May 1718
Elizabeth Ward dau of same b 14 Feb 1719
Anne Taylor dau of Richard & Anne b 30 Jun 1720
Rebecca Sinclar dau of William & Rachell b 19 Jun 1720
John Kimball son of John Junr. & Rebecca b 22 Dec 1719/20
John Cox son of Benjamin & Rose b 3 Oct 1713
Benjamin Cox son of same b 6 Mar 1715/6
Thomas Cox son of same b 18 Jun 1716
Samuell Cox son of same b 5 Mar 1718/9
Henry Cox son of same b 18 Jan 1719/20
Peter Numbers son of Peter & Anne b 11 Mar 1719/20
Elizabeth Caulk dau of Jacob & Mary (illegitemate) b 23 Nov 1716
Richard Dorrall son of Richard & Mary b 4 Jan 1719/20
Sarah Husband dau of James & Alice b 13 Jul 1720
Isaac Foster son of Richard & Sarah b 14 Jan 1719/20
Francis Collins son of John & Jullieanne b 19 Sep 1720
Susana Makey dau of Alexander & Susana b 26 Mar 1715
John Price son of William Senr. & Mary b 9 Aug 1718
Mary Collins dau of James & Ellinor b 20 Nov 1719
Thos. Epthorp son of Francis Epthorp & Ellinor b 8 Sep 1704
Elizabeth Epthorp dau of same b 24 Feb 1707/8
Thomas Crisp son of Thos. & Ellinor b 7 Jun 1710
Mary Hollins dau of John & Abigall b 4 Jul 1719
Esther Latham dau of Arron & Mary b 3 Apr 1712
Anne Latham dau of same b 17 Jan 1715
John Latham son of same b 6 Aug 1720
John Money son of Robert & Margaret b 10 Jul 1714
Robana Money dau of same b 12 Apr 1717
Kathrin Money dau of same b 2 Dec 1719
Augustina Larramore dau of Roger & Augustina b 6 Oct 1720
Rachell Peninton dau of John & Sarah b 24 Mar 1720
John Ingle son of Thomas & Margaret b 3 Dec 1720
Elizabeth Malster dau of Godfrey & Mary b 20 --- 1721
Rebecca Simons dau of John & Rebecca b 9 May 1721
Thomas Pope son of Thomas & Elizabeth b 27 Apr 1718
John Pope son of same b 3 Jan 1720
Hugh Richard Matthiason son of Matthias & Mary b 15 Oct 1721
Solomon Newman son of Daniel & Mary b 17 Oct 1713
Sarah Newman dau of same b 16 Oct 1710
Anne Cox dau of Benj. & Rose b 6 Dec 1721
Elizabeth Kimball dau of John Junr. & Rebecca b 15 Nov 1721
Sarah Price dau of Wm. & Sarah b 21 Sep 1721
Mary Murrain dau of Daniell & Susanna b 4 Sep 1720
Rebecca Ryland dau of John Junr. & Rebecca b 3 Dec 1721
Samuel Bedle son of John Junr. b 25 Dec 1721/2

EARLY ANGLICAN CHURCH RECORDS OF CECIL COUNTY

Benj. Geers son of Daniell & Elizabeth b 22 Oct 1715
John Geers son of same b 19 Feb 1716
Benson Geers son of same b 1 Apr 1720

The Baptizimms of children:

Jno. Gandy son of George & Constance bapt 2 Jul 1692 by Mr. Lawrence Vanderbush
Jno. Ward son of William & Elizabeth bapt 17 Jul 1692
James Waggett son of Jno. & Jaine bapt 17 Jul 1692
Mary Manicozons dau of Michaell & Anne bapt 22 Jul 1692
Elizabeth Crouch dau of Thomas & Mary bapt 22 Jul 1692
Thomas Terry son of Thomas & Rosemond bapt 14 Aug 1692
Robert Machakey son of Alexander & wife bapt 14 Aug 1692
Mary Branklin dau of Wm & Ann bapt 21 Aut 1692
Susanna Morrice dau of Jno. Moris & Margaret bapt 25 Oct 1692
Mary Barker dau of Richard & Mary bapt 4 Sep 1692
Elizabeth Drake dau of Wm. & Margaret bapt 11 Sep 1692
Rachel Peninton dau of Henry & his wife bapt 21 Aug 1692
Mary Moss dau of Richard & Elizabeth bapt 17 Sep 1692
Margaret Dorrle dau of Nicholas & Charisyan bapt 18 Sep 1692
Oliver Caulk son of Isaac & Mary bapt 30 Sep 1692
Mary Wheeler dau of Jno. & Elizabeth bapt -- Oct 1692
Jno. Stoop son of Jno. & Mary bapt 31 Oct 1692
& likewise ye said Mary Stoop dau of Mr. Philip Holeog-r was bapt at ye same time. Sarah Davis dau of Wm. & Angell bapt 6 Nov 1692
Mary Toulson dau of Andrew & Mary bapt 6 Nov 1692
Wm. Babinton son of Jno. & Mary bapt 6 Jan 1694
Johannes son of Nicholas Delamountain & Charistian Roserte All the above bapt by Mr. Lawrence Vanderbush Ffrancis Frisby son of James Esq. & Sarah bapt 7 July 1697 by Mr. Lehiton
Jaine Hynson dau of Mr. Jno. Hynson & Mary bapt 1 Apr 1696 by Mr. Jn. Lehiton
Jno. Hynson son of Mr. Jno. Hynson & Mary bapt 1 Apr 1697
Jno. Bavinton son of Jno. & Mary bapt 1 Aug 1697
Mary Sherwood dau of --- & Mary bapt 1 Aug 1697
Robert Macahee son of Robert & ---- bapt 1 Aug 1697
Anne Watkins dau of James & Mary bapt 1 Aug 1697
Mary Severson dau of Peter & Mary bapt 1 Aug 1697
by Mr. Rich. Sewell Rebecca Penninton dau of Robert & Ann bapt 1 Aug 1697
Thomas Marcus son of Hance & Dina bapt 1 Aug 1697
Mary Marcus dau of same bapt 1 Aug 1697
Esther Browning dau of Thomas & Ann bapt 1 Aug 1697
Abraham Clenson son of Cornelius Clemenson & Junibar bapt 1 Aug 1697
Ephraim Thompson son of Coll Jno. & Judith bapt 3 Oct 1697
Wm. Boyer son of Wm. & Phillis bapt 3 Oct 1697
Thomas Watts son of Thomas & Elizabeth bapt 3 Oct 1697
Sarah Mounce dau of Christopher & Sarah bapt 3 Oct 1697
Rosemond Terry dau of Thomas & Rosemond bapt 12 Sep 1697
Richard Boulden son of Wm. & Thomasen bapt 24 Oct 1697
Elizabeth Bolden dau of Wm. & Thomason bapt 24 Oct 1697

ST. STEPHENS' PARISH (NORTH SASSAFRAS PARISH)

Anne Terry dau of Thomas & Rosemond bapt 24 Oct 1697
John Cock son of Thomas & Katherine bapt 14 Oct 1697
Catherine Herman dau of Coll Casparus Augustin & Catherine bapt Oct 10 1697
Rynerius Vangazely son of Jacob & Gertruly bapt 10 Dec 1697
Richard Barker son of Richard & Rebecca bapt 10 Dec 1697
Isaac Peninton son of Thomas & Alice bapt 16 Jan 1607
Robert Mercer son of Thomas & Elizabeth bapt 5 Dec 1697
Elizabeth Severson dau of Thomas & Catherine bapt 5 Feb 1697 by Mr. R. Sewell Leonard Stoops son of Jno. & Mary bapt 10 Apr 1698
Mary Crouch dau of Thomas & Mary bapt 10 Apr 1698
Catherine Yorkson dau of York & Mary bapt 3 Feb 1697
Mary Fossett dau. of Jno. & Ann bapt 27 May 1701
    about 13 yrs old by Ric. Sewell
Thomas Sewell son of Rich & Jane was bapt 4 Jun 1701 by Rev. Mr. Stephen Bordly minister of Kent Co
Thomas Henrickson son of Christopher & Mary bapt 25 Mar 1701
Nathaniell Hynson son of John & Mary bapt 169 6 by Rev. Mr. Stephen Bordley
Thomas Hynson son of John & Mary bapt 1 Jul 1701
Ann Clifton dau of Thomas & Tabitha bapt 18 Aug 1702
Matthew Matthiason son of Matthias & Mary bapt 20 Aug 1699
Mary Murrain dau of Daniell & Susanna bapt 4 Jun 1722
Jean Robinson dau of Michaell & Margaret b 26 Jan 1732/4
Jacob Archer son of Jacob & Mary b 20 Oct 1689
Catherine Yorkson dau of York & Mary b 18 Nov 169-
Jno. Beadle son of John & Mary b 11 Oct 1695
Thomas Beadle son of Jno. & Mary b 2 Jul 1696
Jaine Beadle dau of Jno. & Mary b 20 Apr 1698
Robert Thompson son of John & Judith b 20 Nov 1699 (Dec 4 1699)
Thomas Sewell son of Richard & Jane b 28 Mar 1700
Thomas Hynson son of John & Mary b Aug 7 1700
Richard Sewell son of Rich. & Jane b 19 Jun 1702
Mary Sewell dau of Rich. & Jane b 15 Apr 1703
Ann Clifton dau of Thos. & Tabitha b 25 Feb 1702
Mary Matthiason dau of Matthias & Mary b 2 Apr 1690
Jacob VanBebber son of Isaac & Fronika b 26 Oct 1692
Hester VanBebber dau of same b 9 May 1693
Peter VanBebber son of same b 25 May 1695
Christian VanBebber dau of same b 15 Aug 1698
Isaac Van Bebber son of same b 5 July 1701
Matthew son of Matthias & Mary b 20 Jul 1699
John Scott son of Walter & Esther b 12 Jun 1695
Eleanor Scott dau of same b 6 Apr 1697
Walter Scott son of same b 15 Dec 1698
George Scott son of same b 24 Oct 1703
Thomas Hynson son of Jno. & Mary b 10 Oct 1702
Rachell dau of same b 17 Apr 1704
Anne Hynson dau. of same b 26 Nov 1705
Wm. Stanley son of Jno. & Jane b 14 Apr 1702
Katherine Stanley dau of same b 28 Jan 1703
David Moll son of Jno. & Elizabeth b 27 Jul 1693
Christian Moll dau of same b 2 Sep 1695
Elizabeth Moll dau of same b 5 Jan 1697

Wm. Davis son of Wm. & Angell b 17 Jan 1690
Fouch David son of same 27 Aug 1693
Thomas Davis son of same b 4 May 1698
Joanna Davis dau of same b 28 Jan 1706
--- Hynson dau of Jno. & Mary b 30 Jan 1706
William ----illegitimate son of Mary Alcock b Apr 14 1707
Christopher Hendrickson son of Christopher & Mary b 23 Mar 1706
Thomasin Crawford dau of Quinton & Dorothy b 21 Feb 1705
Henry Peninton son of Robert & Anne b 8 Jan 1694
Robert Penington son of same b 21 Feb 1700
Anne Penington dau of same b 11 Jul 1704
Rachel Penington dau of same b 31 Jul 1707
Robert Porter son of James & Juniber b 12 Oct 1798
Atkey Copping son of Jno. & Angelica b 10 Aug 1704
Jno. Copping son of same b 2 Mar 1707
Benj. Child son of George & Elizabeth b 16 Oct 1709
Matthias Clementson son of Mathias & Eleanor b 4 Jan 1704
Andrew Clementson son of same b 15 Jul 1707
Mary Smart dau of Jno. & Sarah b 6 Feb 1704
Sarah Smart dau of same b 2 Mar 1705
William Smart son of same b 12 Mar 1708
Matthias Simmonds son of John & Mary b 26 Aug 1708
John Simmonds son of same b 22 Aug 1710
John Owen son of Thos. & Jane b 11 Apr 1709
Thomas Owen son of same b 24 Mar 1710
Francis Child son of Nathaniel & Eleanor b 7 Oct 1710
Wm. Watts son of Thomas & Elizabeth b 10 May 1698
Jacob Watts son of same b 10 Oct 1701
Mary Watts dau of same b 25 Oct 1703
Peter Watts son of same b 15 Apr 1707
Elizabeth Watts dau of same b 3 Nov 1709
Thos Etherington son to Thos. & Elizabeth b 8 Jan 1707
Bartholomew Etherington son of same b 22 Nov 1708
Katherine Cox dau of Thos. & Katherine b 21 Aug 1701
Bridgett Cox dau of same b 2 Jul 1706
Thos. Cox son of same b 13 Feb 1707
Elizabeth Cox dau of same b 19 Oct 1711
Benjamin Marley son of Robt. & Anne b sometime in Aug 1700
John Leak son of John & Jane b 4 Dec 1710
Jacob VanBebber son of Matthias & Haramantia b 2 Feb 1706
Elizabeth VanBebber dau of same b 18 Dec 1708
Christian VanBebber dau of same b 18 Sep 1711
Elizabeth Veazey dau of John Junr. & Mary b 28 May 1727 (error?)
Mary dau of same b 27 May 1731
Hartly Sapenton son of Nathaniel & Mary b 13 Oct 1717
James Sapenton son of same b 24 Aug 1719
William Sapenton son of same b 1 Jul 1721
John Sapenton son of same b 14 Jul 1723
Thomas Sapenton son of same b 29 Oct 1724
Ja Bohaning son of Margaret Bohaning b 1 Jan 1724
Mary Etherington dau of Thos. & Ann b 10 Jan 1733/4
James Campbell son of John & Elizabeth b 5 Nov 1725
James Porter son of Robert & Elizabeth b 6 Nov 1719
Elizabeth Porter dau of same b 6 Apr 1723

ST. STEPHENS' PARISH (NORTH SASSAFRAS PARISH)

Mary Porter dau of same b 23 Oct 1725
Ann Porter dau of same b 25 Mar 1728
Robert Porter son of same b 16 Jun 1730
Sarah Porter dau of same b 16 Jan 1732/3
John Reynolds son of Thomas & Margaret b 14 Apr 1721
Richard Reynolds son of same b 10 Aug 1724
Francis Reynolds son of same b 16 Sep 1726
Rebecca Reynolds dau of same b 21 Feb 1728/9
Thomas Reynolds son of same b 6 Mar 1731/32
Daniel Huckel son of Henry & Eleanor b 30 Oct 1730
James McCay son of Henry & Rebecca b 3 Nov 1726
Sarah McCay dau of same b 25 May 1728
Ann McCay dau of same b 9 Apr 1730
John McCay son of same b 28 Jan 1732/3
William Savin son of Thomas & Elizabeth b 13 Jun 1727
Ann dau of same b 3 Feb 1728/9
Thomas Savin son of same b 3 May 1731
Anne Hack dau of John & Elizabeth b 25 Dec 1720
James Numbers son of Peter & Anne b 3 Feb 1722
Rebecca Watts dau of Thos. & Mary b 24 Mar 1722
Elizabeth Beston dau of Wm. & Sarah b 20 Mar 1719
Susana dau of same b 9 Mar 1722
John Veazey son of Robert & Lucey b 1 Jan 1722
James Murraine son of Daniell & Susana b 5 Jun 1723
Hanah Husband dau of William & Marey b 27 Mar 1721
Elizabeth Veazey dau of James & Mary b 8 Oct 1723
Mary Hynman dau of Garrat & Rachel b 13 May 1719
Hannah Hynman dau of same b 13 May 1721
Anne Ridge dau of Wm. & Curnelia b 4 Feb 1719
Benjamin & James Ridge twin sons of Wm & Curnelia b 9 Jul 1722
Kathrin Cox dau of John & Rose b 1 Nov 1724
John Godmont son of Miles & Mary b 6 Apr 1724
Thomas Green son of Timothy & Elizabeth b 8 Mar 1723
Hanah Latham dau of Joshua & Mary b 15 Jul 1724
Kathrin Walmsley dau of Thomas & Kathrin b 4 May 1722
Elizabeth Child dau of George & Elizabeth b 13 Aug 1723
Mary Kimber dau of John & Rebeca b 1 Oct 1724
John Collins son of John & Julion b 13 Nov 1722
Mary Rippin dau of Henry & Augustine b 12 Aug 1724
Herman Husband son of William & Mary b 3 Oct 1724
Katrin Husband dau of Thos. & Sarah b 1 Sep 1723
John Ryland son of John Junr. & Rebecca b 22 Oct 1724
Lucy Veazey dau of Robert & Lucy b 19 Feb 1724
James Veazey son of James & Mary b 17 Aug 1725
John Husband son of James & Alice b 29 1722
James Taylor son of Richard & Anne b 26 Jan 1717
Richard Taylor son of same b 1 Apr 1722
Samuel Taylor son of same b 16 May 1725
Esther Taylor dau of same b 21 Sep 1727
Elizabeth Taylor dau of James & Elizabeth b 10 Oct 1728
James Price son of Richard & Sarah b 31 Mar 1727
Nicholas Price son of Andrew & Elizabeth b 7 Jan 1725
Perrey Price son of same b 20 Jan 1727
Mary Vandergrift dau of Nicholas & Susana b 25 Jun 1728
Garrat Othoson son of Garrat & Sarah b 17 Mar 1717
Mary Othoson dau of same b 29 Jan 1720

```
Otho Othoson son of same b 20 Apr 1723
John Stoop son of Phillip & Mary b 1 Nov 1722
Margaret Stoop dau of same b 13 Mar 1723
Mary Stoop dau of same b 25 Dec 1724
Phillip Stoop son of same b 4 Apr 1728
Benj. Penington son of John & Sarah b 2 Mar 1728/9
William Caulk son of Jacob & Mary b 11 Feb 1723
Jacob Caulk son of same b 7 Mar 1726
Rogar Barrat son of Phillip & Jane b 6 Mar 1728
Benj. Price son of Wm. & Sarah b 22 Nov 1723
David Price son of Wm. & Sarah b 27 --- 1725
Augustin Price son of same b 26 Oct 1727
James Penington son of Wm. & Mary b 2 Oct 1723
Anne Penington dau of same b 25 apr 1726
Benedict Penington son of same b 13 Sep 1728
Thomas Penington son of Henry & Elizabeth b 28 Oct 1714
Margaret Penington dau of same b 7 May 1718
Wm. Hollet son of John & Elizabeth b 23 Dec 1728
James Thompson son of Robert & Ruth b 28 May 1728
Elizabeth Parsly dau of Richard & Elizabeth b 12 --- 1721
Augustine Parsly son of same b 7 Sep 1725
Augustine Bedle son of John & Mary b 4 Jun 1729
Sarah Mathiason dau of Mathias & Mary b 19 Jul 1728
Peter Jonson son of Garrat & Hester b 12 Oct 1715
Charles Jonson son of same b 16 Jan 1718
Jacob Jonson son of same b 14 Feb 1718
Mary Jonson dau of same b 3 Dec 1723
Rebecca Rully dau of Michael & Anne b 5 Aug 1729
John Benson son of Daniell & Mary b 19 Aug 1724
Mary Benson dau of same b 14 Sep 1726
Daniell Benson son of same b 5 Sep 1728
Benjm. Whittan son of Wm. & Elizabeth b 6 Jan 1729
John Scott son of John & Mary b 15 Feb 1728
Thomas Money son of Robert & Margaret b 26 Jan 1725
Nicholas Money son of same b 14 June 1727
Anne Money dau of same b 22 May 1722
Robert Holton son of George & Mary b 6 Jun 1727
George Holton son of same b 27 Dec 1729
Rebecca Coxell & John Coxell son & dau of John & Sarah b 23 Jan
    1727
Mary Severson dau of John & Sarah b 4 Jun 1725
John Severson son of same b 20 Jan 1727
Simon Severson son of same b 20 Jun 1729
Andrew Price son of Andrew & Elizabeth b 20 Jan 1729
Mary Price dau of Wm. Junr. & Anne b 7 Oct 1728
John Roberts son of Robert & Sarah b 31 Jan 1730
Mary Ward dau of Thomas & Mary b 30 Mar 1731
Susana Ward dau of John & Susana b 14 Oct 1721
Sarah Ward dau of same b 10 Dec 1723
Rachel Ward dau of same b 24 Mar 1725
William Ward son of same b 19 Mar 1727
John Ward son of same b 31 Mar 1730
Susana Watts 3rd dau of Jacob & Mary b 4 Nov 1727
Mary Watts dau of same b 10 May 1729
John Watts son of Wm. & Anne b 26 Sep 1729
```

ST. STEPHENS' PARISH (NORTH SASSAFRAS PARISH)

Elizabeth Latamus dau of James & Anne b 17 Mar 1728
James Latamus son of same b 27 Jul 1730
Mary Rully dau of Michael & Anne b 6 Apr 1732
John Mathiason son of --- Mathiasson & wife b 3 Dec 1731
Christain Prisley dau of Andrew & Anne b 6 Jun 1725
John Volintine Prisley son of same b 3 Jan 1726
Sarah Prisley son of same b 27 Aug 1730
Vinefrite Whitor dau of --- Whiter & Sarah b 1 Jan 1728
John Whiter son of same b 16 --- 17-- William Sweley son of Thomas
    & Milison b 22 Feb 1727
Thomas Bedle son of John Junr. & Mary b 9 Feb. 1735
Thomas Wroth son of James & Anne b 23 Dec 1724
James Wroth son of same b 2 Oct 1727
Mary Wroth dau of same b 15 Mar 1730
Thomas Hamm son of John Junr. & Mary b 26 May 1729
Mary Hamm dau of same b 2 Jan 1731
Rachell Burnham dau of Thos. & Mary b 16 Dec 1730
Susana Foster dau of Wm. & Mary b 25 Aug 1725
Richard Foster son of same b 13 Feb 1727
Anne Foster dau of same b 4 Apr 1728
Mary Cox dau of John & Rosemond b 25 Dec 1731
Cathrine Vanburkeloo dau of Abell & Cathrine b 22 Mar 1717
Margaret Vanburkeloo dau of same b 8 Oct 1719
Herman Vanburkeloo son of same b 28 Jul 1721
Ephraim Vanburkeloo son of same b 25 Aug 1725
William Vanburkeloo son of same b 18 Aug 1728
Mary Sluyter dau of Benj. & Elizabeth b 20 Sep 1723
Henry Sluyter son of same b 11 Jan 1726
John Sluyter son of same b 6 Aug 1728
Rebecca Sluyter dau of same b 17 May 1730
Peter Sluyter son of same b 16 Jul 1731
Benjamin Sluyter son of same b 2 Jan 1734/5
Peter Bouchelle son of Peter & Mary b 28 Mar 1717
Sluyter Bouchelle son of same b 1 Dec 1719
Rachell Bouchelle dau of same b 26 Sep 1725
Mary Bouchelle dau of same b 27 Aug 1727
Benjamin Bouchelle son of same b 31 Apr 1731
Joseph Holt son of ---- & Jane b 5 Dec 1729
Obadiah Holt son of same b 30 Sep 1731
James Taylor son of James & Elizabeth b 6 Mar 1730
Elizabeth Sluyter dau of Benjm. & Mary b 13 Aug 1732
Elizabeth Holten dau of George & Mary b 15 Feb 1731
Richard Boulding son of Richard & Mary b 10 Aug 1720
Thomasin Boulding dau of same b 7 May 1724
Margaret Boulding dau of same b 15 Oct 1726
Thomas Boulding son of same b 1 Apr 1728
John Boulding son of same b 3 Apr 17--
William Ward son of William & Anne b 11 Mar 1718/9
Henry Ward son of same b 3 Dec 1720
John Ward son of same b 31 Jan 1722/3
Joseph Ward son of same b 5 Mar 1725/6
George Ward son of same b 22 Aug 1729
Jane Rippon dau of Henry & Mary b 30 May 1729
William Rippon son of same b 18 Oct 1730
Wm. Foster son of Wm. & Mary b 25 Jan 1731

Wm. Kirtly son of Wm. & Elizabeth b 20 Jul 1732
Nathaniel Ward son of John & Susanna b 25 Mar 1733
Charles Rumsey son of Edward & Margaret b 7 Apr 1728
Edward Rumsey son of same b 26 Oct 1730
Susanah Rumsey dau of same b 13 Apr 1733
Mary Crow dau of Wm. & Mary b 9 Jul 1727
Sarah Crow dau of same b 31 Aug 1729
Rebecka Crow dau of same b 7 Jan 1732
Mary Ham dau of Ephraim & Elizabeth b 9 Apr 1724
Elinor Ham dau of same b 13 Sep 1726
John Ham son of same b 21 Sep 1729
Ephraim Ham son of same b 12 Aug 1732
Rachel Boulding dau of Richard & Mary b 7 Oct 1732
Wm. Terry son of Hugh & Sarah b 29 Nov 1728
Ruth Terry dau of same b 23 Dec 1730
Alisha Terry son of same b 5 Feb 1732/3
John Terry son of Augustine & Elizabeth b 15 Feb 1729/30
Martha Wright dau of John & Sarah b 15 Aug 1732
Joseph Zillafrow son of Andrew & Sarah b 24 Dec 1730
Cathrine Smith dau of Charles & Mary b 2 Jul 1732
Mary Pearce dau of Benjamin & Mary b 18 Feb 1710
Benjamin Pearce son of same b 28 Jun 1711/12
William Pearce son of same b 12 Jan 1718/19
Sarah Pearce dau of same b 1 Dec 1720
Rachel Pearce dau of same b 18 Jan 1722
Andrew Pearce son of same b 15 Feb 1723/4
Daniel Pearce son of same b 25 Jan 1728/9
Mary Cooper dau of Edward & Mary b 16 Mar 1715/16
Joseph Hold son of Obadiah & Jane b 5 Dec 1729
Obadiah Hold son of same b 30 Sep 1731
Elin Vansant dau of Garriet & Susanah b 7 Oct 1721
Cornelius Vansant son of same b 27 Apr 1723
Burenthia Vansant dau of same b 27 May 1725
George Vansant son of same b 3 Mar 1727
Rachel Vansant dau of same b 15 Feb 1729
Benj. Vansant son of same b 23 Mar 1732
Abraham Alman son of Benjamin b 22 Feb 1724/5
Mary Pennington dau of Robert Junr. & Rachel b 7 Sep 1728
Rebecka Pennington dau of same b 19 Dec 1732
Mary Alman dau of Abraham & Margaret b 30 Mar 1723
Rachel Alman dau of same b 2 Feb 1724/5
Amy Alman dau of same b 29 Jan 1726/7
Margaret Alman dau of same b 23 Apr 1728
Abraham Alman son of same b 1 Jan 1730/1
Sarah Alman dau of same b 12 Jun 1733
Thomas Mercer son of Robert & Ann b 5 Feb 1727/8
Sarah Mercer dau of same b 1 Oct 1729
Elizabeth Mercer dau of same b 28 Sep 1732
Peter Harper son of Nicholas & Susanah b 27 Jan 1728
Rebecka Dorrell dau of Nicholas & Elizabeth b 14 Jan 1720
Elizabeth Dorrell dau of same b 14 Feb 1722
Rachel Dorrell dau of same b 24 Apr 1725
Nicholas Dorrell son of same b 2 Oct 1727
Mary Dorrell dau of same b 30 Aug 1730
Sarah Dorrell dau of same b 14 Sep 1732

ST. STEPHENS' PARISH (NORTH SASSAFRAS PARISH)

Jane Lattomus dau of James & Diana b 3 May 1733
Denis Nowland & Daniel sons of Denis & Elizabeth b 24 Jan 1715
Stephen & Rachel Nowland son & dau of Denis & Elizabeth b 7 Jun 1719
James Nowland son of same b 11 Jul 1721
Ann Nowland dau of same b 5 Oct 1725
Henry Miller son of John & Dorrity b 14 Aug 1718
Chilion Miller son of same b 8 Jan 1720
John Miller son of same b 8 Mar 1723
Conrodde Miller son of same b 2 Jun 1725
Adam Miller son of same b 7 Mar 1728
Susanah Miller dau of same b 27 Jun 1730
Peter Miller son of same b 7 Feb 1732/3
Samuel Hendrickson son of Peter & Catherine b 29 Jun 1729
Samuel Hendrickson son of same b 5 Mar 1730
Susanah Hendrickson dau of same b 5 Feb 1732
Elizabeth VanDyke dau of Wm. & Agnuss b 2 Sep 1730
Elizabeth Morgan dau of John & Dority b 28 May 1729
John Morgan son of same b 13 Jun 1731
William Gerrish son of Wm. b 25 Dec 1711
Elizabeth Mercer dau of Thomas Junr. & Jane b 29 Oct 1733
Augustine Bavington dau of John & Mary b 16 Nov 1720
Mary Bavington dau of same b 17 Sep 1722
Rachel Bavington dau of same b 28 Mar 1724
John Bavington son of same b 10 May 1727
William Bavington son of same b 11 Sep 1729
Elizabeth Bavington dau of same b 8 Apr 1731
Martha Stoops dau of Phillip & Margaret b 25 Jun 1732
Abraham Cazier son of Phillip & Catherine b 25 Feb 1732/3
Mary Rodick dau of Robert & Catherine b 19 Apr 1732
Thomas Ogrisey son of Neal & Jane b 4 Jan 1729
Jacob Everdson son of Everd & Elizabeth b 26 Oct 1732
Jeremiah Wattson son of John & Margaret b 31 Jan 1718/9
Mary Smith dau of Wm. & Catherine b 27 Mar 1732
Peter Wattson son of John & Catherine b 30 Jan 1731
Sarah Smith dau of John b 26 Aug 1727
Mary Vanhorne dau of Nicholas & Rebecca b 22 Mar 1725
Nicholas Vanhorne son of same b 5 Apr 1728
Leticia Vanhorne dau of same b 29 Jan 1730
Jacob Vanhorne son of same b 23 May 1732
Charles Cox son of Albord & Ann b 17 Feb 1729
Mary Cox dau of same b 28 Aug 1732
Thomas Reyland son of Thomas & Mary b 27 Sep 1726
John Reyland son of same b 4 Jan 1728/9
Fredus Reyland son of same b 22 Oct 1730
Stephen Reyland son of same b 22 Feb 1732/3
William Merrit son of Thomas & Martha b 6 Sep 1728
Benjamin Merrit son of same b 10 Nov 1731
John Brackenbury son of John & Catherine b 14 Nov 1732
Henry Burnam son of Thomas & Mary b 27 Nov 1732
Sarah Rice dau of David & Elizabeth b 11 Jan 1731/2
Mary Boushel dau of Peter Boushell & Mary b 22 Jun 1733
Abraham Nidey son of Michel & -- b 1 Oct 1719
Dorithy Nidey dau of same b 24 May 1719
Joseph Nidey son of Michel & Ann b 15 Jul 1724

Daniel Nidey son of same b 3 Jan 1727
Catherine Nidey dau of same b 14 Feb 1731
Mary Nidey dau of same b 6 Jan 1729
Susanah Nidey dau of same b 20 Feb 1733
Isaiah Bird son of Thomas & Isabella b 14 May 1725
John Bird son of same b 1 Aug 1727
Thomas Bird son of Thomas & Isabella b 14 May 1725
William Bird son of same b 19 Jun 1732
Susanah Wright dau of John & Hannah b 15 Oct 1709
Margaret Wright dau of same b -- --- 1711
Elizabeth Wright dau of same b -- --- 1713
John Wright son of same b 30 Jun 1716
George Wright son of same b 20 Jan 1718
Mary Wright dau of same b 30 Sep 1722
Ann Wright dau of same b -- --- 1724
Mary Hynes dau of Jonathan & Sarah b 17 Feb 1732
Catherine Everdson dau of Everd & Elionor b 19 Jul 1714
Peter Numbers son of James & Elizabeth b 19 May 1727
James Numbers son of same b 11 Nov 1728
John Numbers son of same b 10 Nov 1730
Joseph Pennington son of Henry & Mary b 4 Oct 1718
Henry Pennington son of same b 6 Dec 1727
Ann Pennington dau of same b 26 Mar 1729
Thomas Bentham son of Richard & Elizabeth b 5 Sep 1730
John Bentham son of same b 24 Nov 1731
Henry Bentham son of same b 19 Jan 1732
Mary Fellows dau of Mathias & Honor b 28 Aug 1726
Rachel Fellows dau of same b 3 Nov 1730
James Fellows son of same b 8 Mar 1732
Sarah Rumsey dau of Charles & Margaret b 8 Oct 1721
William Rumsey son of same b 17 Sep 1724
John Carnan son of John & Margaret b 25 Jun 1728
John Carnan son of same b 21 Aug 1729
William Taylor son of Richard & --- b 1 Jan 1732/3
Lidey Wethers dau of Robert & Mary b 20 Aug 1730
Jane Beaston dau of Thomas & Brigitt b 26 Jun 1724
Thomas Beaston son of same b 17 Aug 1726
George Beaston son of same b 4 Jan 1728/9
Catherine Beaston dau of same b 3 Mar 1731
Elizabeth Taylor dau of James & Elizabeth b 4 Mar 1722/3
Rose Beean(?) dau of Thomas Beean & Ann b 5 Aug 1727
William Beean son of same b 16 Dec 1729
Christian Beean dau of same b 15 Jan 1731
Hannah Cole dau of John & Margaret b 6 Mar 1729/30
Mary Cole dau of same b 10 Jan 1731/2
Maccary Aron son of Francis & Elizabeth b 25 Nov 1726
Phillip Barrat son of Phillip & Jane b 12 Oct 1730
Isabella Wems dau of Thomas & Eleaner b 7 Dec 1729
John Wems son of same b 6 Nov 1731
Andrew Prosler son of Andrew & Ann, grandson of John Vollintine
    Prosler b 4 Feb 1732/3
Charles Rumsey son of William & Sabina b 22 Apr 1729
William Rumsey son of same b 21 Mar 1729/30
Margaret Rumsey dau of same b 28 Apr 1732
Mary Frisby dau of William & Mary b 10 Feb 1723

ST. STEPHENS' PARISH (NORTH SASSAFRAS PARISH)

Sarah Hendrickson dau of --- Hendrickson b 14 Sep 1724
Matthias Hendrickson son of same b 25 Mar 1726
Elizabeth Hendrickson dau of same b 27 Apr 1721
See page 75 for Elizabeth Hendrickson age
Mary Carroll dau of Dominick & Mary b 15 Apr 1727
Julian Carroll dau of same b 3 Jan 1729
Eleanor Carroll dau of same b 23 Mar 1730
Susannah Carroll dau of same b 20 Jun 1733
Mary Kimber dau of John & Mary b 12 Sep 1732
Rachel Rosser dau of John & Jane b - --- 1720
John Rosser son of same b 15 Feb 1721
Catherine Welding dau of Charles & Sarah b 19 Nov 1726
Charles Welding son of same b 26 Aug 1728
John Welding son of same b 24 May 1732
Samuel Pennington son of John & Sarah b 21 Sep 1733
William Smith son of Charles & Mary b 8 Jul 1730
Romaldus Douglas son of Wm. & Mary b 28 Feb 1720
Mary Douglas dau of same b 1 Feb 1723
Clear Douglas dau of same b 21 Mar 1724
Catherine Douglas dau of same b 17 Dec 1726
James Douglas son of same b 20 Feb 1729
John Douglas son of same b 5 Jul 1732
Peregrine Ffrisby son of Peregrine & Elizabeth b 15 Mar 1713/4
Nicholas Ffrisby son of same b -- ----- Susannah Ffrisby dau of same b 9 Jun 1719
James Ffrisby son of same b -- ---- James Ffrisby son of same b 30 Aug 1722
Clear & Ann Ffrisby daus of same b 5 Sep 1727
Elizabeth Ffrisby dau of same b 25 Feb 1729/30
Ann Jackson dau of John & Jane b 1 Jan 1730
William Jackson son of same b 14 Feb 1732
Ephraim Beaston son of Thomas & Bridgett b 5 Sep 1733
Stephen Sayer son of Stephen & Ann b 25 Sep 1730
Daniel Gears son of Daniel & Elizabeth b 30 Jul 1722
Rebecca Gears dau of same b 13 Dec 1725
Sarah Gears dau of same b 16 Oct 1727
Elizabeth Gears dau of same b 19 Jul 1733
Penellapey Martain dau of Nehemiah Martin and Syna b -- Mar 1725
Catherine VanBebber dau of James & Anna b 17 Apr 1721
Anna VanBebber dau of same b 2 Jan 1722/3 Henry VanBebber son of same b -- Nov 1725
Haybartus VanBebber son of same b 22 Jul 1729
Jacob VanBebber son of same b 1 Jul 1731
Abraham Nicholason son of Martin & --- b 29 Apr 1720
Ann Nicholason dau of same b 23 Aug 1724
Peter Nicholason son of same b 30 Jul 1727
Mary Scott dau of John & Mary b 25 Nov 1733
William Bateman son of John & Ann b 13 Jul 1731
Matthias VanBebber son of Matts. & Arriamam b 30 Sep 1729
Henry VanBebber son of same b 13 Jan 1730/1
Jean Robinson dau of Michall & Margt. b 12 Jan 1733/4
Rebecah Abbott dau of William Abbett & Mary b 27 Mar 1732
John Spauldin son of John & Sarah b 7 Mar 1731/2
John Hynson son of Nathll. & Mary 10 Sep 1717
Nathll. Hynson son of same 3 Feb 1719

Thomas Hynson son of same b 20 Aug 1721
Mary Hynson son of same b 15 Jul 1723
Charles Hynson son of same b 15 Mar 1724
Hannah Hynson dau of same b 30 Dec 1727
Rachel Hynson dau of same b 10 Dec 1729
William Hynson son of same b 30 May 1731
Cornelias Wolestain son of Rd. & Cath. b 18 May 1713
Martha Wolestain dau of same b -- --- 1715
Rd. Wolestain son of same b -- Aug 1717
Catherine Wolestain dau of same b -- --- 1722
Ann Wolestain dau of same b 2 May 1728
William Cook son of Corenlias & Ann b 27 Sep 1730
Bartholomew Cook son of same b 28 Oct 1732
Grace Jacobs dau of Barthw. & Mary b 8 Dec 1730
Mart Ffoster dau of James & Hester b 14 Mar 1733/4
Isabella Ffoster dau of same b 6 Jun 1732
John Polson son of Peter & Margaret b 22 Oct 1731
James Mackdowell son of Willm. & Ruth b 4 Jan 1725/6
Jacob Mackdowell son of same b 5 Nov 1727
John Mackdowell son of same b 27 Mar 1730
William Mackdowell son of same b 3 Feb 1731
John Cox son of Jno. & Rosaman b 7 Dec 1733
John Reynolds son of Edward & Mary b 21 Feb 1724
Mary Reynolds dau of same b 10 Mar 1727
Rachel Reynolds dau of same b 29 Oct 1730
Lucretia Reynolds dau of same b 11 Mar 1732/3
Stephen Beedle son of John Junr. & Mary b 1 Mar 1733/4
Esther Scott dau of Walter Junr. & Catherine b 4 May 1734
Mary Scott dau of Charles & Elizabeth b 16 Sep 1733
Mary Holton dau of George & Mary b 18 May 1734
Jacob VanDegriff son of Nicholas & Susanah b 15 Oct 1730
Rebecca VanDegriff dau of same b 31 Oct 1732
Rachel Simmons dau of William & Elizabeth b 9 Apr 1734
Thomas Nowland son of Daniel & Mary b -- Feb 1723/4
Hannah Nowland dau of same b 23 Apr 1727
Benjamin Nowland son of same b 1 May 1731
Barrentdolley Cauls son of Ann Cauls b 3 Jun 1724
John Hart son of John & Ann b 20 Aug 1733
Mary Clements dau of Cornelias & Ann b 22 Jan 1732/3
Mary Zillephro dau of Andrew & Sarah b 19 Feb 1733/4
Sarah Stoops dau of Phillip & Margaret b 2 May 1734
Abraham VanDike son of Wm. & Agness b 14 Apr 1734
Elizabeth Morgan dau of Edward & Eleoner b 11 Feb 1734
Ann Severson dau of John & Sarah b -- ----
Patience Severson dau of same b -- ----
John Matthews son of Patrick & Mary b 11 Feb 1734/5
Benjamin Rumsey son of William & Sabina b 6 Oct 1734
Evan James son of Isaac & ---- b 1 Sep 1726
Persella James dau of same b 23 Sep 1729
Margarett Ross dau of Allen & ---- b 5 Sep 1732
Andrew Clements son of Gabril & Sarah b 4 Jan 1718
Joseph Clements son of same b 12 Apr 1722
Isaac Clements son of same b 9 May 1730
Cornelius Clements son of same b 16 Apr 1732
Sarah Clements dau of same b 18 Jan 1720

ST. STEPHENS' PARISH (NORTH SASSAFRAS PARISH)

Samuel Bayard son of Samuel & Fransinah b 30 May 1730
Peter Bayard son of same b 16 Jun 1732
John Bayard son of same b 29 May 1734
James Holton son of Jessey & Sarah b 30 May 1735
Grace Whittam dau of William & Elizabeth b 2 Mar 1734/5
John Hamm son of John Junr. & Mary b 4 Jun 1734
Mary Davis dau of Thomas & Rebecka b 17 Feb 1735/6
Elizabeth Pearce dau of Benjamin & Margarett b 29 Sep 1735 and baptized 30 Sep 1735 by Th. Jones
Thomas Ward son of Thomas & Mary b 25 May 1734
William Lynch son of Anthony & ELizabeth b 25 Apr 1730
George Lynch son of same b 25 Feb 1732/3
James Lynch son of same b 25 Dec 1735
James Hynes son of Jonathan & Sarah b 22 Nov 1734
Robert Money son of Robert Junr. & Ruth b 8 Jul 1736
Henry Ward Pearce son of Benjamin & Margaretta b 6 Dec 1736
Andrew Croker son of Robert & Rachael b 23 Apr 1736
Sarah Manrean dau of Thomas & Mary b 28 Oct 1735
Catherine Latamus dau of James & Diana b 30 Mar 1736
Susannah Taylor dau of Richard & ---- b 15 Oct 1735
Anthony Ruley son of Michael & Ann b 1 Oct 1735
Richard Price son of Andrew & Elizabeth b 30 Sep 1735
Benjamin Childs son of Benjamin & Martha b 16 Feb 1735
George Childs son of same b 1 Oct 1736
Rebecka Davis dau of Thomas & Rebecka b 17 Dec 1737
Robert Mercer son of Robert & Ann b 22 Dec 1737
Rebecka Penington dau of John Junr. & Ailse b 29 Aug 1736
Thomas Penington son of John Senr. & Sarah b 28 Nov 1736
Margaratt Fillengam dau of John & Margarett b 1 Dec 17--
Rebecka Ham dau of John & Mary b 17 Nov 1736
Elizabeth Price dau of William Junr. & Ann b 13 Feb 1736
Elizabeth Tilton dau of John & ELizabeth b 12 Nov 1736
Benjamin Alman son of Abraham & Margarett b 23 Jan 1736/7
James Hughes son of James & Ailes b 26 May 1735
Rebecca Hughes dau of same b 29 Nov 1736
Kinven Wroth son of Kinven & Sarah b 1 Sep 1730
Benjamin Wroth son of same b 14 Sep 1733
James Wroth son of same b 31 Oct 1736
Mary Lusby dau of John & Margaret b 9 Jun 1736
Samuel Thompson son of John & Mary b 5 Jun 1735
Charles Rumsey fourth son of William & Sabina b Saturday 26 Feb 1736
Jane Zillephro dau of Andrew & Sarah b 26 Dec 1736
Sarah Morgan dau of John & Dority b 7 Jan 1735/6
Ailes Lynch dau of Anthony & Elizabeth b 5 Jan 1737/8
John Wintabury son of John & Mary b 28 Apr 1735
George Wintabury son of same b 27 Sep 1738
Elizabeth Wintabury dau of same b 28 May 1727
William Wintabury son of same b 22 May 1729
Mary Wintabury dau of same b 27 May 1731
Jessey Holton son of Jessey & Sarah b 2 Jul 1738
William Scott son of Charles & Elizabeth b 19 Jun 1737
Jehue Parsons son of William & Garterett b 30 Jan 1736/7
William Parsons son of same b 15 Sep 1737
James Robb son of James & Jane b 10 Dec 1737

Mary Lassells dau of Joseph & Ailes b 10 Aug 1738
William Stoops son of Phillip & Margt. b 2 May 1736
Isabella Stoops dau of same b 20 Jul 1738
Jane Willson dau of William & Jane b 7 Oct 1737
Jacob Ham son of Abraham & Easter b 16 Nov 1737
Catherine Woolestine dau of Cornelias & Martha b 22 Apr 1736
Sarah Scott dau of Walter Junr. & Catherine b 5 Mar 1735/6
Ann Cook dau of Cornelias & Ann b 9 Apr 1736
Richard Meakins son of Joshua & Elizabeth b 17 Feb 1730
Sarah Meakins dau of same b 4 Sep 1733
Joshua Meakins son of same b 19 May 1736
Rebecka Cox dau of Abraham & Ann b 2 Mar 1735/6
Elioner Macmanus dau of John & Elizabeth b 19 Aug 1736
Rebecca Davis dau of Fouch & Jane b 30 Oct 1727
Elizabeth Hendrickson dau of Henry & Elizabeth b 27 Apr 1721
Rachael Severson dau of Thomas & Elizabeth b 23 Jul 1729
Zeckall Severson son of same b 16 Dec 1731
Mary Severson dau of same b 20 Feb 1733/4
Elizabeth Severson dau of same b 7 Jun 1736
Sarah Severson dau of same b 11 Mar 1737/8
William Crow son of William & Mary b 16 Feb 1739
Augustine Beedle son of John Senr. & Mary b 30 Jan 1737/8
Rachel Price dau of Andrew & Elizabeth b 29 Apr 1738
Edward Penington son of John Senr. & Sarah b 1 Apr 1739
Mary Childs dau of Nathll. & Mary b 2 Jun 1738
James Collins Cole son of Matthew & Mary b 7 Sep 1739
Eleanor Cole dau of same b 28 Jul 1741, W. Pearce, Regr.
Elizabeth Price dau of Wm. & Mary b 31 Jul 1739
Robert Wood son of Joseph & Sarah b 12 Aug 1736
Sarah Wood dau of Joseph & Sarah b 10 Jan 1738
Walter Scott son of Walter Junr. & Catherine b 27 Apr 1740
William Bulley son of Matthew & Elizabeth b 11 May 1738
Henry Wroth son of Kinvin & Sarah b 12 Jul 1740
Thomas Davis son of Thomas & Rebecka b 16 Nov 1740
Benjamin Pearce second son of Benjamin & Margarett b 13 Apr 1739
Benjamin Ward Pearce third son of Benjamin & Margarett b 15 Sep 1740
Thomas Walmsley son of Robert & ELizabeth b 27 Mar 1737
John Walmsley son of same b 27 Feb 1739
Ann Wroth dau of James & Ann b 12 Mar (May?) 1738
Thelwell Loftis son of John & Susannah b 5 Nov 1736
John Loftis son of same b 30 Sep 1738
Susanah Loftis dau of same b 31 Jan 1740
Hans Marques Severson son of Thomas & Elizabeth b 23 Feb 1740
John Alman son of Abraham & Margarett b 18 Apr 1740
Henry Penington son of John Junr. & Margtt. b 29 Sep 1737
Hyland Penington son of same b 19 Oct 1739
John Wood son of John & Frances b 19 Sep 1738
Sarah Wood dau of same b 26 Dec 1740
Ruth Morgan dau of Edward & Eleonor b 4 Dec 1736
Sarah Webster dau of William & Ann b 10 May 1735
Rachel Ruley dau of Michael & Ann b 8 Aug 1739
Ann Hughs dau of James Hughes & Alice b 22 Jul 1739
Rachel Money dau of John & Rachel b 18 Feb 1741
Thomas Crocker son of Robert & Rachel b 4 May 1738

ST. STEPHENS' PARISH (NORTH SASSAFRAS PARISH)

William Crocker son of same b 20 Jun 1741
Andrew Steel son of Matthew & Margrett b 3 Feb 1739
Jessey Holten son of George & Mary b 19 Mar 1738
John Ashford son of Jno. & Martha b 5 Jul 1739
John Starling son of Sarah Starling (spinster) b 19 Jan 1738
Mary Murrain dau of Thomas & Mary b 22 Mar 1739
Christian Chick son of Wm. & Catherine b 17 Jan 1739
John Armstrong son of Edward & Martha b 17 Jan 1736
Benjamin Eathrington son of Thomas & Ann b 14 Feb 1735
Thomas Eathrington son of same b 18 Mar 1737
Bartholomew Eathrington son of same b 21 Apr 1740
Rebecca Cox dau of John & Rosaman b 11 Sep 1741
William Boyer Penington son of John & Mary b 26 Oct 1741
Morgain John Roberts and Deboraugh (twins) son & daughter of John
   Morgain and Dority his wife b 3 Jul 1741
Stephen Penington son of Henry Penington minor and Ann b 15 Nov
   1736
Ephraim Penington son of same b 9 Apr 1738
Simon Penington son of same b 15 May 1740
John Skurrey son of Thomas & Mary b 20 Oct 1740
Mary Penington dau of William & Ann b 1 Mar 1734
Rebecca Penington dau of same b 10 Dec 1735
Ebenezer Penington son of same b 9 Jan 1737
William Drake Penington son of same b 29 Sep 1740
Stephen Penington son of Robert Junr. & Rachel b -- --- 1734
John Chaimberlain son of John Junr. & Rachel b 10 Mar 1739
Mary Lusby dau of John & Margret b 5 Aug 1741
Elizabeth Harrison Ward dau of Perege. & Mary b 12 Mar 1738
Anna Chew Ward dau of same b 26 May 1740
Ann Frisby dau of Peregrine & Ann b 2 Mar 1740
James Steal son of Matthew & Margaret b 9 Jan 1741
Hester Zillephro dau of Andrew & Sarah b 6 Jun 1739
Sarah Hollet dau of John & Hannah b 22 Apr 1737
Rebecca and John Hollet son & dau of same b 10 Mar 1739
(twins) Mary Hutcheson dau of The Revd. Alexander Hutcheson b 3 May
   1741
William Cox son of Thomas & Sarah b 12 Jan 1741
Zebulon Hukin son of John & Mary b -- Sep 1735
Sarah Ford dau of Jno. Fford & Mary b 22 Jan 1738
Richard Fford son of same b 31 Jan 1740
Margret Forster dau of Thomas Fforster & Mary b 25 Jan 1738
Sarah Fforster dau of same b 14 Jun 1740
Mary Repose dau of Anthony & Eliza. b 20 Oct 1740
Elias Wood son of John & Rebecca b 26 Mar 1739
Mary Wood dau of same b 7 Jun 1741
Rebecca Taylor dau of James Junr. & Catherine b 8 Dec 1741
William Steward son of Thomas & Miram b 22 Sep 1736
Ann Steward dau of same b 18 Jun 1739
Hannah Steward dau of same b 23 Dec 1741
Nicholas Harris son of Patrick & Margaret born 1738
   and Joseph Harris son of same born 1741
Jacob Alman son of Abraham & Margaret b 30 May 1741
Zechariah Vansandt son of Garriot & Susannah b 21 Apr 1733
Nehemiah Vansandt son of same b 20 Jun 1736
Garriot Vansandt son of same b 24 Oct 1738

Nathan Boulding son of James & Elizabeth b 22 Feb 1737
Augustina Boulding dau of same b 28 Oct 1741
Sarah Cann dau of John & Rachel b 17 Mar 1741
Rebeccah Price dau of Richard & Sarah b 31 Aug 1736
Sarah Price dau of same b 14 Feb 1739
Hyland Price son of same b 17 Nov 1741
Martha Filingam dau of John & Margret b 12 Aug 1738
John Filingam son of same b 9 Apr 1739
Richard Filingam son of same b 14 Apr 1742
Catherine Price dau of William Junr. & Mary b 21 Nov 1741
Sarah Ann Price dau of Robert & Rebeccah b 3 Oct 1740
Rebeccah Rose dau of Thomas & Jean b 31 Jan 1737
Peregrine Rose son of same b 8 Jul 1740
Elizabeth Cooper dau of John Junr. & Rebeccah b 25 Sep 1740
Johannah Chick dau of Joseph & Mary b 23 Oct 1742
William Davis son of Thomas & Rebeccah b 1 Nov 1742
John Ward son of Henry & Hannah b 23 Apr 1740
Sarah Morgan dau of Edward & Elenor b 29 Aug 1742
Andrew Harper son of Jacob & Gartrey b 30 Nov 1742
Mary Carter dau of James & Dinah b 11 Nov 1740
Mary Bouchell dau of Peter & Catherine b 25 Mar 1739
Isabella Bouchell dau of same b 22 May 1741
John Cox son of John Junr. & Susannah b 17 Aug 1741
Thomas Parsley son of Bartholomew & Judith b 21 Sep 1742
Dominick Beetle son of Richard & Augustina b 3 May 1742
William Pearce fourth son of Benjamin & Margret b 8 Apr 1742
James Severson son of John & Sarah b 14 Sep 1740
Peregrine Beetle son of John Senr. & Mary b 20 Nov 1742
Mary Thompson dau of John & Mary b 3 Jun 1742
Benjamin Walmsley son of William & Sarah b 13 Aug 1742
William Crow son of William & Mary b 16 Feb 1736
Rachel Crow dau of same b 14 Feb 1739
William Bradford son of Dr. Benjamin & Margery b 21 Nov 1739
George Bradford son of same 21 Aug 1742
Sarah Thompson dau of Richard Junr. & Mary b 16 Sep 1741
Thomas Mercer son of Thomas & Jean b 30 Oct 1739
Stephen Mercer son of same 19 Dec 1741
Isaac Penington son of Henry minr. (sic) & Ann b 19 Apr 1742
William Carnan son of John & Rachel b 18 Oct 1743
James Bohaning son of Nathaniel & Eleanor b 7 Apr 1743
Jacob Penington son of James & Elizabeth b 5 Jun 1743
Mary Bayard dau of Samuel & Francina b 10 May 1736
Joseph Bayard son of same b 8 Jan 1737
Rebeccah Bayard dau of same b 26 Sep 1739
Susannah Bayard dau of same b 24 Jun 1741
Mary Cowan dau of Thomas & Rosannah b 26 Aug 1735
Margrett Cowan dau of same b 3 Mar 1736
Elizabeth Cowan dau of same b 7 Jul 1739
John Cowan dau of same b 14 Mar 1742
Joseph Bouchell son of Sluyter & Mary b 4 Jul 1739
Susannah Bouchell dau of same b 1 May 1741
Ann Mary Bouchell dau of same b 3 Sep 1743
Daniel Hukin son of Richard & Elizabeth b 24 Mar 1724
Carnelias Hukin son of same b 19 Feb 1726
Elizabeth Hukin dau of same b 30 Jun 1728

ST. STEPHENS' PARISH (NORTH SASSAFRAS PARISH)

Susannah Hukin dau of same b 5 Sep 1730
Richard Hukin son of same b 14 Jun 1733
John Hukin son of same b 10 Aug 1735
Eleanor Hukin son of same b 31 Jan 1738
Henry Hukin son of same b 27 --- 1743
Rebeccah Rider dau of Andrew & Mary b 18 Nov 1724
Peter Rider son of same b 5 Feb 1726
Joseph Rider son of same b 4 Sep 1727
Andrew Rider son of same b 16 Jul 1731
James Rider son of same b 24 Feb 1737
Bassett McCleary son of Samuel & Magdelan b 28 Dec 1741
Rachel Moore dau of Elizabeth Moore b 11 Aug 1733
John Moore son of same b 16 Sep 1736
Samuel Hucheson son of Rev. Alexander Hucheson b 10 Dec 1743
Sarah Hughes dau of James & Alice b 30 Jan 1742
James Ryan son of Edward & Isabella b 22 Apr 1738
Elizabeth Lewis dau of George & Eliza. b 7 Dec 1742
Samuel Ricketts son of Evan & Rachel b 3 Jan 1743
Sarah Penington dau of John Senior & Mary b 29 Dec 1743
John Money son of John & Rachel b 26 Jan 1743
Rebeccah Wood dau of John & Rebeccah b 6 Mar 1743
Thomas Scurrey son of Thomas & Mary b 24 Jan 1742
Susannah Penington dau of John minor & Alice b 3 Apr 1740
Sarah Penington dau of same b 30 Dec 1742
John Ward Penington son of same b 10 Jan 1743
Edward Ward son of Peregrine & Mary b 24 Nov 1744
John Lusby son of John & Margrett b 22 Dec 1743
Margtt. Cox dau of Thomas & Sarah b 10 May 1744
John Hyland Price son of Andrew & Elizabeth b 22 Apr 1744
Mary Fillingham dau of John & Margrett b 20 Apr 1744
Mary Kimber dau of John & Catherine b 4 Dec 1743
Abraham Douglass son of Ann Douglass b 10 Jan 1742
John Chick son of Wm. & Catherine b 14 Jan 1742
Rachel Hollett dau of John & Hannah b 1 Oct 1743
Catherine Chick dau of John Junr. & Susannah b 18 Dec 1736
Christian Chick son of same b 14 Jun 1737
Mary Chick dau of same b 30 Sep 1738
Sarah Chick dau of same b 13 Feb 1740
John Chick son of same b 23 Dec 1742
William Fann son of John & ---- b 15 Feb 1743
Rachel Fann dau of same b -- Nov 1742 (error?)
Rachel Penington dau of John, who was the son of Robert Penington, and Rachel his wife, daughter of William Beadle of Cecil County, b 30 Jan 1752
Thomas Roberson son of Thomas & Frances b 30 Nov 1738
Elizabeth Roberson dau of same b 3 May 1746
Francis Loftis son of John & Susannah b 3 Oct 1749
Thomas Sewall son of John & Mary b 23 Jul 1752
John Price son of John & Mary b 19 Feb 1740
Joseph Price son of same b 12 Dec 1741
Henry Price son of same b 4 Apr 1745
Rebecca Price dau of same b 25 Mar 1754
Elizabeth Parsley dau of Barthol. & Judith b 12 Jan 1747/8
Ann Parsley dau of same b 14 Jun 1750
Rebecca Parsley dau of same b 20 Nov 1752

Sarah Ethrington dau of Bartholomew & Elizabeth b 20 Jan 1751/2
Rebecca Ricketts dau of Evan & Rachel b 23 Jun 1745
Tamar Ricketts dau of same b 9 Nov 1746
William Ricketts son of same b 19 Sep 1748
Rachel Ricketts dau of same b 25 Mar 1752/3
Samuel Filingam son of John & Margrett b 3 Sep 1750
Elizabeth Hutchinson dau of Gavin & Mary b 8 Apr 1751
John Sutton son of Josiah & Mary b 2 Sep 1716
Benjamin Pearce son of Daniel & Sarah b 15 Jul 1753
Mary Money dau of John & Rachel b 17 Jul 1748
Sarah Terry dau of Benjamin & Alifere b 27 Sep 1744
Rebecca Terry dau of same b 16 Nov 1749
Thomas Terry son of same b 12 Jan 1752
Henry Hendrickson son of Henry & Sarah b 24 Jun 1750
William Stoops son of Philip & Margrett b 13 Apr 1744
Elizabeth Morgain dau of John & ---- b 15 Dec 1745
James Morgain son of same b 27 Dec 1748
Elizabeth Edthrington dau of Bartholomew & Elizabeth b 6 Aug 1747
Mary Edthrington dau of same b 23 Jun 1750
John Cox son of John & Margrett b -- May 1748
Thomas Cox son of same b 25 Feb 1749
Hyland Beatle son of John Junior & Rachel b 26 Jun 1738
Henry Beatle son of same b 11 Dec 1742
Sarah Beatle dau of same b 22 Jan 1745
Stephen Beatle son of same b 26 Dec 1749
Mary Beatle dau of same b 12 Mar 1751
Nathaniel Child son of Nathaniel & Sarah b 1 Jan 1741
Sarah Child dau of same b 6 Apr 1747
John Child son of same b 25 Nov 1748
Ann Child dau of same b 23 Nov 1751
Peregrine Ward son of Peregrine & Mary b 15 Jan 1744
Mary Ward dau of same b 12 Dec 1746
Isabella Stockton dau of John & Elisabeth b 23 Feb 1752
John Stockton son of same b 15 Nov 1754
Mary Penington dau of John (who was the son of Robert Penington) and Rachel (who was the daughter of William Beadle) b 16 Apr 1754
Matthias Hendrickson son of Matthias & Sarah b 13 Aug 1750
Bartholemew Hendrickson son of same b 1 Mar 1754
Mary Walmsley dau of Robert & Elisabeth b 1 Jan 1735/6
Thomas Walmsley son of same b 27 Mar 1738
John Walmsley son of same b 27 Feb 1740
William Walmsley son of same b 20 Apr 1742
John Walmsley second son of same of that name b 8 Mar 1743
Nicholas Walmsley son of same b 3 Oct 1747
James Walmsley son of same b 28 Jun 1750
Anne Walmsley dau of same b 8 May 1752
Mary Walmsley dau of same b 2 Jan 1754
Grace Hewston dau of James & Rachel b 23 Dec 1755
John Edthrington son of Bartholomew & Elizabeth b 16 Dec 1755
Stephen Severson son of Thomas & Mary b 1 May 1751
Rebeccah & Sarah Severson (twins) daus of same b 27 Nov 1752
James Lynch son of Anthony & Elizabeth b 21 May 1755
John Stoops son of John & Mary b 25 Dec 1748

ST. STEPHENS' PARISH (NORTH SASSAFRAS PARISH)

```
Edward Stoops son of same b 22 Jan 1751
William Stoops son of same b 22 Sep 1752
Sarah Stoops dau of same b 14 Feb 1756
Peter Golat son of John & Mary b 17 Jun 1740
John Golat son of same b 13 Jan 1745
Mary Pearce dau of Benjamin & Margret b 28 Aug 1751
Sarah Price dau of William & Mary b 16 Jun 1750
Tamar Wroth dau of Thomas & Mary b 8 Feb 1748
Mary Ann Wroth dau of same b 12 Jan 1751
Julian Wroth dau of same b 20 May 1754
George William Frederick Wroth son of same b 19 Jan 1757
Samuel Money son of John & Rachel b 22 Jul 1751
Robert Money son of same b 4 Aug 1753
Mary Price dau of William Junr. & Mary b 9 Feb 1752
John Mulster son of John & Martha b 19 Jul 1752
John Cann son of Robert & Sarah b 21 Sep 1753
Mary Ann Cann dau of same b 31 Dec 1754
Peregrine Marcer son of John & Sarah b -- Sep 1754
Ann Marcer dau of same b 1 Jul 1756
Ann Hall dau of John & Rachel b 29 Sep 1747
John Hall son of same b 4 Oct 1750
Andrew Beadle son of William & Sarah b 6 Jan 1748
Sarah Beadle dau of William & Jane b 7 Feb 1753
Rebecca Ryland dau of John & Rebecca b 18 Apr 1746
Mary Ryland dau of same b 12 Jan 1751
Mary Ann Ryland dau of same b 12 Jan 1753
Rachel Ozier dau of John & Sarah b 23 May 1753
Jacob Ozier son of same b 22 Nov 1754
Ephraim Ozier, illegitimate son of John Wiley and Mary Ozier b 4
    May 1743
Mary Millegan dau of George & Catherine b 20 Jul 1752
Robert Millegan son of same b 11 Jun 1754
Margret Millegan dau of same b 30 Jun 1756
Hugh Gribben son of Hugh & Rachel b 16 Apr 1757
Mary Bordley dau of William & Sarah b 21 May 1758 midnight
Catherine Milligan dau of George Esqr. & Catherine b 23 Jul 1759
George Milligan son of same b ----
Henry Gribbin son of Hugh & Rachel b 13 Sep 1759
Stephen Bordley son of William & Sarah b 13 Mar 1761 about nine
    o'clock in the morning
Susannah Pearce dau of Daniel & Sarah b -- --- 17--
Mary Pearce dau of same b 19 Mar 1756
William Pearce son of same b 13 Dec 1757
Mary Pearce dau of same b ---- Andrew Pearce son of same b ----
Mary Gibbs dau of Joseph & Esther b 7 Apr 1757
John Coppen Cowarden son of Peter & Ann b 11 Jun 1755
James Coppen Cowarden son of same b 11 Dec 1757
Peter Ambros Cowarden son of same b 11 Apr 1759
Benson Gears son of Daniel & Sarah b 15 Oct 1748
Jacob Gears son of same b 2 Feb 1751
William Gears son of same b 3 Dec 1753
Rebecca Gears dau of same b 10 Sep 1754
Daniel Gears son of same b 29 Oct 1758
Elisabeth Benson dau of Benjamin & Mary Ann b 1 Jun 1751
```

Ruth Benson dau of same b 7 Aug 1757
Casandra Susannah Driscole dau of John & Catherine b 17 Mar 1750
Catherine Driscole dau of same b 17 Mar 1756
Ann Driscole dau of same b 17 Mar 1757
John Driscole son of same b 17 Mar 1759
Ann David dau of James & Catherine b 25 Jan 1747
Rachel David dau of same b 10 Oct 1749
Rebeccah Matthews dau of Dr. Hugh & Catherine b 1 May 1752
Catherine Matthews and William Matthews dau and son (twins) of Dr. Hugh & Catherine b 26 Apr 1755
Elizabeth Matthews dau of same b 5 Mar 1758
James Egnatious Matthews son of same b 30 Jul 1760
Hugh Matthews son of same b -- Apr 1762
Sarah Vansandt dau of Cornelias & Hester b 30 Aug 1749
Hester Vansandt dau of same b 2 Feb 1751
Garardes Vansandt son of same b 15 Dec 1752
Susannah Vansandt dau of same b 12 Feb 1755
Hitteybell Vansandt dau of same b 5 Sep 1757
Haulwel Chamberlain son of William & Elizabeth b 3 Apr 1745
Rebeccah Money dau of Thomas & Elizabeth b 26 Apr 1749
Thomas Money son of same b 4 Jun 1752
Benjamin Money son of same b 21 Feb 1756
Sarah Morgan dau of William & Elizabeth b 26 Sep 1752
Ann Morgan dau of same b 12 Nov 1754
James Kimber Price son of Nicholas & Elizabeth b 16 Jan 1755
Andrew Price son of same b 24 Apr 1757
John Cox son of Benjamin & Margrett b 30 Apr 1760
Peregrine Noxon Frisby son of James & Sarah b 21 Feb 1758 about 12 o'clock at night Heszia Price dau of William & Mary b 17 Aug 1757
Jervis Filingham son of John & Margrett b -- Sep 1754
Benjamin Filingham son of same b 1 Aug 1756
Benjamin Cox son of Benjamin & Margret b 4 Aug 1758
Mary Hutchinson dau of Gavin & Mary b 18 May 1756
Sarah Hutchinson dau of same b 6 Feb 1758
Henry Ward Pearce son of Henry Ward Pearce & Anna b 23 Jun 1760
Margaret Stoops dau of John & Mary b 3 Aug 1761
Henry Ward son of Henry Ward & Hannah b 19 Jul 1757
Rebecca Veazey dau of Edward & Elisabeth b 13 Sep 1756
Elisabeth Veazey dau of same b 14 Feb 1759
Edward Veazey son of same b 12 Nov 1761
John Currier Campbell son of James & Elisabeth b 15 Sep 1753
William Campbell son of same b 17 Feb 1755
Mary Campbell dau of same b 26 Oct 1757
Mary Pearce dau of Henry Ward Pearce & Annastatia b 22 Oct 1762
Ann Barroll dau of Revd. William & Ann b 16 Sep 1762
John Currier Jones son of Jacob & Teney b 20 Mar 1761
Millicent Jones dau of same b 14 Aug 1762
Anne Hall dau of John & Rachel b 29 Sep 1747
John Hall son of same b 4 Oct 1750
George Hall son of same b 1 Apr 1753
Henrietta Hall dau of same b 2 Jan 1756
William Hall son of same b 30 Dec 1758
Francies Mary Hall dau of same b 7 Mar 1760
Kisiar Price dau of William & Mary b 17 Aug 1757

ST. STEPHENS' PARISH (NORTH SASSAFRAS PARISH)

Sarah Holt dau of George & Cathrine b 8 Nov 1763
Edward Henry Veazey son of Edward & Elisabeth b 20 Sep 1762
Elisabeth Stockton dau of John & Elisabeth b 3 Sep 1763
Susanna Ward dau of William & Rebecca b 28 Dec 1757
William Ward son of same b 28 Sep 1760
Rebecca Ward dau of same b 2 May 1762
Ann Money dau of John & Rachel b 4 Nov 1755
Isaac Money son of same b 2 Apr 1758
Rachel Money dau of same b 31 Dec 1761
Mary Stoops dau of John & Mary b 22 Jan 1764
Mary Craige dau of Capt. Robert & Blanchey b 15 Dec 1765
Franciney Beedle dau of William Jnr. & Sarah b 5 Oct 1754
Elisabeth Beedle dau of same b 23 Dec 1755
John Beedle son of same b 5 Mar 1758
Augusteen Beedle son of same b 17 May 1761
Jane Holt dau of Geo. & Cathrine b 30 Jan 1766
Ann Veazey dau of Edward & Elisabeth b 9 Apr 1766
Mary Thompson dau of John & Mary b 23 Apr 1767
Bartholomew Etherington son of Barthow. & Elisabeth b 14 Nov 1759
Rebecca Etherington dau of same b 16 Apr 1765
Rebecca Childs dau of Nathaniel & Tamma b 9 Aug 1765
Mary Wallace dau of Richard & Cathrine b 20 Nov 1757
James Wallace son of same b 12 May 1760
John Craige and Henry Craige, twin sons of Robert and Blanchey, b 17 Sep 1767
Robert Ward son of John & Elisabeth b 12 Sep 1765
Hester Veazey dau of Jno. Ward Veazey & Sarah b 6 Sep 1766
John Bauldin Veazey son of same b 8 Feb 1767
Alce Price dau of Ann Price b 12 Feb 1769
George Holt son of George & Cathrine b 16 Oct 1769
Joshua Ward son of John & Elisabeth b 31 Jul 1769
William Barroll son of William & Ann b 6 Aug 1764
Ann Henderson dau of Anthoney & Elisabeth b 1 Nov 1757
Hannah Henderson dau of same b 25 Nov 1762
Rebecca Henderson dau of same b 27 Aug 176-
Mary Henderson dau of same b 7 May 1769
Thomas Browning Price son of William & Elisabeth b 3 Jun 1760
William Price son of same b 20 Oct 1766
Sarah Veazey dau of Edward & Elisabeth b 2 Dec 1769
Mary Holt dau of George & Cathrine b 18 Jul 1772
Thomas Ruley son of Anthoney & Ann b 7 Jun 1763
Anthoney Ruley son of same b 7 Aug 1765
William Ruley son of same b 15 May 1768
John Ruley, twin with William, born the same time.
Ann Ruley dau of same b 28 Dec 1769
Benjamin Ruley son of same b 11 Apr 1771
Rachel Ruley dau of same b 25 Nov 1772
Elisabeth Yarley dau of William & Ann b 4 Jun 1773
Elisabeth Pennington dau of Samuel & ---- b 6 Sep 1764
William Pennington son of same b 20 Oct 1766
Robert Pennington son of same b 9 Oct 1768
Samuel Pennington son of same b 11 Nov 1770
Samuel Woodbury son of Samuel & Mary b 5 Nov 1688
Jonathan Woodbury son of same b 5 May 1685

Jonathan Woodbury son of Samuel & Margaret b 11 Apr 1722
Samuel Woodbury son of same b 1 Nov 1726
Thomas Ward Veazey son of Edward & Elisabeth b 31 Jan 1774
Elisabeth Lusby dau of Joseph & Rebecca b 27 Feb 1776
Ann Yardley dau of William & Ann b 28 Aug 1775
Ann Price dau of Rebecca Price b 1 Nov 1774
Eloner Can dau of Robert & Sarah b 23 Oct 1774
Jonas Stoops son of John & Mary b 22 Sep 1766
Peregrine Stoops son of same b 31 Dec 1768
James Stoops son of same b 10 Mar 1771
James Dorrell Fitchgarrell b 15 Dec 1767
Hyland Fitchgarrell b 14 Dec 1770
Shradrach Dorrell b 27 Feb 1774
Lewis Price Holt son of George & Cathrine b 31 Oct 176-
Michael Ruley son of Anthoney & Ann b 20 Apr 1772
Samuel Ruley son of same b 16 Mar 1774
Rebecca Ruley dau of same b 11 Feb 1778
Thomas Veazey Lusby son of Joseph & Rebecca b 10 Feb 1779
Edward Veazey Miller son of John & Elizabeth b 4 Aug 1780
Benjamin Francis Pearce son of Henry Ward Pearce and Rachel b 20 Oct 1780
Elizabeth Veazey Miller dau of same b 11 Jul 1782
Anne Maria Lusby dau of Joseph & Rebecca b 8 Oct 1780
John Davis son of John & Frances b 16 Oct 1776
John Thompson Veazey son of Thomas Brocus Veazey and Mary b 22 Jul 1783
Elizabeth Price dau of Lewis & Mary b 8 Oct 1781
Ann Price dau of same b 21 Sep 1783
Hannah Gordon dau of Charles & Elizabeth b 6 Nov 1765
Elizabeth Ann Gordon dau of same b 19 Feb 1767
Sarah Nicholson Gordon dau of same b 24 Oct 1768
Anna Maria Gordon dau of same b 18 Jan 1770
Joseph Gordon son of same b 9 Oct 1775
John Gordon son of same b 7 Sep 1777
Charles Gordon son of same b 14 Nov 1778
John Henry Lusby and Sarah Veazey Lusby (twins) son and daughter of Joseph & Rebecca b 16 May 1784
Mary Williamson dau of Alexander & Millicent b 20 Sep 1766
Elizabeth Williamson dau of same b 11 Oct 1770
Meliscent Williamson dau of same b 8 Jul 1772
John Williamson dau of same b 13 Oct 1775
James Williamson son of same b 19 Oct 1777
Rebecca Davis dau of John & Elizabeth b 30 Jan 1785
Sarah Porter dau of Benjamin & Anne b 21 Oct 1776
John Porter son of same b 23 Dec 1777
Benjamin Porter son of same b 25 Sep 1780
William Porter and Anne Porter (twins) son and daughter of Benjamin & Anne b 8 Oct 1783
Thomas Penington son of John & Cathrine b 24 Feb 1782
John Thompson son of John Dockrey Thompson & Hester b 1 Aug 17--
George Ward son of John & Elizabeth b 19 Apr 1778
Deborah Ward dau of same b Monday 15 Jan 1781
Nancy Logan dau of John & Cathrine b Friday 2 Sep 1780 about 15 minutes after 3 o'clock in the morning
Henry Conoley son of John & Rebecca b 2 Nov 1782

ST. STEPHENS' PARISH (NORTH SASSAFRAS PARISH)

Mary Price dau of Noble & Cathrine b 28 Dec 1782
William Henry Ward son of William & Anne b 21 Nov 1785
Robert Porter son of Benjamin & Anne b 3 Aug 1786
William Roberts Price son of Lewis & Mary b 11 Nov 1785
Joseph Stockton Davis son of John & Elizabeth b 9 Mar 1787
Elizabeth Ward dau of William & Ann b 23 Oct 1787
Ann Ward dau of same b 8 Feb 1790
Elizabeth Nowland dau of Peregrine & Rebecca b Friday P.M. 28 Sep 1787
Maria Nowland dau of same b 14 Feb 1789
at two o'clock A.M. Harriot Bonde Naglee dau of Samuel & Rebecca b 1 Mar 1786
James Caskey Naglee son of same b 5 Jun 1788
John Davis and Sarah Davis (twins) son and daughter of Richard & Elizabeth b 9 Feb 1790
Thomas Savin Nowland son of Peregrine & Rebecca b 27 Jan 1791
at 10 o'clock P.M. Elizabeth Davis dau of Richard & Elizabeth b 28 Aug 1791
Alethea Cosden dau of Jerh. & Catherine b 11 Jul 1790
Miliscent Jones dau of Thomas & Margaret b 1 Nov 1778
William Savin Fulton son of David & Elizabeth b Tuesday A.M. 2 Jun 1795
Robert Walmsley Junr. son of Robert & Alethea b 11 Oct 1765
William Walmsley son of Robert & Margaretta b 20 Sep 1788
John Gording Walmsley son of same b 12 Jul 1790
Eliza Walmsley and Isaac Walmsley (twins) daughter and son of Robert & Margaretta b 16 Feb 1793
Rebecca Walmsley dau of same b 30 Apr 1795
Margaretta Gooding dau of Isaac & Phillis b 1 Aug 1773
Margaretta Walmsley dau of Robert & Margaretta b 3 Jul 1798
Edward Larrimore Lusby son of Edward & Ann b 28 Jul 1778
Elizabeth Lusby dau of same b 2 Sep 1780
John Lusby son of same b 30 Aug 1782
Acel Cosden Lusby son of same b 17 Aug 1784
Margaretta Lusby dau of same b 30 Jul 1786
Sarah Lusby dau of same b 11 Oct 1788
Nicholas Lusby son of same b 4 Jan 1791
Samuel Cosden Lusby and Joseph Lusby (twins) sons of Edward and Ann b 17 Dec 1792
William Lusby son of same b 1 Jun 1795
Augustine Larimore Lusby dau (sic) of same b 28 Sep 1797
Sarah Price dau of Mary Price b 22 Jun 1779
Jane Price dau of same b 21 Feb 1781
John Price son of same b 8 Apr 1784
George Price son of same b 11 Mar 1787
Julia Ann Price dau of same b 21 Jan 1796
Samuel Ruley Price dau (sic) of Sarah Price b 20 Feb 1796
Henny Ritty Mary Penington dau of Sal. & Sarah b 28 Aug 1790
Samuel Price Penington son of same b 1 Nov 1792
Wm. Spencer Lassell son of Wm. C. & Ann b 19 Feb 1797
Sarah Mercer wife of Thos. Severson b 22 Apr 1765
John Walmsley son of John & Rebecca b 21 Mar 1777
Anne Mariah Price dau of Lewis & Mary b 20 Dec 1787
Deborah Price dau of same b 24 Jul 1792
Lewis Price son of same b 8 Oct 1794
Elizabeth Price dau of same b 14 Dec 1796

Thomas Walmsley son of William & Susanna b 14 May 1790
William Walmsley son of same b 30 Jun 1791
Margaretta Walmsley dau of same b 2 Apr 1794
Warner Walmsley son of same b 28 Dec 1796
Richard Walmsley son of same b 27 Feb 1799
John Hague son of Joseph & Priscella b 9 May 1782
John Lusby son of William & Pamelia b 23 Feb 1782
Susannah Lusby dau of same b 25 May 1783
Robert Clothier Lusby son of same b 12 Apr 1785
James Lusby son of same b 16 Jun 1787
Ruth Lusby dau of same b 12 Oct 1789
Elizabeth Lusby dau of same b 25 Oct 1792
Sarah Lusby dau of same b 18 May 1796
Zebulon Lusby son of same b 14 Jan 1798
William Lusby son of same b 1 Nov 1800
Hyland Biddle Penington son of Robert (of William) and Mary b 5 Mar 1777
Edith Hendrickson dau of Augustine & Rozamond (and now wife of the above Hyland B. Penington) b 17 Feb 1779
Vachel Terry Price son of John & Terry b 17 Jul 1777
Joshua Pearce son of Henry & Mary Ann b 29 Oct 1779
Sons and daughters of Augustine Hendrickson and Rozamond Hendrickson his wife (All those marked thus * are dead at this time, 1801):
    1st Mary Hendrickson b 26 Nov 1774 *
    2nd Mary Hendrickson b 29 Sep 1776
        Edith Hendrickson b 17 Feb 1779
    1st Hosea Hendrickson b 7 Apr 1782 *
    1st Peregrine Henrdickson b 5 Apr 1784 *
    1st Noble Hendrickson b 19 Feb 1786 *
    2nd Peregrine Hendrickson b 22 Mar 1788
    2nd Noble Hendrickson b 13 Feb 1790 *
        Ann Hendrickson n 3 Mar 1792
    2nd Hosea Hendrickson b 7 Apr 1782 (sic) *
Edward Cox son of William & Mary b 4 Apr 1774
Augustine Hyland Penington son of Hyland B. & Edith b 29 May 1801 between the hours of 10 & 11 o'clock P.M. Sons and daughters of John Cox (of Benjamin) and Rebecca Cox his wife:
    Elias Cox b 30 Oct 1783
    Thomas Cox b 2 Oct 1785
    Elizabeth Cox b 15 Jul 1787
    Henrietta Cox b 8 Apr 1795
    Edward Cox b 18 May 1799
Phebe Penington dau of Hyland B. & Edith b Sunday 8 May 1803 about 10 o'clock A.M. John Sullivan son of Henry & Mary b 22 Apr 1796
Peregrine Sullivan b 1 Jan 1798
Henry Sullivan b 30 Jan 1800
Elijah Sullivan b 23 Sep 1801
Joseph Biggs son of Richard & Sarah b 13 Mar 1786
Elizabeth Biggs dau of same b 11 Feb 1788
Mary Biggs dau of same b 6 Oct 1789
Araminta Biggs dau of same b 9 Oct 1791
William Biggs son of same b 4 May 1794

ST. STEPHENS' PARISH (NORTH SASSAFRAS PARISH)

John Biggs and Richard Biggs sons of same b 20 Jan 1796
Rachel Biggs dau of same b 21 --- 1797
Henry Biggs son of same b 28 Oct 1799
Benjamin Biggs son of same b 9 Apr 1802
John Roberts son of Lewis & Elizabeth b 19 Jan 1787
Isaac Gooding Roberts son of same b 4 Oct 1788
James Roberts son of same b 10 Oct 1790, d 5 Oct 1791
Lewis Clothier Roberts son of same b 17 Aug 1792
William Roberts son of same b 25 Apr 1794
Elizabeth Roberts dau of same b 2 May 1796
James Roberts son of same b 1 Feb 1798
Anne Roberts dau of same b 15 Dec 1799
Robert Roberts son of Lewis Roberts and Rebecca his second wife b 6 Jan 1803
William Thomas Veazey first son of Dr. John L. & Sarah born between 3 & 4 o'clock in the morning on 29 Oct 1815
John Thompson Veazey second son of same b 22 Nov 1817 in the morning
George Ross Veazey third son of same b 17 Jan 1820 between 2 & 3 o'clock in the morning
Thomas Brocus Veazey fourth son of same b 28 Feb 1822 in the morning
Sarah Severson dau of Thomas & Sarah b 28 Jan 1801
John Severson son of same b 1 Jan 1804
Samuel Severson son of same b 10 May 1807
Arabella Ann Veazey dau of Thomas B. & Ann b 4 May 1818
John Leach Knight son of Dr. John & ---- b 27 Mar 174-
Ann Mercer dau of Thomas & Jean b 28 Mar 1745
Joshua Thompson son of John & Mary b Wednesday 26 Jan 1744 about 7 o'clock in the morning
Jean Loftis dau of John & Susannah b 27 Sep 1743
Charles Loftis son of same b 17 Nov 1745
William Walmsley son of William & Sarah b 8 Oct 1744
John Cox son of John Junior & Susannah b 17 Aug 1741
Hester Cox dau of same b 10 Nov 1743
Edward Cox son of same b 1 Jun 1746
James Marcer son of Robert & Ann b 16 Dec 1742
Samuel Ricketts son of Evan & Rachel b 1 Aug 1744
Rebecca Ricketts dau of same b 23 Jun 1745
Tamar Ricketts dau of same b 9 Nov 1746
Rachel Davis dau of Thomas & Rebecca b 23 Feb 1746
James Money son of John & Rachel b 22 Apr 1746
Elizabeth Porter dau of James & Rebecca b 20 Sep 1746
---- Davis son of Thomas & Rebecca b 5 Apr 1745
Richard Obriant son of Daniel O'Briant of Kent County and Mary O'Briant (spinster) b 1 Jan 1738
William Price son of William Junr. & ---- b 5 Nov 1744
John Tulley son of Edward & Sarah b 1 May 1745
Mary Thompson dau of John & Mary b 3 Jun 1742
John Dockra Thompson son of same b 16 Dec 1743
Joshua Thompson son of same b 26 Jan 1745
Rebecca Shelley dau of ---- Shelley & Mary Gibson b -- Jan 1741
John Hyland Price son of Andrew & Elizabeth b 22 Apr 1744
(Note: Name "John Hyland" written in a different hand.)
Ann Taylor dau of James Junr. & Catherine b 16 Sep 1743

Silas Taylor son of James Senr. & Elizabeth b 18 Apr 1743
James Scurrey son of Thomas & Mary b 1 Jan 1744
Richard Taylor son of James Senior & Elizabeth b 18 Sep 1745
Robert Steal son of Matthew & Margarett b 24 Jan 1745
Mary Ann Price dau of Richard & Sarah b 9 Mar 1743
The Baptisms of Children (by Mr. Laurance Vanderbush) as followeth: Jno. Gandy son of George & Constance bapt 2 Jul 1692
Jno. Ward son of William & Elizabeth bapt 7 Jul 1692
James Waggett son of Jno. & Jaine bapt 17 Jul 1692
Mary Manicozons dau of Michaell Manycozons & Anne bapt 22 Jul 1692
Elizabeth Crouch dau of Thomas & Mary bapt 22 Jul 1692
Thomas Terry son of Thomas & Rosamond bapt 14 Aug 1692
Robert Mackahay son of Alexander & ---- bapt 14 Aug 1692
Mary Branklin dau of William & Ann bapt 21 Aug 1692
Susanna Morrice dau of Jno. Morris & Margrett bapt 23 Oct 1692
Mary Barker dau of Richard & Mary bapt 4 Sep 1692
Elizabeth Drake dau of Wm. & Margaret bapt 11 Sep 1692
Rachel Penninton dau of Henry & ---- bapt 21 Aug 1692
Mary Moss dau of Richard & Elizabeth bapt 17 Sep 1692
Margrett Dorrle dau of Nicholas & Christina bapt 18 Sep 1692
Oliver Caulk son of Isaac & Mary bapt 30 Sep 1692
Mary Wheeler dau of Jno. & Elizabeth bapt 30 Oct 1692
Jno. Stoop son of Jno. & Mary bapt 31 Oct 1692, and likewise the said Mary Stoop daughter of Mr. Phillip Hollogr. was baptized at the same time.
Sarah Davis dau of Wm. & Angell bapt 6 Nov 1692
Mary Toulson dau of Andrew & Mary bapt 6 Nov 1692
Wm. Babinton son of Jno. & Mary bapt 6 Jan 1694
Johannes Delamountain son of Nicholas Delamountain and Christian Roserta ------.

Registered by Thomas Powell, Clerk of the Vestry of North Sassafras Parish, as followeth (Baptisms by Mr. Richard Sewell unless otherwise indicated after each entry):
Ffrancis Frisby son of James Esq. & Sarah bapt 7 Jul 1697 by Mr. Leliston
Jaine Hynson dau of Jno. & Mary bapt 1 Apr 1696 by Mr. Jno. Liliston
Jno. Hynson son of Jno. & Mary bapt 1 Apr 1697 by Mr. Jno. Liliston
Jno. Bavinton son of Jno. & Mary bapt 1 Aug 1697
Robt. Macahee son of Robt. & ---- bapt 1 Aug 1697
Mary Sherwood dau of Wm. & Mary bapt 5 Aug 1697
Anne Watkins dau of James & Mary bapt 1 Aug 1697
Mary Severson dau of Peter & Mary bapt 1 Aug 1697
Rebecca Penninton dau of Robt. & Ann bapt 1 Aug 1697
Thomas Marcus son of Hance & Dina bapt 1 Aug 1697
Mary Marcus dau of Hance & Dina bapt 1 Aug 1697
Esther Browning dau of Thomas & Ann bapt 1 Aug 1697
Abraham Clemenson son of Cornelius & Junibar bapt 18 Aug 1697

ST. STEPHENS' PARISH (NORTH SASSAFRAS PARISH)

Ephraim Thompson son of Coll. Jno. Thomson & Judith bapt 29 Sep 1697
William Horne son of Darby & Sarah bapt 3 Oct 1697
Wm. Boyer son of William & Phillis bapt 3 Oct 1697
Thomas Watts son of Thomas & Elizabeth bapt 3 Oct 1697
Sarah Mounce dau of Christopher & Sarah bapt 3 Oct 1697
Rosamond Terry dau of Thomas & Rosamond bapt 12 Sep 1697
Richard Boulden son of Wm. & Thomason bapt 24 Oct 1697
Elizabeth Bolden dau of Wm. & Thomason bapt 24 Oct 1697
Anne Terry dau of Thomas & Rosamond bapt 24 Oct 1697
John Cock son of Thomas & Katherine bapt 14 Oct 1697
Cathrine Herman dau of Coll. Casparus Augustine Herman and Catherine bapt 10 Dec 1697
Rynerius Vangagely son of Jacob & Gertruij bapt 10 Dec 1697
Richard Barker son of Richard & Rebecca bapt 10 Dec 1697
Isaac Penninton son of Thomas & Alce bapt 16 Jan 1697
Robert Mercer son of Thomas & Elizabeth bapt 5 Dec 1697
Elizabeth Severson dau of Thomas & Catherine bapt 3 Feb 1697
Leonard Stoop son of Jno. & Mary bapt 10 Apr 1698
Mary Crouch dau of Thomas & Mary bapt 10 Apr 1698
Catherine Yorkson dau of York & Mary bapt 3 Feb 1697
Mary Fossett dau of Js. & Ann bapt 27 May 1701 abt 13 yr old
Thomas Sewell son of Richard & Jane bapt 4 Jun 1701 by Revd. Mr. Stephen Bordley, minister of Kent County
Thomas Henrickson son of Christopher & Mary bapt 25 Mar 1701
Nathaniell Hynson son of John & Mary bapt 1698 by Revd. Mr. Stephen Bordley
Thomas Hynson son of John & Mary bapt 1 Jul 1701
Ann Clifton day of Thos. & Tabitha bapt 18 Aug 1702

Registered by Jno. Wellinger. Register as follows:
Matthew Matthiason son of Matthias & Mary bapt 20 Aug 1699 by Mr. Richd. Sewell, minister of this parish
Mary Murrain dau of Daniel & Susanna bapt 4 Jun 1722 by the Revd. Richd. Sewell, minister of St. Stephen's Parish in Cecil County
Jean Robinson dau of Michael & Margt. born 26 Jan 1733/4.

Burialls of Men, Women and Children Registred by Thomas Powell, Clerke of North Sassfras Parish:
Annica Prise wife of Jno. died in Bohemia 28 Nov 1695
Mr. Daniell Smith of Bohemia bur 30 Nov 1695
Mr. George Stevens bur 30 Dec 1695
Ann Hill wife of William bur 23 Nov 1695
Mr. Jno. Hyland died 17 Jan 1695
Elizabeth Ward wife of William bur 14 Nov 1696
Mary Morgan wife of James bur 13 Jan 1696/7
Ann Severson dau of Thomas & Katherine bur 31 Feb 1696/7
Mr. Robert Crooke bur 23 May 1697
Thomas Nicholson of Bohemia bur 30 Jul 1697 by Rev. Sewell
Ephraim Thompson son of Coll. Jno. & Judith bur 1 Oct 1697
Edward Johnson bur 29 Oct 1697
Elizabeth Lapage dau of Edward & Joan bur 12 Dec 1697
Peter Severson bur 10 Jan 1697/8 Mary Worgan wife of Joseph bur 24 Apr 1698
Catherine Harkin wife of Cornelius bur 12 May 1698

Registered by Jno. Wellinger:
Matthias Matthiason of Sassafrass Parish bur 7 May 1702
Esther Scott wife of Walter of Bohemia River bur 17 Dec MDCCVI
    (Note: Year 1706 is written in Roman numerals.)
Thomas Watts of Sassafrass River bur 11 Apr MDCCXI (1711)
Jacob VanBebber Sr. of Bohemia River bur -- Sep MDCCV (1705)
Christiana VanBebber wife of Jacob Sr. of Bohemia River bur 4 Sep MDCCX (1710)
Elizabeth Cox wife of Benjamin of Sassafrass River bur 28 May MDCCXI (1711)
Edwd. Laramore bur 1 Feb MDCCX (1710)
John Robinson son of Capt. Thos. & Sarah bur 30 Nov 1712
Frisby Knight son of Stephen & Sarah bur 26 Apr 1712
Anne McKeye dau of Alexander & Susana bur 14 Jun 1711
Christopher Mounce of the ponds bur -----
Christopher Mounce son of Christopher bur 12 Sep 1713
Casparus Mounce son of Christopher bur 16 Dec 1713
Peter King of Bohemia River bur -- Dec 1713
---- King wife of Peter bur -- Dec 1713
Elias Marques of Bohemia River bur 25 Nov 1713
Thomas Currey of Bohemia River bur 7 Dec 1713
Richard Smith of Sasafrax River bur 7 Nov 1713
Thomas Price son of Wm. Junr. & Kathrin bur -- Jan 1712
Martha Barrat wife of Phillip of Bohemia River bur 28 Mar 1713
Elizabeth Griffeth wife of John bur 12 Oct 1713
Thomas Cox son of Thomnas of Sasafrax River bur 7 Oct 1712
Elizabeth Cox dau of Thomas Senr. of Sasafrax & Kathrin bur 28 Oct 1712
Thomas Cox Senr. of Sasafrax River bur 21 Mar 1712/3
Sarah Smart dau of John & Sarah bur 23 Oct 1712
Curnelus Clements of the ponds bur 7 Nov 1713
Mary Price wife of John of the ponds bur 11 Aug 1713
Sarah Price dau of John & Mary bur 20 Oct 1713
Anne Allin wife of Paul of Sasafraz River bur 24 Nov 1713
Richard Morgan son of James of the ponds & Elizabeth bur 2 Nov 1712
Rebecca Peninton dau of Robert & Anne of Sasafraz River bur 3 Jan 1712
Alice Veazey wife of George of Bohemia River bur 28 Nov 1712
John Wellinger of Sasafrass River bur 13 Jul 1713
Jellian Crow wife of Charles of Bohemia Mannor bur 18 Dec 1713
Aron Degrote of Bohemia River bur 23 Feb 1713
William Hill of Sasafrax River bur 10 Feb 1712
Rebecca Griffeth dau of John & Elizabeth bur 4 Sep 1712
Thomas Steele son of Francis & Rebecca bur 17 Nov 1708
George Thompson of Sasafrax River bur 25 Apr 1713
James Bray of Bohemia River bur 24 Apr 1713
Nathaniell Child of Sasafrax River bur 25 Sep 1712
Mary Sapinton wife of Nathll. of Sassafrass River bur 2 May (no year given)
Nathaniell Sapinton of Sasafrass River bur 2 May ----.
James Sapinton son of Nathll. of Sasafrass River bur 12 Jul 1713
    Samuel Holyday of Sasafrass River bur 2 Mar 1710
Samuel Hews of Bohemia River bur 11 Jul 1713
Sarah Davis dau of Morris & Sarah bur -- --- 1712

ST. STEPHENS' PARISH (NORTH SASSAFRAS PARISH)

Sarah and James Davis (twins) son and dau of Morris & Sarah bur -- --- 1712
Elizabeth White son (sic) of John & Mary bur 12 Nov 1713
Mary White dau of John & Mary of Bohemia River bur 14 May 1714
Mary Hollins spinster of Bohemia River bur 1 May 1714
Mary Hollins dau of John & Abigall bur 20 Oct 1713
Gilder Huckin son of Danll. & Elizabeth bur 28 Aug 1713
William Huckin son of Daniell & Elizabeth bur 20 Jan 1712
Susan Foster wife of Richd. of Elk River bur 15 Jul 1714
William Davis of the ponds bur 3 Oct 1714
Walter Newman son of John bur 20 Nov 1714
Jonathan Newman son of Walter & Mary bur 20 Oct 1714
Walter Crow son of John & Elizabeth bur the last of Nov 1714
George Bristow son of Wm. & Mildred bur 26 Feb 1714
Sophia Child dau of Nathll. & Helinor bur 7 Jan 1714
Francis Ozey of Sasafrax River bur 6 Jul 1714
Samll. Boulding son of William & Thomasin bur 27 Feb 1714
Daniell Wells of Bohemia River bur 6 Mar 1714
John Rye of the ponds bur 15 Mar 1714
Susana Pooley dau of Nicholas & Sarah bur ----.
John Burgis son of Francis & Mary bur 12 Feb 1710
Robert Morgan son of James & Elizabeth bur 11 May 1715
Samll. White son of John & Mary bur 24 Jul 1716
Mary Larramore dau of Rogr. & Margrett bur 28 Apr 1715
Sarah Larramore dau of Rogr. & Margret bur 27 Aug 1716
Elizabeth Price dau of Thos. & Mary bur 6 Sep 1716
Mary Price dau of Thos. & Mary bur 16 Sep 1716
Thomas Foster son of Richd. & Sarah bur the last of Aug 1715
Thomas Pearce Senr. of Bohemia River bur 20 Feb 1716
Anne Latham wife of Joshua of Bohemia River bur 7 Mar 1715
Thomas Kare of Bohemia River bur 13 Mar 1715/6
John Stanly of Bohemia River bur 7 Jun 1716
Mary Stanly dau of John & Jane bur 16 Jan 1716
Thomas Parsley son of Thomas & Elizabeth bur 23 Jan 1716/7
Anne Broxon wife of Thomas of Bohemia River bur 23 Jan 1716
John Brace son of John & Elizabeth bur 28 Jan 1716
Mary Watts dau of Thomas & Elizabeth bur 11 Feb 1716/7
James Etherinton son of Thomas & Eliz. bur 12 Feb 1716
Bartholomew and Elizabeth Etherinton son and dau of Thos. & Elizabeth bur 17 Feb 1716
John Price son of Wm. & Mary bur 7 Mar 1716
Sarah Clements dau of Henry & Sarah born (sic) 22 Oct 1707
Edward Robinson son of James & ---- bur 27 Feb 1716/7
John Sedberrey bur 11 Mar 1716/7 Susana Makey wife of Alexander bur 11 Mar 1716/7
Mary Cox dau of Thos. & Kathrin bur 11 Mar 1716/7
Kathrin Cox of Sasafrax River bur 20 Mar 1716/7
Rebecca Price dau of Wm. & Mary bur 18 Mar 1716/7
John McKandrick son of ---- & Kathrin bur 23 Mar 1716/7
Kathrin Price wife of Wm. Junr. bur 23 Mar 1716/7
John and James Gibbons sons of James & Elizabeth bur 28 Feb 1716/7
James Gibbons of Bohemia River bur 5 Jul 1717
Sarah Beeston dau of William & Sarah bur 28 Apr 1716
Elizabeth Huckin wife of Daniell bur 2 May 1718

Elizabeth Beck dau of Jonathan & Mary bur 5 Apr 1714
Benj. Beck son of same bur 28 Aug 1716
Jonathan Beck of Bohemia River bur 23 Sep 1718
Margret Larramore wife of Rogar bur 16 Sep 1718
Capt. James Ffrisby of St. Stephens Parish bur 6 Jan 1719/20
    Samuell Bedle son of John bur ----. Nathaniel Ward son of
    William Senr. of Sasafrass River bur 29 Apr 1718
William Ward of Sasafrass River bur 17 Apr 1720
Rebecca Sinclar dau of William & Rachell bur 19 --- ----.
Kathrin Barrat dau of Phillip & Kathrin bur 11 Feb 1720
Mary Pope dau of Thomas & Elizabeth bur 26 Aug 1719
Rogar Larramore of St. Stephens Parrish bur 24 Oct 1721
William Beston of Bohemia River bur 2 Feb 1722
John Collins son of John & Julian born (sic) 12 Nov 1722
Rebecca Watts dau of Thomas & Mary bur 31 Oct 1723
Thomas Walmsley cordwiner bur 23 Aug 1722
Denis Seeney bur 28 Jun 1725
John Peirce son of Thos. & Mary bur 16 Nov 1722
Mary Veazey dau of James & Mary born (sic) 13 Jan 1728
Richard Ffoster Senr. of Bohemia Hundred bur 6 Apr 1732
Rachell Burnham dau of Thos. & Mary bur 8 Sep 1731
John Oats shoemaker bur 14 Apr 1732
Ephraim Vanburkeloo son of Abell & Cathrine bur 9 Oct 1725
Thomas Boushall son of Peter & Mary bur 8 Sep 1732
Mary Boushall dau of Peter & Mary bur 11 Sep 1732
Registered by Col. Benjamin Pearce, Regr. Elected and duly qualified on Tuesday the first day of May 1733:
Elizabeth Key widow bur 25 Apr 1733
William Veazey died 15 Apr 1733
Isabella Herman wife of Ephraim Augt. Herman bur 29 --- 1732
Casparus Herman son of Ephraim Augt. & Isabella bur 24 Sep 1732
Rachel Huchison wife of Alexander died 22 Jan 1732/3
Joseph Sealey died 16 Sep 1732 and bur 19 Sep 1732
Augustine Terry died 29 Jan and bur 1 Feb 1731/2
Jacob Caulk died 11 Feb 1724/5
Eleoner Everdson wife of ---- died 26 Apr 1730
Charles Rumsey died -- --- 1726
Charles Carnan son of John & Margaret died 12 Aug 1728
Charles Rumsey son of Wm. & Sabina died 16 May 1729
Mary Kimber dau of John & Rebecca died 24 Dec 1727
Rebecca Kimber wife of John died 1 Mar 1727/8
Rebecca Kimber dau of John & Rebecka died 27 Jun 1729
Mary Beedle Senr. (sic) died 29 Sep 1733
Martha Beedle wife of William died 3 Oct 1733
Ann Sayer wife of Stephen died 14 Apr 1733
Thomas Merret son of ---- & Elizabeth died 12 Nov 1733
Thomas Husband son of Jno. & Sarah died 9 Jan 1733/4
Rachell Davis wife of Thomas died 14 Jan 1733/4
Benjm. Bennit died 10 Dec 1733
Thomas Crouch died -- Dec 1733
Elizabeth Campbell wife of John died 12 Dec 1732
Rachel Campbell dau of John died 7 Mar 1732/3
William Bryan died 14 Aug 1732

ST. STEPHENS' PARISH (NORTH SASSAFRAS PARISH)

Coll. Benjamin Pearce of Cecil County son of Coll. William Pearce & Isabella of Kent County died 4 Apr 1734 about 12 o'clock at night

Registered by Benjamin Pearce, Regr. Elected and duly quallified on Tuesday 14 May 1734:
John Beedle Senr. died 16 May 1734
Henry Ward died 9 May 1734
Mary Matthews wife of Patrick died 17 Feb 1734/5
Elizabeth Sluyter wife of Benjamin died 2 Jan 1734/5
Garriot Othoson died 8 Feb 1735
Fouch Davis died 19 May 1738
Peter Numbers died -- May 1737
John Thompson died 7 Dec 1735
John McManus died 2 Feb 1737/8
James Young son of Joseph died 20 Jan 1738/9
Christopher Beedle son of John Senr. died 20 Jan 1738/9
Augustine Beedle son of John died 9 Sep 1735
Benjamin Pearce second son of Benjamin & Margarett died 30 Nov 1739
Sarah Penington wife of John died 3 Sep 1739
Robert Weithers died 20 Mar 1739
and was buryed by the Revd. Hugh Jones Dianna Lattymus wife of James died 29 Aug 1739
Mary Harper wife of John Harper blacksmith died 22 Jul 1741
Margret Parsons dau of William died 25 Jan 1739
Mary Parsons widow of William died 13 Feb 1739
William Parsons son of William died 1 Dec 1741
Gartrick Parsons widow of William Junr. died 20 Dec 1741
Rachel Money dau of John & Rachel died 25 Jan 1743
William Pearce fourth son of Benjamin & Margtt. died 14 Sep 1743
Benjamin Ward Pearce third son of same died 30 Sep 1743
John Knight of Cecil County chyurgeon otherwise called Doctr. John Knight son of Mr. Stephen Knight of Cecil County died ----.
Mary Pearce widow of Colonel Benjamin Pearce of Cecil County died 14 Nov 1753 aged 61 years and interred the 17th.
Benjamin Pearce son of Col. Benjamin Pearce of Cecil County died 19 Apr 1756 at Philadelphia in his 45th year.
Mary Ann Wroth died 11 Nov 1756 nd Julia Wroth died 26 Nov 1756, both daughters of Thomas & Mary Wroth.
Sarah Beedle wife of William died -- Oct ----.
Catherine Milligan wife of George Milligan, Esquire, died Christmas Eve, 24 Dec 1760.
William Bordley son of Thomas Bordley, Esquire, died 17 Feb 1762 in the 47th year of his age.
Sarah Beedle wife of William Jur. died 28 Aug 1764.
Rebecca Veazey wife of Coll. John Veazey died 24 Apr 1761 with the smallpox. Coll. John Veazey died with the smallpox in his 77th year on 4 May 1777. Edward Veazey son of Colonel John & Rebecca died 24 Apr 1784
Robert Porter Senr. son of James & Junibar died 28 Sep 1775 aged 77 years wanting 15 days.
Mrs. Mary Ann Jones of Sassafras River buried 12 Apr 1822.
John Benson buried 21 Apr 1822.

54 EARLY ANGLICAN CHURCH RECORDS OF CECIL COUNTY

Marriages in St. Stephens Parish, 1828, Henry N. Hotchkiss:

Joshua Ward to Rebecca Veazey, 31 Jan 1828
Thomas Taylor to Margarett Low, 9 Mar 1828
Sylvester Magee to Catherine Welsh, 27 Mar 1828
John H. Price to Deborah Coulyer, 1 Apr 1828
Peregrine F. Lloyd to Letticia Smith (nothing else written)
Morgan A. Price to Harriott Veazey, 20 May 1828
Robert Hayes to Nelly Etherington, 25 May 1828

Funerals, 1827-1828: Benjamin Walmsley 5 May 1827

Highland J. Pennington 10 May 1827
Mrs. Ann Price 8 Jul 1827
Judge Wm. Ward 20 Jul 1827
Samuel Otterson 21 Jul 1827
Wm. Davis, -- Jul ----
Philip Lloyd by Mr. Smith (no date)
George Ward 4 Sep 1827
John Hall 7 Sep 1827
Mrs. Fisher (no date)
Mr. George Reese 6 Nov died 17 Aug ----
Mrs. Ann Reese 6 Nov 1827
Mrs. Greenwood 19 Sep 1827
Mrs. James 15 Nov 1827
Joseph Morse 5 Dec 1827
Mrs. Sophia Hendrickson 9 Dec ----
Mrs. Roth 10 Dec 1827
Alphonso Comegys -- Jan 1828
Mrs. Lloyd wife of P. F. Lloyd 31 Jan 1828
Elizabeth Hays 31 Jan 1828
Wm. Morgan 1 Feb 1828
Mrs. Pennington 18 Mar 1828
James Nowland 22 Mar 1828
Henry W. Pearce 16 Apr 1828
Peregrine Biddle 18 Apr 1828
An infant of Williamson 8 May 1828
Miss Biddle 11 May 1828

Baptisms by Rector Robert Piggot (1837):

James Henry Dorset, a colored child and son of Perry Dorset, slave of Widow Wickes, & Sarah his wife, slave of General Forman.
James Henry Dorset born 15 or 16 Jan 1837, bapt 16 Apr 1837, sponsor: mother.
Ann Eliza Crage, dau of Levi Crage & Rebecca his wife, born 31 Apr 1837, bapt 30 Jun 1837, sponsor: mother.
Delia Griffins, a colored child and dau of Abraham Griffins, slave of Benedict Jones, & Mary Ann his wife, slave of Doctor John Veazey. Delia Griffins born 3 Jan 1837, bapt 30 Jun 1837, sponsor: mother.
Laura Cornelia Briscoe, dau of John T. Briscoe & Amelia Ann Elisabeth his wife, born 3 Mar 1837, bapt 16 Jul 1837, sponsors: parents.

ST. STEPHENS' PARISH (NORTH SASSAFRAS PARISH) 55

John Chandler Crookshanks, son of Francis B. Crookshanks & Mary E. his wife, born 16 Feb 1837, bapt 23 Jul 1837, sponsors: parents. John Edward Walmsley, son of Robert Walmsley & Mary his wife, born 9 Jun 1837, bapt 28 Jul 1837, sponsor: mother. Alethea Lavinia Woodland Ireland, dau of William Pope Ireland & Hannah Wallace Woodland his wife, born 24 Oct 1826, bapt 27 Aug 1837, sponsors: Mrs. Alethea Wickes and Mrs. Emmeline Lavinia Davis.
Thomas Young, son of Samuel Young & Rachel his wife, born 10 Apr 1837, bapt 8 Oct 1837, sponsor: mother.

Jeremiah Cosden Price son of Fredus Price, Nov. 1822
a black child of Mr. Pearce's Cook   Dec. 1822
                    Henderson son of   Jan. 1823
                        black adult   Jan. 1823
Edward Thomas Veazey of Dr. Ed. & Eliza.   Feb. 1824
At the consecration of the new church   29 June 1824
James Birckhead Weller, son of Rev. G. & H. C. Weller, born Oct 1823.
James Ruley, son of Saml. & ---- Ruley, born ----.
Elizabeth Ann Ruley, dau of the same, born ----.

Marriages:
John Rawleigh of Dela. to ---- Coulyer, C.Co.   -- Nov 1822
Andrew Price to ---- Coulyer, both of C. C.   -- Dec 1822
Robert Hall to ---- Hague, both of C. C.   -- Dec 1822
---- Pennington to ----   -- Jan 1822
---- Copes to ---- Copes   -- Jan 1822
Geo. Walmsley to Sarah Hall   -- Jan 1822
& 5 blacks.
---- Gence (Genee?) to ---- Comegys   -- --- 1824
John Cruikshanks to Mary Ellis   -- --- 1824
James Magee to Ann Hellnay   -- Feb 1824
John Ruley to Julianna Ruley   -- Feb 1824

Marriages by Rector Robert Piggot:
John Savin, slave of George Davis, Esq., to Jane Wilson, slave of Hyland Price, Saturday 3 Jun 1837.
Abraham Kinnard, slave of John H. Lusby, to Rachel Moore, a free woman, in the presence of Commodore Jones & Lady and Lieutenant Jones & Lady, Saturday, 8 Jul 1837.
Stephen Savin, slave of George Davis, Esq., to Susan Medford slave of Alfred C. Nowland, Esq., 12 Aug 1837.
Mr. William S. Hessey to Louisa Hayes, both of Cecil County, Tuesday, 31 Oct 1837.
Stephen Bayard, slave of General Forman, to Fanny Wilson, a free colored woman, Saturday, 11 Nov 1837.
Henry Nindson, slave of Commodore Jacob Jones, to Ann, slave of Thos. B. Veazey, Esq., Thursday, 28 Dec 1837.
Jacob Sewall to Nancy Yorkman, free persons of color, 28 Dec 1837.

Communicants: Mrs. Comegys, W. Ward, Anne Ward, Eliza Ward, Sally Lusby, M. Pearce, Anna Pearce, Dr. J. T. Veazie, S. Veazie, Mrs. T. B. Veazie, P. Biddle, Mrs. Biddle, Miss S. Davis, Miss & --- Veazie of Edward, Col. F. W. Veazie (Whitsundie 1823), G. Ford (March 1824), Susan Biddle (July 1824), Julianna Ward.

(End of vital records of St. Stephen's Parish, 1689-1837)

ST. MARY ANNE'S PARISH (NORTH ELK PARISH)

St. Mary Ann's Parish Register, 1709-1799

John Lewis Jr. b 4 May 1729
Izabella Lewis b 13 Mar 1731
John Lewis m Heston Phillips 10 Nov 1727
Catherine Phillips b 28 Apr 1734
Margaret Brunfield b 20 Feb 1733
Richard Bond b 4 Oct 1728
Sarah Bond b 9 Feb 1729
Margaret Bond b 4 Oct 1732
Mary Ellet b 27 Feb 1733
William Deoran son of James and Jean b 18 Sep 1718
James Deoran Jr. son of same b 15 Aug 1721
Mary Deoran dau of same b 9 Oct 1725
Elizabeth Deoran day of same b 16 May 1729
Temperance Touchstone b 11 Sep 1725
Katherine Touchstone b 6 Nov 1727
Christian Touchstone b 22 Oct 1729
Andrew Touchstone b 1 Jul 1732
Richard Touchstone b 21 May 1734
Thomas Jones b 15 Jun 1734
Alexander Mackeny bur 3 May 1722
Mary Mackeny m Mathew Kemp 1 Oct 1724
Miriam Justice b 18 Apr 1731
Peter Anderson b 2 Nov 1726
Mary Anderson b 22 Jan 1727
Ann Anderson b 5 Oct 1734
Elizabeth Watson bur 25 Oct 1733
Abrm. Watson m Susannah Bishop 12 Apr 1733
Jacob Watson b 20 Aug 1734
Prudence and Ephraim Bishop bur 13 Sep 1733
Margaret Brumfield b 20 Feb 1733
John Green b 30 Jan 1732
Mary Powlson b 15 May 1734
John Powlson d 15 Oct 1733
Samuel Whittiker b 17 Mar 1729
Thomas Whittiker b 29 May 1731
Mary Whittiker b 21 Mar 1734
Elizabeth Guilder d 24 Oct 1734
Moses Justice m Sarah Morgan 4 Sep 1737
Moses Justice m Ann Wilds 18 Aug 1734
Sarah Justice bur 10 Nov 1733
John Justice b 4 Jun 1733
Edward Cartmill b 27 Jan 1722
Thomas Cartmill b 14 Jun 1728
Nathan Cartmill b 25 Dec 1731
William Daws b 2 Dec 1734
Benjamin Daws b 10 Jun 1734
Rebecca Blake b 12 Sep 1730
Margaret Blake b 28 Aug 1729
Sarah Blake d 22 Oct 1729
John Stump b 6 May 1728
Henry Stump b 1 Sep 1731
Mary Hendrick b 14 Aug 1732

John Piggot b 18 Apr 1717
Samuel Piggot b 11 Jul 1718
Elizabeth Piggot b 10 Jun 1720
Abigal Piggot b 30 Jan 1721
Susannah Piggot b 13 Mar 1723
William Piggot b 8 Jul 1726
Jeremiah Piggot b 26 Sep 1730
Benjamin Piggot b 29 Oct 1732
William Smith m Sarah Pearson 20 Jan 1734
Joseph Young m Ann Johns 24 Dec 1732
Mary Young b 1 Dec 1733
Mary Young bur 30 Aug 1733
(sic) Mathew Turner m Sarah Maybury 14 Aug 1734
Jonas Touchstone b 10 Nov 1724
Nathan Cleaves b 18 Jan 1731
Benjamin Cleaves b 17 Jan 1734
Mary Harnons (Hamons?) b 21 Sep 1732
Margaret Stephens --- 16 Aug 1716
John Patterson b 13 Jun 1732
Mary Patterson b 11 Apr 1733
John Kasay b 28 Feb 1732
Mary Polson bur 15 Dec 1720
Andrew Polson bur 14 Dec 1726
Hannah Lofty b 28 Jan 1732
Izabella Lofty bur 14 Dec 1731
----- dau of Izabella Lofty bur 15 Jan 1731
Abraham Teague b 1 May 1721
Charity Teague b 14 Dec 1722
Elijah Teague b 1 May 1726
Susannah Teague b 3 Jan 1730
William Teague b 30 Jul 1733
Elijah Teague bur 1 Sep 1720
Prudence Amary b 14 Oct 1719
Stephen Amary b 15 Oct 1720
Lidia Amary b 14 Apr 1724
Rachel Amary b 7 Apr 1726
John Parker m Sarah Amary 3 Nov 1732
Jonathan Parker b 18 Aug 1734
John Ewing b 10 Jun 1732
Rachel Ewing b 2 Jan 1734
John Husbands b 31 Mar 1729
Thomas Husbands b 10 Mar 1731
Mary Husbands b 20 May 1734
---- dau of William Husbands b 10 Mar 1732
William Teague b 16 May 1734
Charles Berry b 25 Sep 1726
Elizabeth Berry b 15 Jul 1729
Mary Berry b 2 Apr 1734
Daniel Dunofin b 14 Oct 1730
Izabella Clift b 4 Feb 1732
Cornelius Dunofin bur 4 Oct 1730
Elizabeth Manheny b 1 May 1723
Thomas Manheny b 14 Oct 1722
Margaret Manheny b 1 May 1728
Cornelius Lessly b 12 Sep 1734

ST. MARY ANNE'S PARISH (NORTH ELK PARISH)

Samuel Young m Elenor Johnson 2 Feb 1730
Sarah Watson b 25 Jan 1724
Elizabeth Watson b 12 Apr 1721
Patience Watson b 28 Sep 1718
John Watson b 15 Dec 1723
John Watson d 26 Dec 1723
Alicia Denlon m William Watson 12 Feb 1731
Rebecca Bristow dau of William and Elizabeth b 25 Aug 1743
Elizabeth Bristow dau of same b 5 Jul 1731
John Watson b 3 Apr 1731
Mary Denton died 14 Mar 1730
Anthony Maughor b 10 Feb 1716
Patrick Maughor b 10 Nov 1719
Edward Maughor b 10 Sep 1723
Catherine Maughor b 23 May 1726
Mary Maughor b 20 Mar 1728
Ann Maughor b 14 Feb 1733
George Thompson b 29 Jun 1730
Jacob Johnson b 14 Feb 1722
Rachel Johnson b 15 Jan 1721
Margaret Johnson b 13 Jul 1723
Phebe Johnson b 21 Jul 1726
Ann Johnson b 25 Jan 1728
Caleb Carman b 30 Aug 1711
Sarah Penington bur 18 Jan 1730
John Penington m Elizabeth Umberson 25 Nov 1733
Susannah Cox b 19 Nov 1726
John Umberson Jr. bur 9 Jan 1732
John Umberson bur 17 Jan 1732
Reuben Gilder b 14 Apr 1719
James Manypeny b 28 Jan 1733
Robert Turner m Mary Friend 3 May 1727
Jane Ledgwood b 10 Dec 1734
Ann McKentire b 27 May 1725
John McKentire b 10 Oct 1728
Nicholas McKentire b 24 Feb 1729
James McKentire b 14 Jan 1734
Alexander McKentire b 10 Dec 1732
Laughlin Winter m Jennet McKentire 14 Nov 1734
John Sartil bur 1 Mar 1730
Leiah Kelly bur 7 Mar 1731
Thomas Kelly m ----- 31 Jan 1733
Sarah Kelly b 24 Nov 1734
Murty Maughan m Ann Leshly 28 Jun 1733
William Maughan b 30 Nov 1734
William Maughan bur 4 Dec 1734
Randall McDaniel b 24 Feb 1731
Sarah McDaniel b 2 Apr 1733
Joshua Hartshorn bur 20 Nov 1731
Samuel Hartshorn bur 10 Dec 1733
Samuel Patten b 11 Feb 1723
Jane Kilpatrick b 25 Feb 1732
Mary Penington b 30 Oct 1720
Catherine Jacobs b 7 Jan 1713
John Jacobs b 16 Feb 1715

Joseph Jacobs b 26 Aug 1720
Grace Jacobs b 17 Apr 1718
Mary Jacobs b 29 Nov 1721
Sarah Jacobs b 2 Feb 1722
Thomas Jacobs b 18 May 1725
Ann Jacobs b 17 Jan 1727
Hannah Jacobs b 7 Sep 1730
Mary Jacobs d 17 Sep 1730
Oliver Johnson b 15 Aug 1714
Mary Johnson b 17 Jun 1716
Margaret Johnson b 23 Jun 1718
Peter Johnson b 31 May 1720
Andrew Johnson b 25 Jun 1722
Thomas Dean b 4 Jan 1729
Thomas Dean bur 14 Aug 1729
Agnes McMaughan b 15 Apr 1730
Jacob Johnson m Elizabeth Drake 5 Apr 1730
Elizabeth Johnson b 17 Jan 1730
Elenor Johnson b 18 Feb 1731
Sarah Young b 14 Nov 1734
Jacob Young m Margaret Carmack 10 Dec 1729
Francis Mauldin d 30 Jan 1734
James Dason b 27 Mar 1735
Richard Greedy b 10 Mar 1735
Phebe Pewe b 16 Apr 1735
Richard Thompson m Hester Miller 20 Sep 1735
Benjamin Culver m Ann Dutton 16 Feb 1732
William Culver b 14 Mar 1733
Job Ruston m Mary Baker 6 Jul 1735
John Hackney m Phebe ---- 28 Sep 1735
Sarah Currer dau of William and Mary b 17 Feb 1734/5
George Death son of Randell and Honoria b 28 Mar 1735
William Vesey son of James and Mary d 4 Dec 1735
John George son of Nicholas and Mary d 10 Aug 1735
Rebekah Johnson dau of Thomas and Rebekah b 11 Oct 1735 about ten o'clock in the morning
Abram Watson son of William and Elizabeth b 29 Jul 1735
Isaac Hyland son of Nicholas and Elizabeth b 29 Feb 1735/6 about 5 o'clock in the afternoon
Jacob Hyland son of Nicholas and Elizabeth b 29 Feb 1735/6 about 7 o'clock in the afternoon
William Vesey son of James and Mary b 26 Sep 1736
Charity Wattson dau of Abram and Susannah b 20 Sep 1735
Elinor Howdle dau of John and ---- b 4 Mar 1729
John Urine son of John and ---- b 1 Mar 1732
Abel Bristow son of William and Elizabeth b 16 Jun 1736
Nathan Baker m Joyce Yardley 12 Jan 1736/7
Samuel Peryman son of Roger and Mary b 30 Apr 1735
Robert Milburn m Elinor ---- 25 Jan 1735/6
Edward Taylor m Mary ---- -- May 1735
Hannah Taylor dau of Edward and Mary b 25 Feb 1735/6
Catrin Ward dau of ----- b 10 Apr 1736
Francis Maybury m Rose Irwin 11 May 1736
Beriah Maybury son of Francis and Rose b 17 Mar 1736/7
Francis Turner son of Matthew and Sarah b 24 Dec 1735

ST. MARY ANNE'S PARISH (NORTH ELK PARISH)

Mathew Turner m Sarah Maybury 15 Aug 1734
William Redman son of James and ---- b 1 Nov 1733
Thomas Redmon son of same b 4 May 1735
James Cummings son of Robert and Elizabeth b 18 May 1736
Mary Young dau of Samuel and Elinor b 19 Oct 1735
Samuel Gilpin son of Samuel and Jane b 20 Oct 1734
Rachel Gilpin dau of same b 31 Aug 1736
Mary Phillips dau of John and Elizabeth b 29 May 1737
Mary Roberts dau of James and Ann d 10 May 1735
John Roberts son of James and Ann b 4 May 1737
John Jones son of Will Jr. and Mary b 21 Mar 1735/6
William Stanley son of Luke and Mary b 7 Sep 1725
Hannah Jones dau of James and Patience b 29 Apr 1737
Susanah Grady dau of James and Mary b 27 Oct 1737
John Grady son of same b 17 Feb 1735/6
Sarah Simcoe dau of George and Elizabeth b 15 Dec 1737
Abram Watson son of Abram and ---- b 14 Feb 1737/8
Mary Culver dau of Benjamin and Ann b 15 Apr 1736
Ann Culver dau of same b 22 Apr 1738
Mercy Pecot dau of Peter and Hannah b 5 May 1737
John Kankey son of John and Ann b 16 Sep 1738
Antony Roos m Jane Miller 24 Jul 1738
Zebulon Hollingsworth m Ann Mauldin 18 Apr 1727
Elizabeth Hollingsworth dau of Zebulon & Ann b 6 Feb 1727/8
Steven Hollingsworth son of same b 13 May 1730
Jesse Hollingsworth son of same b 12 Mar 1732/3
Zebulon Hollingsworth son of same b 17 May 1735
Elizabeth Owens b 18 Feb 1718
Joseph More m Kisiah Rutter 15 Jul 1737
Ruth More dau of Joseph and Kisiah b 15 Oct 1737
Ann Bristor dau of William and Elizabeth b 25 Feb 1738
Silvin Jones dau of William and Mary b 30 Jul 1738
Elizabeth Robards dau of Joseph and Margret b 11 Aug 1737
Mary Hambleton dau of John and Elizabeth b 21 Apr 1733
John Hambleton bur 24 Jan 1737
Garrit Mekeney m Margret Curyeur 26 Jan 1738/9
Ann Currer dau of John and Sarah b 16 Aug 1735
John Currer bur 10 May 1738
Peter Justice son of Peter and Catherine b 3 Mar 1735
Rebecca Justice dau of same b 25 Jul 1737
Peter Justice m Catherine Crew 28 Jan 1731
Thomas Johnson son of Mathias and Magdellin b 6 Jul 1735
Joseph Johnson son of same b 19 Jan 1739
Thomas Johnson Jr. son of Thomas and Rebecca b 29 Sep 1737
Thomas Johnson Jr. bur 5 Nov 1738
Thomas Johnson father of Thomas Johnson Jr. bur 7 Jan 1738
Nicholas Cursine son of John and Deborah b 22 Sep 1734
John Cursine son of same b 12 Jul 1736
George Cursine son of same b 18 Aug 1738
Samuel Yunge bur 3 Feb 1738/9
Prudence Yunge dau of above Samuel and Elennor b 31 May 1739
Michael Lum m Mary Makenne 9 Jul 1739
William Denne son of Simon and Margret b 15 Aug 1739
James Denne son of same b 1 Feb 1739/40
Margret Picot dau of Peter and Hannah b 7 Jul 1739

EARLY ANGLICAN CHURCH RECORDS OF CECIL COUNTY

Ann Beazely dau of Jethro and Elizabeth bur 10 Aug 1739
Elizabeth Beazely dau of same bur 20 Sep 1739
Isaac Phillips son of Samuel and Ann b 7 Jan 1738/9
Isaac Phillips bur 7 Aug 1739
Jecobas Poulson son of Jecobus and ---- b 8 Oct 1739
John Hyland m Martha Tilden 29 Apr 1739
Rebecca Hyland dau of John and Martha b 19 Jan 1739/40
Nicholas Hyland son of same b 15 Oct 1742
Steven Hyland son of same b 26 Dec 1744
John Hyland son of same b 27 Nov 1746
Charles Hyland son of same b 26 Mar 1749
Lambeart Hyland son of same b 24 Jul 1751
Millicent Hyland dau of same b 12 Feb 1754
Captain John Hyland departed this life 3 Nov 1756
Martha Hyland widow & relict of Capt. John d 28 Aug 1766
Samuel Clerk son of John and Elizabeth b 13 May 1735
Cathrine Clerk dau of same b 14 Aug 1737
Mary Clerk dau of same b 26 Oct 1738
Rachel Bristow dau of William and Elizabeth b 25 Oct 1739
William Starkey m Catherin Voice 28 Nov 1739
Ealce Taylor dau of Benjamin and Hannah b 20 Dec 1736
Sarah Taylor dau of same b 27 Sep 1738
Alexander Orton bur 14 Dec 1739
Ann Orton wife of Alexander bur 31 Mar 1740
Rebecca Johnson dau of Bartholomew and Sarah b 12 Sep 1736
Joseph Johnson son of same b 28 Jan 1738
Mary Currer bur 23 Sep 1739
Sarah Currer bur 1 Nov 1739
John Currer m Millicent Johnson 16 Jun 1740
Nicholas Hyland son of Nicholas and Elizaebth b 21 May 1738
Millicent Hyland dau of same b 31 Jul 1740
Rebecca Johnson dau of Edward and Mary b 25 Apr 1736
Edward Johnson son of same b 15 Nov 1738
Mary Johnson above bur 13 Jun 1741
Francina Robarts dau of James and Ann b 26 Feb 1740/1
Susannah Jacob dau of Thomas and Ann b 11 Jan 1735/6
Frances Jacob dau of same b 2 Jul 1739
Henry Hollingsworth son of Zebulon and Ann b 17 Sep 1737
Levi Hollingsworth son of same b 29 Nov 1739
Steven Hollingsworth son of same bur 8 Nov 1740
Ann Hollingsworth bur 13 Nov 1740
Zebulon Hollingsworth m Mary Jacob 21 Jul 1741
Ralf Whitaker son of Robart and Mary b 22 Sep 1739
Rachel Whitakar dau of same b 22 Jul 1741
Thomas Currer son of John and Millicent b 25 Jul 1741
Moses Jones son of William and Mary b 25 Apr 1741
Abraham Whatson Jr. son of Abraham & Susannah b 20 Dec 1738
Charity Whatson dau of same b 20 Dec 1735
Isaac Deone Whatson son of same b 4 Jan 1741
Bryan Grady son of James and Mary b 9 Feb 1740/1
Hanah Rutter wife of Jon. (sic) Rutter bur 10 Feb 1739
Jno. (sic) Rutter above bur 25 Mar 1740
Jno. Rutter Jr. m Catherine Jones 19 Jul 1740
Mary Rutter dau of Jno. and Catherine b 29 Jul 1741
John Mekinne son of Garret Mekenne and Margret b 5 May 1742

ST. MARY ANNE'S PARISH (NORTH ELK PARISH)

Jacob Death son of Randal and Honoure b 7 Oct 1742
John Crouch son of Thomas and Rebecca b 6 Jul 1743
Zebulon Hollingsworth m Mary Jacob 1 Jul 1741
Jacob Hollingsworth son of Zebulon and Mary b 30 Jul 1742
Thomas Jones son of Samuel and ---- b 15 Dec 1737
Samuel Jones above bur 17 Nov 1743
Simon Johnson m Catherine Vandeveare 4 Nov 1738
Mary Johnson dau of Simon and Catherine b 10 Oct 1739
Rachel Johnson dau of same b 14 Mar 1743
Ann Robards dau of James and Ann b 9 Jan 1742
Elizabeth Starkey dau of Will and ---- b 26 Mar 1742
Catherine Starkey wife of Will bur 25 Apr 1742
William Starkey m Susannah Cox 7 Jan 1742/3
John Starkey son of William and Susannah b 7 Feb 1743/4
Jonas Powlson bur 5 Mar 1743/4
Mary Jones dau of William Jr. and Mary b 15 Jun 1744
James Nevil son of Edward and Mary b 24 Mar 1732/3
John Nevil son of same b 18 Mar 1740
Joseph Corte m Margret Ricketts 25 Sep 1741
John Corte son of Joseph and Margret b 19 Jul 1742
Rebecca Corte dau of same b 3 Jun 1744
Amus Fogg m Elenor Yung 15 Jul 1742
Elizabeth Fogg dau of Amus and Elenor b 17 Mar 1742/3
Febey Whiteaker dau of Robert and Mary b 18 Feb 1743
Richard Hitchcok son of Milicent Hitchcok b 22 Apr 1738
Elizabeth Lum dau of Michel and Mary b 2 Jul 1743
Ann Lum dau of same bur 17 Nov 1743
Alexander Mekeney m Susannah Forster 3 Jun 1742
Sarah Mekeney dau of Alexander and Susannah b 3 Apr 1744
Nicholas George son of Nicholas and Mary b 3 Nov 1738
The Reverend John Brady departed this life 22 Mar 1745/6
John Stockton m Elizabeth Alldredg 5 Nov 1745
Joseph Stockton and Benjamin Stockton sons of John and Elizabeth
    b 24 May 1746
Rachel Crouch dau of Thomas and Rebecca b 18 Jan 1745
Milicent Hyland dau of Nicholas and Elizabeth b 31 Jul 1740
Samson Hyland son of same b 11 Nov 1742
Michael Hyland son of same b 23 Dec 1744
Jessey Mekeney son of Garrit and Margret b 14 Oct 1746
Harman Arronie son of Johanas and Sarah b 4 Apr 1746
about ten o'clock at night George Rock m Mary Story 28 Mar 1743
Marrabella Rock dau of George and Mary b 27 Oct 1745
William Rock son of same b 9 Jun 1747
Thomas Story son of Robert and Mary b 21 Jun 1739
Marcey Story dau of same b 26 Dec 1741
William Cronagan m Frances Jenins 25 Aug 1741
William Cronagan Jr. son of William & Frances b 29 Aug 1741
William Cronagan Jr. bur 4 Sep 1741
Frances Cronagan wife of William bur 1 Dec 1744
William Cronagan m Jane Swann 9 Feb 1745
Sarah Cronagan dau of William and Jane b 10 Apr 1747
Sarah Poulson dau of Peter and Mary b 31 Jan 1746
Thomas Hollingsworth son of Zebulon and Mary b 2 Aug 1747
Rachel Starkey dau of William and Susannah b 3 Dec 1745

William Starkey son of same b 13 Dec 1747
Susannah Starkey wife of William bur 23 Dec 1747
Richard Williams son of Robert and Catherine b 3 Aug 1743
Thomas Williams son of same b 31 Mar 1745
Robert Williams Jr. son of same b 5 Apr 1747
Amelia Pattin dau of Richard and Rebecca b 31 Dec 1747
Mary Waugh Baxter dau of James and Elizabeth b 22 Feb 1742/3
Rachel Baxter dau of same b 22 Nov 1745
William Mekeney son of Alexander and Susannah b 26 Sep 1746
Samuel Brown m Milicent Hitchcok 30 Oct 1746
Thomas Brown son of Samuel and Milicent b 14 Oct 1747
Milicent Brown bur 23 Feb 1748/9
Jesse Mekeney son of Garrit and Margret bur 12 Dec 1749
Rebecca Lum dau of Michael and Mary b 8 Feb 1745
Isaac Lum and Jacob Lum sons of same b 1 Aug 1748
Isaac Lum above bur 5 Oct 1748
Mary Darlington dau of John and Sarah b 29 Oct 1740
John Darlington son of same b 28 Jan 1742
Mary Mekeney dau of Alexander and Susannah b 8 May 1750
Will Grace m Mary Keatly 25 Apr 1747
Elizabeth Grace dau of Will and Mary b 16 Nov 1747
William Hamilton son of John and Littice b 11 Feb 1748
Steven Hollingsworth son of Zebulon & Mary b 21 Feb 1749/50
Jane Pryer dau of Thomas and Christian b 26 May 1740
Thomas Pryer son of same b 28 Jul 1745
John Brown bur 11 May 1748
Daniel Picot m Elizabeth Brown 17 May 1750
Mary Bull dau of Constantine and Catharine of Charlestown b 6 Oct 1750
Alexander Dugging m Ann Miller 30 Jun 1750
Sarah Dugging dau of Alexander and Ann b 5 Feb 1752
Rachel Hyland dau of John and Mary b 4 Sep 1751
Catharine Bull dau of Constantine & Catharine b 18 Nov 1752
Elizabeth Mekeney dau of Garrit and Margret b 4 Apr 1752
John Hollingsworth son of Zebulon and Mary b 12 May 1752
Elizabeth Hyland dau of John Jr. and Mary b 19 Feb 1753
Nicholas Foster son of John and Margret b 25 Dec 1740
Elizabeth Foster dau of same b 29 Dec 1742
John Foster son of same b 8 Oct 1744
Nathan Foster son of same b 30 Oct 1746
Jesse Foster son of same b 28 Jan 1751/2
John Stalkup m Mary Treadway 30 Oct 1752
Henry Stalkup son of John and Mary b 5 May 1753
David Hollingsworth son of Capt Zebulon & Mary b 12 Aug 1754
Ann Mekeney dau of Alexander and Susannah b 1 May 1752
William Pennock son of William and Mary b 20 May 1753
Edward Hyland son of John and Mary b 10 Jan 1755
James Crouch son of Thomas and Rebecca b 25 Feb 1753
Rebecca Crouch dau of Thomas and Rebecca b 24 Dec 1755
Thomas Rutter son of Moses and Ann b 15 Oct 1755
William Mainly m Rebecca George 24 Sep 1747
Ann Mainly dau of William and Rebecca b 15 May 1749
Jesse Mainly son of same b 9 Jul 1751
Elizabeth Mainly dau of same b 27 Aug 1753
Mary Mainly dau of same b 25 Dec 1756

ST. MARY ANNE'S PARISH (NORTH ELK PARISH)

Jacob Mainly son of John and Elizabeth b 18 Apr 1747
Sarah Mainly dau of same b 19 Feb 1748
William Mainly son of same b 26 Feb 1751
Rachel Mainly dau of same b 15 Jul 1753
Jacob Hyland son of John and Mary b 4 Aug 1757
Reverend Jones Avren m Keady Justice dau of William and Mary Justice 16 May 1709
Benedictes Avren son of Jones and Keady b 3 Mar 1711
William Avren son of same b 9 Jul 1713
Reverend Jones Avren minister from Sudeland d 15 Aug 1713
Keady Avren wife of Rev. Jones Avren d 29 Aug 1713
William Avren son of Jones and Keady d 3 Sep 1713
Benedictes Avren m Sarah Kitely dau of John 7 Nov 1738
Jonas Avren son of Benedictes and Sarah b 8 Oct 1739
Henry Avren son of same b 1 Nov 1740
Thomas Avren son of same b 7 Aug 1744
Rebekah Roter dau of John and Catran b 28 Oct 1727
Johannes Arrants m Sarah Phillips 25 Nov 1745
Herman Arrants son of Johannes and Sarah b 4 Apr 1746
Nathan Arrants son of same b 23 Aug 1748
William Arrants son of same b 22 Aug 1750
Sarah Arrants wife of Johannes d 9 Dec 1750
William Arrants son of Johannes and Sarah d 21 Aug 1752
Johannes Arrants m Elizabeth Veazey dau of James 12 Mar 1751
Mary Arrants dau of Johannes and Elizabeth b 29 Mar 1752
Julia Arrants dau of same b 15 Aug 1753
Sarah Arrants dau of same b 17 Jun 1756
William Arrants son of same b 19 Feb 1758
John Arrants son of same b 29 Oct 1760
James Arrants son of same b 24 Sep 1762
Er. Arrants son of same b 10 Dec 1764
Samuel McCauly son of Bryan and Ann b 22 Apr 1754
Thomas Owens and Mary his wife was -----.
David Owens son of Thomas and Mary b 19 Sep 1766
Lavender Owens b 27 Jan 1769
Glenn Owens b 1 Aug 1775
Blanchey Owens dau of same b 4 Oct 1774
Jonas Avron b 23 Nov 1763
Thomas Avron m Keesy Clark 5 Sep 1776
Elizabeth Avren dau of Thomas and Keesy b 12 Jan 1777
Jonas Avren son of same b 23 Jul 1779
William Avren son of same b 27 Mar 1781
Kady Avren dau of same b 17 Oct 1783
John Avren son of same b 14 Mar 1785
Mary Avren dau of same b 7 Mar 1786
Joseph Clark and Francis Clark sons of Mary Clark, dau of Samuel and Elizabeth Clark, b 20 Mar 1781
Robert Broom m Frances Jacobs 7 Jun 1756
Elizabeth Broom dau of Robert and Frances b 11 Aug 1757
William Beck son of William and Mary b 7 May 1746
John Bristow son of William and Rachel b 4 Nov 1750
Meliscent Bristow dau of same b 19 Sep 1760
James Bristow b 19 Oct 1762
William Barns m Margret Schott 2 Nov 1758
John Barns son of William and Margret b 16 Aug 1759

William Barns son of same b 19 Mar 1761
Sarah Barns dau of same b 15 Feb 1763
Andrew Barrett m Mary Shepperd dau of Thomas and Ann Shepperd 11 Dec 1749
Ann Barrett dau of Andrew and Mary b 25 Nov 1752
Mary Barrett dau of same b 18 Apr 1755
Jane Barrett dau of same b 11 Apr 1757
William Barrett son of same b 19 Jul 1759
Elizabeth Barrett dau of same b 15 Dec 1761
Catherine Barrett dau of same b 26 Apr 1764
Shepperd Barrett son of same b 1 Aug 1766
Amelia Barrett dau of same b 19 Mar 1772
Mary Barrett dau of same b 6 Aug 1775
Mr. John Boulting, merchant of Chestertown in Kent County, m Mrs. Ellenor Daugherty dau of Mr. Edward Daughty (sic) of Cecil County in Maryland by Rev. John Hamilton 30 Dec 1771
Ann Boulting dau of John and Ellenor b 8 Oct 1772
Thomas Brown son of Robert and Frances b 4 May 1760
William Bristow son of William and Rachel b 28 Jan 1765
Tabitha Bristow dau of same b 4 Aug 1769
Ann Brown b 21 Sep 1752
Henry Beedle m Mary Bunkerd 19 Jan 1768
Stephen Beedle son of Henry and Mary b 18 Oct 1769
Grace Baythorn dau of James and Catherine b 1 Sep 1766
Ann Baythorn dau of same b 20 Apr 1769
Mary Baythorn dau of same b 15 Jun 1771
Margret Baythorn dau of same b 1 Apr 1773
James Baythorn son of same b 4 Jul 1775
Cathran Baythorn dau of same b 29 Aug 1779
Sarah Baythorn dau of same b 25 Apr 1784
George Baal (Ball?) m Sarah Blew 9 May 1766
Elizabeth Ball (Baal?) dau of same b 29 Aug 1767
Rachel Baal (Ball?) dau of same b 26 Jan 1770
Ezra Ball son of same b 31 Jul 1772
Mary Ball dau of same b 10 Oct 1774
George Ball m Ann Kely 1 Dec 1776
Isiah Ball and Jeremiah Ball and Ester Ball, sons and dau of George and Ann, b 20 Apr 1778
Richard Brookings son of Charles Brookings & Margret Gordon his wife b 15 Jun 1766
Susannah Brookings dau of same b 4 Jul 1767
Elizabeth Brookings dau of same b 26 Feb 1773

Entries made by Samuel Thomson, Clerk, 28 May 1774.
John Wells son of John Wells, m Mary Riley of County Donegal Ireland 26 Jan 1773
John Carr m Arimento Carr 12 Jan 1776
Hannah Arant son to same (sic) b 13 Nov 1771
Mary Carr dau of same b 4 Aug 1773
Nathaniel Littell m Mary Jackson 1 Nov 1774
Mary Littell dau of Nathaniel and Mary b 26 Mar 1775
Henry Touchstone m Margret Mahen 12 Nov 1749
Elizabeth Touchstone dau of same b 6 Oct 1745
Richard Touchstone son of same b 25 Sep 1749
Temperance Touchstone dau of same b 16 Mar 1769
William Touchstone son of same b 19 Jul 1772

ST. MARY ANNE'S PARISH (NORTH ELK PARISH)

Robert Crouch son of Thomas and Rebeccah b 1 Jul 1758
Benonee Currer son of John and Milicent b 12 Oct 1756
Elizabeth Crouch dau of Thomas and Rebecca b 25 Nov 1760
Richard Cazier son of Richard and Susanna b 16 Aug 1762
Andrew Coulter m Hannah Killpatrick 20 Feb 1750
John Coulter son of Andrew and Hannah b 30 Nov 1751
Samuel Coulter son of same b 6 Feb 1754
Andrew Coulter son of same b 9 Apr 1756
Alexander Coulter son of same b 16 Apr 1760
Elizabeth Coulter dau of same b 15 Nov 1762
Abraham Cazier son of Richard and Susanna b 13 Jul 1764
Richard Cazier m Susannah Kirkpatrick 15 Apr 1760
Isaac Crouch m Ann Johnson 3 May 1760
Mary Crouch dau of same b 24 Dec 1760
Edward Crouch son of same b 29 Jun 1762
Johnson Crouch son of same b 3 Jan 1764
John Crouch son of same b 25 Feb 1766
Nathan Crouch son of same b 3 Feb 1768
Susannah Cazier dau of Richard and Susannah b 26 Feb 1772
William Donergin (Dunigan?) b 15 Feb 1752
Ellener Donergin dau of ditto (sic) b 15 Feb 1754
Elener Dunigan wife of Rodger Dunigan of Charlestown died 22 Apr 1775 age 55 years
Augustine Herman Ensor son of Joseph and Mary b 28 Jan 1761
Thomas Elliott of Charlestown d 27 Jul 1763
Elizabeth Elliott widow of Thomas d 9 Apr 1764
Thomas Elliott son of Thomas and Elizabeth m Mary dau of Benjamin and Sarah Chew 29 Jul 1765
Frances Brumfield m Edward Brumfield son of Francis Brumfield and Sarah Jackson 9 Mar ----.
Elise Brumfield b 14 Mar 1764
Mary Brumfield b 7 Feb 1766
Agness Brumfield dau of ditto (sic) b 13 Mar 1768
Sarah Brumfield dau of same b 7 Mar 1768
Ed. Francis Brumfield son of same b 9 Feb d the year 1775
Patrick Downey born in Ireland 24 Jun 1753
William Brumfield m Mary Brumfield 25 Dec 1765
Zeblon Oldron b 14 Feb 1762
Ann Oldron b 4 Mar 1764
John Brumfield b 14 Jul 1766
Elizabeth Brumfield b 8 Jun 1768
Cathrine Brumfield b 23 Sep 1772
John Brumfield m Elizabeth Gibson -- Aug 1767
Philess Brumfield son of John and Elizabeth b 2 Mar 1768
Edward Brumfield son of same b 14 Jan 1770
Rachel Brumfield dau of same b 25 Aug 1772
John Brumfield son of same b 25 Oct 1773/4
Zebulon Foster son of William and Ellener b 21 Oct 1755
Richard Foster son of John Sr. and Margret b 18 Apr 1754
James Foster son of same b 16 Aug 1758
Benjamin Fergueson m Mary Rutter 1 Apr 1761
Ann Fergueson dau of Benjamin and Mary b 8 Mar 1763
William Foster m Elener Poulson 2 Jan 1753
Elijah Foster b 24 Apr 1768
James Alon d 23 Apr 1775

William Alon son of James m 9 Jul 1773 -----.
William Alon son of William and ---- b 25 Jun 1774
Edward Beasley m Elizabeth Beasley -- --- 1766
Ann Beasley dau of Edward and Elizabeth b 16 Mar 1768
Sarah Beasley dau of same b 16 Nov 1769
Elizabeth Beasley dau of same b 14 Aug 1771
John Greenland Beasley son of same b 29 Aug 1773
Edward Beasley m Ann ---- 19 May 1774
Abraham Beasley (Bazley) born of Ann Bazley 28 Nov 1774
Ann Bazley wife of Edward Bazley (Beasley) b 28 Oct 1753
William Burke m Jean Campbell 16 Jun 1774
Margret Burke dau of William and Jean b 6 Mar 1775
Nathan Brumfield m Ann Foster 5 Dec 1774
Mary Brumfield dau of Nathan and Ann b 24 Nov 1775
Nicholas George d 8 Aug 1760
Sampson George son of Nicholas d 13 Jul 1760
Hannah Greedy dau of Richard and Alice b 10 Mar 1760
Aaron Grace m Ann Boyar dau of Peter and Esther 27 Jan 1758
Rebecca Grace dau of Aaron and Ann b 8 Mar 1762
John Grace son of same b 3 Sep 1767
Peter Boyar Grace son of Aaron and Ann b 16 Apr 1778
Alexander Gray m Margrett Galeher 12 Apr 1759
Sarah Gray dau of Alexander and Margrett b 10 Jan 1760
Rebecca Gray dau of same b 9 Dec 1761
Mary Gray dau of same b 9 Oct 1763
James Gray son of same b 6 Dec 1767
Thomas Gray son of same b 10 Oct 1770

Rev. John Hamilton late of Strabane of the County of Tyrone in
  Ireland became Rector of this Parish 1746 and his wife
  Lettice daughter of Charles Short arrived here 6 Sep 1746 &
  with them their son John born in Ireland 24 Feb 1743/4.
Mary Hamilton dau of John and Lettice b 28 May 1747 and died the
  September following.
William Hamilton son of Rev. John and Lettice b 6 Feb 1748/9
Charles Hamilton son of same b 24 Jul 1750
Lettice Hamilton wife of Rev. John Hamilton died 2 Aug 1750.
Rev. John Hamilton m Jane Peck dau of Mr. Benjamin Peck of New
  York, merchant, and widow of Rev. Richard Currer (or Caner?)
  7 Sep 1757.
Angel Hamilton dau of Rev. John and Jane Hamilton b 6 Jan 1758
  in New York.
John Hamilton m Catherine Margaretta Forester dau of Rev. George
  William Forester of Kent County, MD 2 Jul 1772.
Rev. John Hamilton departed this life 13 Apr 1773.
Catherine Lettice Hamilton dau of John and Margaretta b 16 Apr
  1773
Ann Sophia Hamilton dau of same b 3 Nov 1774, d 6 Nov 1774
Samuel Hollingsworth son of Zebulon and Mary b 17 Jan 1757
Elizabeth Hyland dau of John and Mary b 1 Aug 1760
Sampson George Hyland son of John and Mary b 17 Jan 1763
James Henderson son of John Henderson and Jane Henderson b 9 May
  1750
John Henderson son of same b 6 Mar 1754
Jacob Handerson (Henderson) son of same b 8 Sep 1756
William Handerson (Henderson) son of same b 21 May 1759

ST. MARY ANNE'S PARISH (NORTH ELK PARISH)

Robert Handerson (Henderson) son of same b 14 Aug 1761
John Hall m Jane Greary in the County of Ardmagh in Parish of
 Mollabrach (Ireland) 6 Dec 1747
Ann Hall dau of John and Jane b 20 Sep 1748
Sarah Hall dau of same b 12 Sep 1754
John Hall first son of John and Jane b 1 Jul 1756
Jane Hall dau of same b 21 Apr 1759
Thomas Hall son of same b 22 Oct 1762
Robert Hart son of James and Ann b 20 Apr 1759
James Hart son of same b 17 Nov 1761
Jennet Hart dau of same b 29 Jan 1764
Nicholas Hyland son of Col. Nicholas Hyland m Margery Kankey dau
 of John and Ann Kankey 2 Aug 1764
Ann Hyland dau of Nicholas and Margery b 28 Aug 1756
William Howell son of George and Mary, both from Cork in Ireland,
 m Ruth Smith dau of William and Sarah 9 Nov 1755
James Howell son of William and Ruth b 22 Sep 1756
John Howell son of same b 22 Sep 1758, d 27 Sep 1758
William Howell son of same b 5 Nov 1759
George Howell son of same b 16 Jan 1762
Elisha Howell son of same b 13 Feb 1764
Levi Howell son of same b 2 Jun 1766
Benjamin Howell son of same b 13 Sep 1767
Stephen Hyland m Rebecca Tilden -- Dec 1774
John Hyland son of Stephen and Rebecca b 1 Oct 1775
Mrs. Rebecca Hyland wife of Stephen d -- Oct 1775
Stephen Hyland m Araminta Harnon (Hamm?) 20 Mar 1777
Nicholas Hyland son of Stephen and Araminta b 15 Jul 1779
George Johnson m Ann Shepard 23 Jan 1755
Thomas Johnson first son of George & Ann b Thurs 11 Mar 1756
Mary Johnson dau of same b Thursday 10 Nov 1757
William Johnson son of same b Monday 22 Oct 1759
Melecin Johnson dau of same b 20 May 1761
Benjamin Johnson son of same b 26 Aug 1763
Thomas Jones of Baltimore County m Elizabeth Baxter dau of Col.
 James Baxter and Elizabeth his wife, 14 Dec 1761
Edward Johnson d 9 Nov 1760
Philip Barton Key son of Francis and Ann Arnold Key b 12 Apr 1757
John Kankey m Rebecca Hyland 6 Jun 1738
John Kankey son of John and Rebecca b 6 Mar 1759
Elizabeth Key first daughter of Francis and Ann Arnold Key b
 Friday 10 Aug 1759 in Charlestown, Cecil County.
Samuel Killpatrick m Jannet Good 16 Nov 1761
Robert Killpatrick first son of Samuel and Jannet b 26 Oct 1762
John Kankey son of Harman and Elizabeth b 17 Oct 1757, d 30 Sep
 1760
Ann Kankey dau of same b 6 Aug 1759
John Kankey son of same b 15 Dec 1761, d 4 Sep 1766
David Kankey son of same b 4 Dec 1767, d 17 Dec 1767
Mary Kankey dau of same b 16 Feb 1769
March 8, 1775 - Samuel Kilpatrick was married to the late Elener
 Foster - Elias Kilpatrick - (sic)
Hannah Killpatrick dau of Samuel Killpatrick and Jean Good b 12
 Feb 1768

John Killpatrick son of same b 26 Mar 1766
Samuel Killpatrick son of same b 3 Jan 1768
Mary Lowry b 4 Aug 1730
James Lowry m Mary Vezey 27 Apr 1748
John Lowry son of James and Mary b 27 Apr 1750
Ann Lowry dau of same b 7 Oct 1753
Mary Lowry dau of same b 20 Feb 1756
William Lowry son of same b 10 Jun 1759
James Lowry son of same b 4 Apr 1762
Elijah Lowry son of same b 11 Sep 1764
Robert Lowry son of same b 8 Mar 1766
Stephen Lowry son of same b 21 Dec 1768
Alley Crowley b 12 Sep 1770
Truman Crowley son to ditto (sic) b 29 May 1774
William Bryan son of Edward and Lydia born in 1768
Emilia Bryan dau of same born in the same year 1768
John Bryan son of same born in the year 1771
Michael Lum son of Michael and Mary b 7 Mar 1751
Mary Lum dau of same b 27 Jul 1753
Rachel Lum dau of same b 21 Mar 1756
Michael Lum d 29 Jun 1756
Mary Lewis dau of John and Sarah b 10 Sep 1763
Titan Leeds Kimble m Mary Avery 22 Jan 1765
and he was born 27 Jul 1747
Mary Avery dau of Peter and Elijah (sic) b 8 Oct 1744
Elizabeth Kimble dau of Titan Leeds Kimble and Mary Avery b 27
    Oct 1766 about 6 o'clock in the morning
Sarah Kimble dau of same b 22 Apr 1769 about 8 o'clock in the
    morning
Leeds Kimble son of same b 27 Feb 1773 about 7 o'clock in the
    morning and d 17 Jun 1774 about 4 o'clock in the morning
    aged 1 year 3 months and 21 days
Jane McDougall dau of Charles and Mary b 4 Jan 1765
Catherine Abigail McKeown dau of John McKeown and Partiana Lake b
    5 Jun 1767
Jacob Manly m Rebecca Lum 15 Dec 1768
William Manley son of Jacob and Rebecca b 3 Jul 1769
Mary Manly dau of same b 26 Mar 1771
John Manly son of John and Elizabeth b 10 Oct 1762
James McClure son of William and Margaret, both of this parish, b
    8 Nov 1764
Jacob Northerman m Mary ---- 4 Jun 1753
Margret Northerman dau of Jacob and Mary b 11 Sep 1755
John Northerman son of same b 9 Mar 1757
Ann Northerman dau of same b 9 Nov 1760
William Vandike b 1 Sep 1749
Benjamin Nelson shipwright m Margaret Hedrick, real daughter of
    Elizabeth Elliott and daughter in law to Thomas Elliot 8 Dec
    1763
William Thomas b 6 Jun 1729
Sarah Kennerly wife to William Thomas b 4 Apr 1742 and they were
    married 2 Mar 1762
William Thomas son of William and Sarah b 18 Sep 1763 at half
    after 11 o'clock at night

ST. MARY ANNE'S PARISH (NORTH ELK PARISH)

Charles Thomas son of same b 7 Apr 1765 at 12 o'clock at night and d 19 Apr 1765
Sarah Thomas dau of same b 6 Sep 1766 at 2 o'clock in the morning
Edward Thomas son of same b 18 Jul 1768 at 11 o'clock in the morning
Charles Thomas son of same b 9 Aug 1770
Elizabeth Thomas dau of same b 6 Feb 1774 at half after 6 o'clock in the evening
John Conery m Elizabeth Anderson his present wife 17 Jul 1774
Silvester Newgent m ----- 5 Dec 1756
John Newgent son of Silvester and ---- b -- Dec 1756
George Newgent son of same b 5 Dec 1763
Mary Newgent dau of same b 24 Oct 1760
William Newgent son of same b 23 Jan ----
Daniel Newgent son of same b 24 Oct 1765
Andrew Newgent son of same b 23 Jan ----
Silvester Newgent son of same b 29 Jan 1775
Campbell Newgent born in the year 1774
Thomas Patton son of Richard and Rebecca b 12 Oct 1758
Peregrine Rose m Ellenor Potter 31 Oct 1760
Augusteny Rose dau of Peregrine and Ellenor b 26 Mar 1762
Hannah Pritchard dau of Samuel and Mary b 21 Aug 1759
Elizabeth Pritchard b 15 Jan 1762
Thomas Palmer m Hannah Norton 29 Oct 1751
Elizabeth Palmer dau of Thomas and Hannah b 20 Oct 1752
Grace Palmer dau of same b 23 May 1761
Thomas Palmer m Mary Sommersell 23 May 1761
Rebekah Palmer dau of Thomas and Mary b 25 Nov 1762
Mary Penington dau of Boyar and Hesther b 16 Feb 1764
Sheckaniah Sommersill m Mary Haderick 19 Oct 1752
Thomas Palmer widower m Mary Somersill widow of Sheckaniah Sommersill 1 Jun 1761 by Rev. John Hamilton
Mary Elliott Palmer dau of Thomas and Mary b 14 Sep 1764 at 4 o'clock in the morning
Ann Elizabeth Palmer dau of same b 25 Oct 1766 at 4 o'clock in the morning
Joseph Palmer son of same b 14 Dec 1768 after 3 o'clock in the afternoon
Mary Rutter dau of Moses and Ann b 30 Dec 1757, d 21 Sep 1762
Thomas Rutter son of same b 15 Oct 1755
Samuel Rutter son of same b 24 Jun 1760
Rebecca Rutter dau of same b 13 Feb 1763
John Rialy son of Mathew and ---- b 9 Dec 1750
William Booth b 25 Dec 1754
Mathew Rialy son of Mathew and ---- b 5 Feb 1763
Joseph Rock late Walshall baker and son of Thomas and Sarah Rock of Brerwood in the County of Stafford in Old England died 12 Jun 1764
William Rooke m Ann Maybury dau of Francis and Rosannah Maybury 30 Sep 1762
Richard Rutter son of Moses and Ann b 1 Nov 1765
Ann Rickets Roberts dau of James and Levina b 16 Apr 1750
William Rutter m Ann Rickets Roberts 5 Jun 1766

William and Ann Rutter had a son born alive 22 Oct 1766 but died unbaptized.
William Rutter son of John and Catherine b 8 Mar 1745
William Rutter died 2 May 1775
Mary Rutter dau of Moses and Ann b 21 Aug 1768
Francis Rock m Mary Pryer widow, dau of Robert and Elizabeth Cummings of North East, 27 Jul 1759
Benjamin Rumsey of Cecil County m Mary Hall dau of Col. John Hall and Hannah his wife of Baltimore County, 24 Mar 1768
James Redman son of James and Jane b 28 Dec 1756
Thomas Redman son of same b 6 Sep 1760
Benjamin Redman son of same b 29 Sep 1763
Hannah Rumsey dau of Benjamin and Mary b 30 Mar 1770
Moses Rutter m Ann Ricketts dau of Thomas Ricketts and Mary his second wife 15 Jan 1752
Ann Rutter dau of Moses and Ann b 25 Mar 1771
John Thomas Ricketts son of John and Rebecca b 8 Apr 1754
Paul Ricketts son of same b 30 Jun 1755
Jane Ricketts dau of same b 26 Aug 1758
Rebecca Ricketts d 6 Jan 1760
John Ricketts m Sarah Penington 2 Jun 1760
Even Ricketts son of John and Sarah b 12 Oct 1761
John Ricketts son of same b 11 Nov 1763
David Ricketts son of same b 13 Nov 1765
Mary Ricketts dau of same b 14 Dec 1767
Catherine Ricketts dau of same b 18 Mar 1770
Thomas Russell m Ann Thomas 17 Feb 1774
Mary Russell dau of Thomas and Ann b 17 Nov 1774
Frances Russell dau of same b 23 Sep 1776
Thomas Russell son of same b 5 Apr 1779
Thomas Hughes m Frances Forrester of Georgetown, Kent County 16 May 1774
Edward Forrester Hughes son of Thos. & Frances b 8 Jun 1776
Elizabeth Margaret Hughes dau of same b 6 Apr 1777
Deborah Hughes dau of same b Wednesday 18 Feb 1778
Catherine Hughes dau of same b Saturday 9 Sep 1780
Nathaniel Sympers son of Thomas and Amey Sympers m Ann Lewis dau of Richard and Amey Lewis 10 Oct 1759
Amey Sympers dau of Nathaniel and Ann b 9 Sep 1760
Richard Sympers son of same b 21 Feb 1763
Thomas Sympers son of same b 21 Mar 1765
Nathaniel Sympers d 4 Nov 1766
Nathaniel Sympers son of Nathaniel and Ann b 15 May 1767
Richard Simpers m Catherine Howell 1 Jun 1751
George Simpers son of Richard and Catherine b 18 May 1752
Thomas Simpers son of same b 4 Dec 1754
Isaac Simpers son of same b 29 Dec 1756
Jacob Simpers son of same b 4 Feb 1759
Mary Simpers dau of same b 31 Oct 1761
Richard Simpers son of same b 23 Oct 1764
Richard Simpers Sr. d 14 Sep 1766
William Howell Simpers son of Richard and Catherine b 20 Nov 1766
Sarah Howell dau of Sarah Howell b 25 Jun 1758

ST. MARY ANNE'S PARISH (NORTH ELK PARISH)

Benjamin Stockton son of John & Elizabeth Stockton m Martha
    Altricks dau of Peter & Mary Altricks 14 Dec 1769
Catherine Seger dau of Joseph and Mary b 20 Dec 1760
Jeremiah Seger son of same b 20 Feb 1763
Francis Seger son of same b 31 Mar 1765
Joseph Seger son of same b 23 Aug 1767
Ruben Seger son of same b 22 Oct 1769
Old Rock alias George Rock in the 64th year of his life was
    married to Katherine Simpers aged 40 by Rev. Hamilton in the
    merry month of April, 16th day, 1772
Catherine Short dau of Adam and Jane b 6 May 1722
Adam Short son of same b 10 Jan 1723
John Short son of same b 11 Nov 1725
Thomas Short son of same b 27 Sep 1727
William Short son of same b 22 Sep 1729
Elizabeth Short dau of same b 1 Jan 1731
The ages of Thomas and Elizabeth Short's children:
    Araminta Short dau b 9 Sep 1761
    Elizabeth Short dau b 28 Apr 1765
    Rebecca Short dau b 25 Jan 1767
    Sarah Short dau b 24 Apr 1769
    John Short son b 24 Jan 1771
    Thomas Short son b 5 Feb 1773
    William Short son b 21 Aug 1774
    Mary Short dau b 8 Aug 1778
    Jean Short dau b 25 Feb 1781
    Rachel Short dau b 17 Feb 1783
Rebecca Short dau of John and Elizabeth b 4 Oct 1798
John Thomas Short son of Thomas and Marty b 20 Oct 1797
Richard Thomas m Mary Waugh Baxter 7 Oct 1767
Edward Jackson m Sarah Greenland 12 Jan 1773
Betsey Jackson dau of Edward and Sarah b 11 Apr 1775 about seven
    o'clock in the morning
Sarah Cooper dau of Joanes and Elizabeth b 13 Aug 1774
John Cooper son of same b 2 Dec 1756
Thomas Cooper son of same b 16 Mar 1760
Nathaniel Cooper son of same b 23 Feb 1763
Patrick Bourn, Clerk William Short b 21 Aug 1774
William Thomson, son to the Reverend Mr. Samuel Thomson, was born
    22 May 1735 and was ordained Deacon and Priest in the Church
    of England at the Bishop of London's Palace in Fullam,
    December, 1759.
Susanna Ross dau of Rev. George Ross, Rector of North Elk alias
    St. Mary Ann's Parish, b 17 Jan 1738.
The above William and Susanna were married by the Reverend Thomas
    Barton at Lancaster in Pennsylvania 28 Oct 1762.
Ross Thomson son of William and Susanna b 27 Oct 1763
Mary Thomson dau of same b 9 Jan 1765
Gertrude Thomson dau of same b 31 May 1766
Samuel Magaw Thomson son of same b 25 Oct 1767
Elizabeth Thomson dau of same b 16 Nov 1768
Sarah Howard Thomson dau of same b 16 Mar 1770
Susanna Warrel Thomson dau of same b 13 Dec 1772
Written by Samuel Thomson, Clerk, 21 Feb 1774

Jane Ramsey Thomson dau of William and Susanna b 13 Mar 1774
William Biddle Thomson son of same b 27 Feb 1776
Thomas Baker m Margret Pheland in 1763
Hanah Yeardley Baker dau of Thomas and Margret b 17 Sep 1764 at 2 o'clock in the evening
Thomas Whittaker son of Robert and Mary m Elizabeth Rogers dau of Rowland and Ann 2 Jan 1760
Samuel Whittaker son of Thomas and Elizabeth b 29 Nov 1761
Ann Whittaker dau of same b 24 Oct 1760
Thomas Whittaker son of same b 17 Jun 1763
Isaac Vanbibber son of James and Ann Vanbibber of Bohemia Mannor m Ann Chew dau of Benjamin and Sarah Chew near Susquehannah 27 Nov 1768
Baruch Williams late of Prince George's County, Maryland m Rachel Baxter of Cecil County, Maryland dau of Col. James Baxter and wife Elizabeth, by the Rev. Mr. John Hamilton 7 May 1776
Mary Waugh Williams dau of Baruch and Rachel b 26 Apr 1772
Baxter Williams son of same b 13 May 1774
Basil Williams m Jane Barret dau of Andrew Barret 6 Apr 1775
James Pritchard m Elisabeth Carr dau of Walter and Elizabeth 8 Jul 1768
Samuel Pritchard son of James and Elizabeth Pritchard b 12 May 1769, d 6 --- 1769
George Pritchard son of same b 16 Aug 1770
Catherine Keitly dau of Henry and Mary b 22 Jul 1767
Mary Keitly dau of same b 20 Jul 1770
James Campbell m Sarah Rutter 11 Jan 1764
John Campbell son of James and Sarah b 13 Nov 1764
James Campbell son of John Campbell and Jane Campbell otherwise Ogelvie his wife, b 16 Mar 1748 in Smithsborough in the County of Monaghan in Ireland.
David Corbit m Ester Corbit 12 Jun 1770
James Corbit son of David and Ester b 12 Apr 1772 at four o'clock in the morning
Margret Cowdan Corbit b 6 Jul 1774
John Willham born in Ireland 12 May 1750 John White m Sarah White his present wife 16 Oct 1776
James White son of John and Sarah b 13 Sep 1772
Thomas White son of same b 5 Sep 1774
James Hill son of Samuel and Ann born 13 Apr 1751 in Cecil County, North Milford Hundred
Ann White born in Ireland 17 Mar 1752
Moses Jones m Rebecca Ruten 14 Jan 1766
John Jones son of Moses and Rebakah b 10 Dec 1768
Amey Jones dau of same b 28 Oct 1776
Moses Jones son of same b 7 Dec 1774
William Ruten Jones son of same b 9 Nov 1776
Aliga Jones son of same 17 Nov 1778
Thomas and Maly Jones son and dau of same b 17 Aug 1781
Nancy Jones dau of same b 14 Sep 1783
Richard Jones son of same b 7 Mar 1787. This is the family of Moses Jones and Rebakah his wife.
Philip Javyr m Ledia ---- 31 Sep 1768, New Castle, Delaware
Cornelia Javyr dau of Philip and Ledia b 3 Feb 1772
Frances Rodin b 9 Apr 1760/1
James Hunter m Sarah Walch 28 Sep 1761
Ann Hunter dau of James and Sarah b 14 Mar 1763

ST. MARY ANNE'S PARISH (NORTH ELK PARISH)

Andrew Hunter son of same b 8 Nov 1764
James Hunter son of same b 8 Aug 1767
Sarah Hunter dau of same b 22 Apr 1770
Edward Jackson m Margret Memullen 26 Jan 1768
James Jackson son of Edward and Margret b 6 Jul 1786
John Jackson (Jekson) son of same b 27 Jul 1770
Edward Jackson (Jeckson) son of same b 31 May 1773
William Bogs m Margaret Blair 24 --- 1746
Elizabeth Bogs b 31 --- 1776
Jeremiah Baker m Hannah Thackey 14 Dec 1769
Marcy Baker dau of Jeremiah and Hannah b 20 Sep 1776
Francis Baker son of same b 17 Jul 1774
Elizabeth Baker dau of same b 17 Aug 1776
Sarah Baker dau of same b 25 Mar 1778
John Wood m Rachel Death 20 Jan 1755
Elizabeth Wood dau of John and Rachel b 2 Aug 1757
Bennonia Wood son of same b 16 Sep 1760
Sarah Wood dau of same b 16 Sep 1763
Jean Wood dau of same b 8 Sep 1765
John Wood son of same b 20 Feb 1769
Robert Williams (aged 28) m Jean Meek -----.
Easter Williams dau of Robert and Jean b 20 Feb 1769
Cathrin Williams dau of same b 26 Aug 177
Thomas Williams son of same b 26 Aug 1773
James Hunter Conwa (sic) b 2 Aug 1775
Jane Daws Watson (sic) m Ann Welsh 29 Aug 1762
Moses Nevill b 5 Mar 1763
Jeans Morrisse b 2 Dec 1764
Cathren Finney b 27 Jul 1774
John Finney b 1 Jun 1752
Mary Finney b 7 Aug 1750 (sic)
Susannah Finney b 30 Jun 1761
Elizabeth Finney b 16 Mar 1765
Elonar Finney d 14 May 1777
William Veazey m Mary Carr 16 May 1758
George Veazey son of William and Mary b 26 May 1759
Elizabeth Veazey dau of same b 7 Oct 1760
John Veazey son of same b 22 Jan 1763
Mary Veazey dau of same b 17 Jun 1765
James Veazey son of same b 22 Dec 1767
Mary Veazey wife of William Veazey died 20 Nov 1770
William Veazey m Mary Rock 1 Mar 1776
John Miller m Rachel Paulson 11 Oct 1756
Henry Miller son of John and Rachel b 1 Sep 1758
John Miller m Sarah Allen 16 May 1773
Ann Miller dau of John and Sarah b 22 Aug 1774
Rachel Miller dau of same b 26 Nov 1776
John Miller son of same b 10 Feb 1779
John Currier son of John and Sarah b 17 Mar 1717/8
William Currier son of same b 28 Feb 1719
Mary Currer dau of same b 6 Nov 1722
Thomas Currer son of same b 13 Jan 1724
Michael Currier son of same b 18 Jan 1727
Elizabeth Currer dau of same b 4 Feb 1729
Sarah Currier dau of same b 5 Mar 1731
Catharine Currier dau of same b 9 Mar 1733
William Currier m Mary Bird dau of Empson & Susanna Bird 17 Jul

1774
Sarah Currier dau of William and Mary b 11 Apr 1775
Thompson Bird son of Empson and Mary b 21 Oct 1770 a Sunday at 6 o'clock
James Avren son of Benedictus and Sarah Avran b 3 Oct 1739
Henery Avren son of same b 1 Nov 1740
Thomas Avren son of same b 7 Aug 1744
Jonas Avren son of Henry and Catrener b 23 Nov 1766
Henry Avren d 17 Feb 1775 Jones Avren d 18 Jul 1775
Ann Avren d 18 Aug 1775 Benedictes Avren d 3 May 1777
Ann Trew dau of D. Trew b 11 Jul 1776
Thomas Trew son of same b 30 Sep 1773
James Dugin m Sarah Avren 11 Jan 1775
Ann Dugan dau of James and Sarah b 8 Oct 1776
Sarah Avren d 17 Nov 1784
Thomas Dugin son of James and Sarah b 6 Jan 1779
Mary Dugin dau of same b 3 Sep 1781
Lady Dugin dau of same b 9 Feb 1784
Patrick Grimes m Elizabeth Charter 9 Oct 1779
Joseph Grimes son of Patrick and Elizabeth b 18 Oct 1780
John Grimes son of same b 12 Nov 1782
George Ball m Sarah Blue his first wife 9 May 1766
Elizabeth Ball dau of same b 29 Aug 1767
Rachel Ball dau of same b 26 Jan 1770
Ezra Ball son of same b 13 Jul 1772
Mary Ball dau of same b 10 Oct 1774
 George Ball m Ann Keely 1 Dec 1777
Isaiah Ball and Jeremiah Ball and Easter Ball sons and dau of
    George and Ann b 20 Apr 1778
Sarah Ball dau of same b 27 May 1780
Noah Ball son of same b 22 Apr 1782
Margrat Ball dau of same b 25 Mar 1784
Josiah Jonson m Hannah Merrall 26 Mar 1777
Levi Jonson son of Josiah and Hannah b 10 Jul 1777
Robert Johnson son of same b 3 Feb 1779
Hezekiah Jonston son of same b 8 Mar 1781
Hannah Jonson dau of same b 27 Jan 1783
John Jonson son of same b 10 Apr 1773
Isaac Johnson m Sarah Dickson 2 Nov 1770
John Johnson son of Isaac and Sarah b 16 Apr 1772
Mary Johnson dau of same b 22 Mar 1774
 Simon Johnson son of Josiah and Hannah b 1 Feb 1785
Jeane Hall dau of John Hall and Mary Brown b 25 Jan 1777
Joseph and Francis Clark sons of Mary Clark, dau of Samuel and
    Elizabeth Clark b 20 Mar 1781
John Johnson son of Josiah and Hannah Jonson b 27 Nov 1787
Rachel Johnson dau of same b 6 Jan 1790
Thomas Avren m Keesy Clark 5 Sep 1776
Elizabeth Avren dau of Thomas and Keesy b 12 Jan 1778
Jonas Avren son of same b 23 Jul 1779
William Avren son of same b 17 Mar 1781
Lady Avren dau of same b 17 Oct 1783
John Avren son of same b 14 Mar 1785
Mary Avren dau of same b 7 Mar 1786
Sarah Avren dau of same b 25 Jun 1791
Joseph Campbell son of James and Mary b 17 Apr 1773
John Campbell son of same b 31 Aug 1775

ST. MARY ANNE'S PARISH (NORTH ELK PARISH)

Mathew Campbell son of same b 12 Feb 1780
Mary Campbell dau of same b 26 Feb 1782
Ruth Campbell dau of same b 4 Mar 1784
James Campbell son of same b 26 Feb 1786
Richard Burke m Grace Farrier 10 Aug 1766
William Fyfe son of James and Grace b 18 Apr 1782
Elizabeth Fyfe dau of same b 12 Dec 1785
Patrick Grimes m Elizabeth Charty 9 Oct 1779
Joseph Grimes son of Patrick and Elizabeth b 18 Oct 1780
John Grimes son of same b 12 Nov 1782
Thomas Avren m Keesy Clark 5 Sep 1776
Elizabeth Avren dau of Thomas and Keesy b 12 Jan 1778
Jonas Avren son of same b 23 Jul 1779
William Avren son of same b 27 Mar 1781
Leady Avren dau of same b 17 Oct 1783
John Avren son of same b 14 Mar 1785
Mary Avren dau of same b 7 Mar 1786
Joseph and Francis Clark sons to Mary Clark, dau of Samuel and
    Elizabeth Clark, b 20 Mar 1781
Rachel Johnson dau of Isaac and Cateren b 17 Mat 1786
Rebecca Johnson dau of same b 26 Dec 1770
Sarah Avren dau of Thomas and Keesy b 25 Jun 1791
Nickles Hitchcock m Sarah Polsen 12 Oct 1775
John Hitchcock son of Nickeles and Sarah b 5 Aug 1776
Rotch Hitchcock dau of same b 13 Apr 1780
Augusta Hitchcock dau of same b 29 Apr 1785
Samson Hitchcock son of same b 5 Jan 1787
John Nite son of Elizabeth Nite b 20 Jun 1778
Ann Moore Hitchcock dau of Nickles and Sarah b 11 Apr 1794
John Cummings son of John and Remento Cummens b 12 Oct 1793
Jesse McCullogh son of George and Sina b 7 Dec 1767
Levi McCullogh son of same b 5 Nov 1770
Mary McCullogh dau of same b 24 Feb 1773
George McCullogh son of same b 4 Jun 1776
Rebecca McCullogh dau of same b 14 Jun 1779
John Cummings son of John & Araminta Cummings b 12 Oct 1793
William Cummings son of same b 23 Aug 1795
Thomas Cummings son of same b 20 Feb 1797
Robert Cummings son of same b 24 Feb 1799. Taken from loose sheets
    in the Register: [Note: It is apparent from these entries that
    more of these loose pages may be missing from the register.
    Editor]
Elizabeth Jones dau of ditto (sic) and Mary b 1 Jan 1725
Catherine Jones dau of same b 6 Sep 1732
Mary Lang dau of John and Sarah b 5 Mar 1725
John Lang son of same b 20 May 1728
Daniel Lang son of same b 30 May 1734
Catherine Lang dau of same bur 15 Mar 1722
Timothy Stedam son of Luliff and ---- b 30 Jun 1733
William ---- m Jane Stevens 4 Aug 1734
Jonas Brown m Elizabeth Paine 5 Aug 1734 [Ed. Note: Line drawn
    between these two entries.]
Mary Fedry dau of ditto (sic) 12 May 1734
Mary Parsley dau of Richard and Sarah b 29 Aug 1739
Nathaniel Parsley son of same b 16 Feb ----
Sarah Parsley bur 17 Aug ----
Elizabeth Morgan dau of Hugh and Ann Catherine b 13 Jun ----

Margaret Morgan dau of same b 14 Jul ----
Mary Morgan dau of same b 26 Jan ----
John Morgan son of same b 1 Mar ----
Ann Morgan dau of same b 28 May ----
William Morgan son of same b 13 Feb ----
Margaret Morgan bur 15 Feb ----
Henry Morgan m Catherine Dehoes 17 Apr ----
Rebecca Pecoe dau of Peter Pecoe b 25 Apr 17--
Daniel Pecoe b 25 Sep 1727
Hannah Pecoe b 14 Feb 1730
Lady Pecoe b 26 Sep 1732
Guilbert Guilder m Elizabeth Casine 11 Aug 1728
Ann Guilbert b 14 Oct 1734
Agnass Miller bur 21 Feb 1733
Elizabeth Casteever b 30 Jun 1732
Elizabeth Casteever bur 29 Oct 1732
Daniel Orton b 1 Jan 1723
Alexander ----- b 8 Feb 1728
Susannah ----- b 10 Feb 1729
Joseph Nevall b 12 Mar 1729
Sarah Nevell b 2 Feb 1727
Margaret Johnson b 13 Jul 1734
Thomas Nevell b 23 Jun 1721
James Nevell b 25 Mar 1732
Elenor Miller b 27 May 1731
John Rutter b 15 Nov 1713
Kenabah Rutter b 15 Nov 1719
Hannah Rutter b 18 Oct 1722
Whitton Rutter b 10 Sep 1724
Margaret Rutter and Ann Rutter b 14 Jul 1729
Moses Rutter bur 10 Jul 1726
Edward Omullen m Mary Maclegun 23 Dec 1733
Abigal Hall bur -- Sep ----
Jonas Lum m Mary Massy 4 Feb ----
Elinor Dilon b 18 May ----
Daniel Dilon b 17 Feb ----
Hannah Dilon b 24 Feb ----
Richard Forster m Sarah Manely 20 Aug ----
William Forster b 29 Nov 1729
John Forster b 30 Jun 1730
William Forster bur 20 Aug 1730
Lewis Jones bur 14 Nov 1727
John Nelson m Mary Loath 17 Sep 1731
James Greely m Mary Roach 8 Jul ----
James Roberts b 23 Sep ----
Jacob Roberts b 9 Oct ----
Mary Roberts b 15 Feb ----
Elizabeth Roberts bur 18 Dec ----
Lidia Roberts bur 3 Apr ----
Jacob Roberts bur 2 Mar ----
James Roberts m Ann Rickets 1 Jan ----
---- Turnbull dau of John and Ann -----
John Dorsey m Silvia Heathcoat 2 Aug 1724
Mary Dorsey dau of John and Silvia b 2 Oct 1725
Silvia Dorsey wife of John Dorsey bur 2 Mar 1733
Charles Duffey son of Charles and Sarah b 18 Apr 1729
Sarah Duffey dau of same b 4 Aug 1723

ST. MARY ANNE'S PARISH (NORTH ELK PARISH)

Margaret Duffey dau of same b 20 Apr 1726
Duffey McClure dau of William and ---- b 29 Jun 1729
Charles McClure son of same b 21 Feb 1731
Ann McClure dau of same b 15 Feb 1733
Charles McClure bur 12 Apr 1729 (sic)
Charles Duffey bur 22 Apr 1729
James Duffey bur 17 Feb 1732
Elizabeth McClure wife of William bur -- --- 1733
Thomas Johnson b 20 Nov ---- Mary Johnson b 5 May ----
Sarah Johnson b 25 Sep ----
Ann Johnson b 24 Jan ----
George Cazine b 10 Aug ----
Thomas Shepherd son of Thomas and Ann b 1 Jan ----
Mary Shepherd dau of same b 26 Dec ----
Judith Purify dau of Nicholas and ---- b 17 Dec ----
Elizabeth Purify dau of same b 23 Jan ----
Nathan Phillips m Jane Simcoe 18 Apr ----
Nathan Phillips son of Nathan and Jane b 27 May ----
Nathan Phillips bur 15 Sep ----
Sarah Phillips dau of Nathan and Jane b 1 Jan ----
James Wilson b -- --- 1734
Roger Peryman m Mary Burrage 15 Apr 1728
Mathias Johnston m Magdalene Poulson 30 Oct 1716
Jacob Johnston son of Mathias and Magdalene b 9 Mar 1730
John Johnston son of same b 19 Jun 1732
Elenore Rea dau of Andrew and ---- b 24 May 1734
John Bristow son of William and ---- b 18 Apr 1734
---- Carter dau of William and ---- b -- --- 1731
Richard Clerk son of John and Jane b 23 Jan 1732
William Clerk son of same b -- --- 1734
Richard McClure m Catherine Mackeve -- --- 1727
James McClure son of Richard and Catherine b 21 Nov 1728
Sarah McClure dau of same b 8 Dec 1730
Elizabeth McClure dau of same b 8 Apr 1733
Sarah Clerk dau of John and Elizabeth b 7 Sep 1733
John Clerk m Elizabeth ---- 1732
John Jones m ---- 16 Apr 1732
Samuel Jones b 18 Oct 1733
Elizabeth Phillips b 16 Apr 1725
Samuel Phillips b 19 Mar 1727
Nathan Phillips b 21 Feb 1732
Samuel Phillips m Elizabeth Brooks 19 Mar 1724
Sarah Hodgson b 13 Feb 1728
Rachel Hodgson b 3 Jul 1730
John Hodgson b 16 Dec 1733
William White b 1 Jul 1727
Samuel White b 7 Sep 1728
Nathan White b 19 Jan 1730
Hannah White b 18 Mar 1734
Nathan White bur 16 Jul 1732
Rebeccah George b 1 Jun 1727
Sampson George b 3 Oct 1729
Ann George b 10 Dec 1731
John George b 27 Mar 1734
Edward Gazine (Cazine?) bur 14 Jul 1728
Jacob Vanpool m Amy Cazine 23 Oct 1726
Jacob Vanpool b 11 Sep 1729

EARLY ANGLICAN CHURCH RECORDS OF CECIL COUNTY

John Vanpool b 16 Jan 1731
Peter Vanpool b 3 Jul 1734
John Keedly m Susannah Gray 14 Jul 1734
Sarah Ozman b ----
Phillis Ozmon b 30 Sep ----
Rachel Ozmon b 24 Sep ----
Ann Ozmon b 24 Sep ----
Moses Rutter son of Richard and Mary b 17 Nov 1731
Ann Rutter wife to Moses Rutter b 18 Jan 1734
Richard Rutter d 10 Mar 1748
Mary Rutter wife to Richard Rutter d 12 May 1749
Thomas Johnson m Milliscent Hyland 1 Jul 1722
Elizabeth Johnson dau of Thomas and Milliscent b 6 Apr 1723 d 6 Sep 1723
Milliscent Johnson dau of same b 14 Oct 1724 about 8 of the clock in the evening
Edward Johnson son of same b 20 Mar 1726
Milliscent Johnson wife of Thomas Johnson d 6 Aug 1734, bur 9 Aug 1734
Rachel Johnson dau of Thomas Sr. and Jane b 29 Jan 1723
Daniel Johnson son of same b 6 Sep 1726
George Johnson son of same b 24 Jun 1730
Joseph Young bur 11 Apr 1732
Catherine Young wife of Joseph Young bur 28 Dec 1732
Joseph Young son of Samuel and Elenor b 15 Feb 1733
---- Phillips son of John and Elizabeth b 3 Mar 1732
Mary Wilds dau of Joshua and Ruth b 28 May 1733
Ann Simpers dau of Thomas and Emy b 28 Apr 1730
William Simpers son of same b 12 Mar 1732
Thomas Simpers bur 28 Jan 1733/4
Hukill Guilder m Emy Simpers 30 Dec 1733/4
Sarah Carmack dau of William and ---- b 2 Jul 1733
Abraham Short son of Adam Jr. and ---- b 7 Apr 17-- about the break of day
Robert Cummins m Elizabeth Baker 15 Oct 1732
Nicholas Hyland son of Nicholas and Elizabeth b -- --- 1733
Martha Death wife of Randall Death bur -- --- 1732
Randall Death m Honour Kersy -- --- 1733
William Currier m Mary George 26 Dec 1713
Katherine Currier dau of William Currier bur -- --- 1732
William Veasy son of James and Mary b -- --- 1734
Allen Robins m Martha Banner 11 Feb 1724
Jasper Robins son of Allen and Martha b 6 --- 1728

The End of St. Mary Ann's Register, 1709-1799. The following typed page compiled by William B. Steel, 22 Nov 1922, was also included in the record.

Tombstone Records, Old West Nottingham Cemetery, Rising Sun:
Rebecca Meek wife of John d 5 Jul 1760 aged 45 years
Matew Meek d 22 Mar 1758 aged 11 years
John Glasgow d 23 May 1769 aged 47 years
Jean Finley d 30 Apr 1812 aged 82 years
Robert Finley d 12 Oct 1807 aged 42 years
Robert Finley Sr. d 21 Apr ---- aged 88 years
Rebecca Hynman d 14 Aug 1765 ----
Margaret Simpson wife of John d 20 Feb 1812 aged 30 years

ST. MARY ANNE'S PARISH (NORTH ELK PARISH)

William McCay son of John and Frances d 12 Apr 1797 age 36
Frances McCay wife of John d 5 Oct 1795 aged 58 years
John McCay d 17 Mar 1794 aged 66 years
William Buchanan d 29 Nov 1769 aged 63 years
William McCullough Logan d 8 Sep 1851 aged 24 years
Martha Smith d 9 Nov 1808 aged 67 years
David Smith Sr. d 15 Sep 1815 aged 74 years
Mary Currethers wife of William d 23 Dec 1762 aged 42 years
David Moor d 30 Nov 1793 age 75 years
Elizabeth Linton wife of William d 1 Feb 1790 aged 28 years
John Patterson d 1 Dec 1798 aged 67 years
S. P. 1779
D. P. 1781
Rev. John Paul d 30 Sep 1739 aged 32 years
Andrew Leeper d 15 Apr 1776 aged 70 years
William Rowland (no headstone) d 1784

Unlawful Cohabitations, St. Mary Ann's Parish (From the Parish Vestry Proceedings, 1749-1776)

John Key (Keyes) and Mary Skurry (Scurry), wife of Thomas Scurry, admonished in May, 1749 and again in Nov., 1751, but they were still unlawfully cohabiting in March, 1752.
John Howard and Alice Walley were admonished in July, 1750. Alexander McIntosh and Alice Howard admonished in Dec. 1752.
Lewis Lee and Rebecca Childs were admonished in Aug., 1756, but they were still unlawfully cohabiting in March, 1757.
Charles Ragon and the widow Death were cited in August, 1756 but they appeared with a marriage certificate signed by Mr. William Lindsay, a minister living in Pennsylvania.
Jonas Cooper of Charles Town, cordwainer, and Elizabeth Jackson were cited in March, 1759, but Rev. John Hamilton informed the Vestry that he had since married them.
Walter Rodgers and Martha his supposed wife were cited in March 1759, but Rev. Hamilton stated he had married them.
William Lashell and Elizabeth Ryan cited in November, 1761, and ordered to produce a marriage certificate by Easter.
Ralph Rutter of Charles Town and Liddy Wells (widow), she being with child, were admonished in November, 1761.
Joseph Ellot of Charles Town and Sarah Brumfield (Brumfeld), she being big with child, were cited in November, 1761.
William Merchant and Jane Armstrong were cited in November, 1761, but reportedly had moved out of Maryland.
Thomas Beetle and Sylvia Jones were admonished in Dec. 1765.
Samuel Faris and Elizabeth White were cited in November, 1765 and appeared in March, 1766, reportedly married.
John Magruder and Elizabeth Jackson were cited in November, 1765 and by March 1766 he had reportedly left the county.
Charles Brookins and Margaret Gordon were cited, Sept. 1766.
Jacob Johnson and Rebecca Hawkins were cited in Sept., 1766.
James Wareham and Sabina McDowell (widow) were cited in June 1767. They appeared and were admonished in August 1767.
Mordecai Cloud and Elizabeth Connolly were cited, Oct. 1767.
Alexander Butler and Hester Hughes were cited in Oct., 1767.
Edward Bryan and Lydia Wells were cited in August, 1786 and subsequently appeared and were admonished by the Veatry.
Edward Welden and Mary Campbell were cited in October, 1768.

James Orrick and Eve Baker were cited and he produced the following certificate in September, 1770: "These are to certified all concerned that Mr. James Orrick and Miss Eve Baker were some considerable time agoe married by me by virtue of a license from his Excellency Robert Eden, Governor of Maryland. Given under my hand this 2nd Sep. 1779. (Signed) John Beard."

Edward McVinish (McVinchie) and Sarah Noland (Nowldham) were cited and admonished by the Vestry in April, 1771.

Samuel Logan and Jane Bing were cited and subsequently were reported to have left the county in June, 1771.

William McCullough and Susannah Connolly were cited in Dec., 1774 and he appeared in January, 1775 before the Vestry to inform them that the charge was based on information which proceeded from malice and ill will of some of his neighbors and he assured the Vestry that "the girl with whom he was supposed unlawfully to cohabit is not in the province nor has not been at his house since harvest."

Patt Hamilton and Jane Lee (alias Shaw) were cited in April, 1776, and he responded by letter, informing the Vestry that "they had been treated with unbecoming rudeness" because Jane has had several children which are still being provided for by him. The Vestry then responded by informing Hamilton that "Jane had been seen in bed with him and often leaving and entering his house late and early, and they presume his own conscience if duly attended to with candor will be a sufficient apology for the tender notice they had given him, though as Hamilton had said in his letter it may be difficult to prove co-habitation they still in the spirit of meekness recommend that he be circumspect in his walking with this woman." Charles Whitelock and Susanna Emmitt cited in April, 1776. Edmund Warimer and May Baker cited in April, 1776.

INDEX

ABBETT Mary 33
  William 33
ABBOTT Rebecah 33
  William 6
ADAMS Sarah 6
ALCOCK Mary 26
  William 26
ALLDREDG Elizabeth 63
ALLEN Sarah 75
ALLIN Anne 10
  Anne 50
  Daniell 4
  Paul 10
  Paul 50
ALMAN Abraham 7, 8, 21, 30, 35, 36, 37
  Abram 3
  Amy 30
  Benjamin 30, 35
  Jacob 37
  John 36
  Joseph 21
  Margaret(t) 21, 30, 35, 36, 37
  Mary 7, 30
  Rachel 8, 30
  Sarah 8, 30
ALON James 67
  James 68
  William 68
ALTHAM Mary 6
ALTRICKS Martha 73
  Mary 73
  Peter 73
AMARY Lidia 58
  Prudence 58
  Rachel 58
  Sarah 58
  Stephen 58
ANDERSON Ann 57
  Christopher Mounce 16
  Elizabeth 71
  Mary 57
  Peter 57
ARANT Hannah 66
ARCHER Jacob 2, 14, 20, 25
  Mary 14, 20, 25
ARMSTRONG Edward 37
  Elizabeth 8
  Jane 81
  John 37
  Martha 37
ARNOLD Ann 69
ARON Maccary 32
ARRANTS Elizabeth 65
  Er. 65
  Herman 65
  James 65
  Johannes 65
  John 65
  Julia 65
  Mary 65
  Nathan 65
  Sarah 65
  William 65

ARRONIE Harmon 63
  Johanas 63
  Sarah 63
ASHFORD Jane 2
  John 37
  Martha 37
ASHLEY Rachel 7
ATKEY Angelico 1
  John 1
  Mary 2
ATKINS John 17
  Mary 17
  Rebecca 4
  Rebecca 17
AVERY Elijah 70
  Mary 70
  Peter 70
AVREN Benedictes (Benedictus) 65, 76
  Catrener 76
  Elizabeth 65, 77
  Henry 65, 76
  James 76
  John 65, 77
  Jonas 65, 76, 77
  Jones 65, 76
  Kady 65
  Keady 65
  Keesy 65, 77
  Leady 77
  Mary 65, 77
  Sarah 65, 76, 77
  Thomas 65, 76, 77
  William 65, 76, 77
AVRON Jonas 65
  Thomas 65

BAAL Elizabeth 66
  George 66
  Rachel 66
BABINTON John 24, 48
  Mary 24, 48
  William 24, 48
BAKER Elizabeth 75, 80
  Eve 82
  Francis 75
  Hanah Yeardley 74
  Hannah 75
  Jeremiah 75
  Marcy 75
  Margret 74
  Mary 60
  May 82
  Nathan 60
  Sarah 75
  Thomas 74
BALDWIN Catherine 8
  John 8
BALL Ann 66, 76
  Easter 76
  Elizabeth 66, 76
  Ester 66
  Ezra 66, 76
  George 66, 76
  Isaiah 66, 76
  Jeremiah 66, 76
  Margrat 76

  Mary 66, 76
  Noah 76
  Rachel 66, 76
BANNER Martha 80
BARKER Elizabeth 14
  Mary 14, 24, 48
  Rebecca(h) 14, 25, 49
  Richard 14, 24, 25, 48, 49
BARNS John 65
  Margret 65
  Sarah 66
  William 65, 66
BARRAT Jane 28, 32
  Kathrin 12, 19, 52
  Martha 10, 19, 50
  Phil(l)ip 2, 4, 8, 10, 12, 19, 28, 32, 50, 52
  Rogar 28
BARRATT Jane 8
BARRET Andrew 74
  Jane 74
BARRETT Amelia 66
  Andrew 66
  Ann 66
  Catherine 66
  Elizabeth 66
  Jane 66
  Mary 66
  Shepperd 66
  William 66
BARROLL Ann 42, 43
  William 9, 42, 43
BARTON Thomas 73
BASSETT Arnold 8
  Magdelem 8
BATEMAN Abigale 3
  Ann 33
  John 33
  William 33
BAVINGTON Augustine 31
  Elizabeth 31
  John 8, 19, 31
  Mary 19, 31
  Rachel 31
  Thomas 19
  William 31
BAVINTON Augustina 8
  Elizabeth 21
  Hugh 17
  John 17, 21, 24, 48
  Jonathan 17
  Mary 17, 21, 24, 48
  Rose 17
BAXTER Elizabeth 64, 69, 74
  James 64, 69, 74
  Mary Waugh 64, 73
  Rachel 64, 74
BAYARD Anna Marya 16
  Francina 38
  Fransinah 35
  Jacobus 16
  John 35
  Joseph 38

Mary 8, 38
Peter 35
Petrus 16
Rebeccah 38
Samuel 6, 8, 16, 35, 38
Stephen 55
Susana 16
Susannah 38
BAYLEY Mary 7
BAYTHORN Ann 66
  Catherine 66
  Cathran 66
  Grace 66
  James 66
  Margret 66
  Mary 66
  Sarah 66
BAZLEY Abraham 68
  Ann 68
  Edward 68
BEADLE Andrew 41
  Benjamin 16
  Jaine 25
  Jane 41
  John 16, 25
  Mary 16, 25
  Samuel 16
  Sarah 3, 13, 16, 41, 53
  Thomas 3, 25
  William 13, 16, 39, 40, 41, 53
BEARD John 82
  Kathrin 3
BEASLEY Abraham 68
  Ann 68
  Edward 68
  Elizabeth 68
  John Greenland 68
  Sarah 68
BEASTIN Elizabeth 8
  William 8
BEASTON Bridgett (Brigitt) 32, 33
  Catherine 32
  Ephraim 33
  George 32
  Jane 32
  Thomas 32, 33
BEATLE Henry 40
  Hyland 40
  John 40
  Mary 40
  Rachel 40
  Sarah 40
  Stephen 40
BEAUMONT Anne 22
  John 22
BEAZELY Ann 62
  Elizabeth 62
  Jethro 62
BECK Benjamin 17, 52
  Elizabeth 12, 17, 52
  Jane 17
  Jonathan 12, 17, 52
  Mary 4, 12, 17, 52, 65

William 65
BEDLE Augustine 28
  Christopher 23
  Elizabeth 21
  John 4, 12, 23, 28, 29, 52
  Mary 23, 28, 29
  Samuel(l) 12, 23, 52
  Thomas 21, 29
  William 21
BEEAN Christian 32
  Rose 32
  Thomas 32
  William 32
BEEDLE Augusteen 43
  Augustine 13, 36, 53
  Christopher (Christofore 13, 53
  Elisabeth 43
  Franciney 43
  Henry 66
  John 13, 34, 36, 43, 53
  Martha 13, 52
  Mary 13, 34, 36, 52, 66
  Richard 8
  Sarah 43, 53
  Stephen 34, 66
  William 13, 43, 52, 53
BEEDLES John 7
BEESTON Benjamin 17
  George 20
  Jane 20
  Mary 18
  Sarah 12, 17, 21, 51
  William 2, 12, 17, 21, 51
BEETLE Augustina 38
  Dominick 38
  John 38
  Mary 38
  Peregrine 38
  Richard 38
  Thomas 81
BEKER Thomas 5
BELL Jane 16, 22
  Jean 8
  John 16
  Rachel 22
  Richard 3, 8, 16, 22
  Thomas 16
BELLOWS Martha 6
BENNIT Benjamin 52
BENSON Benjamin 41
  Daniell 28
  Elisabeth 41
  John 28, 53
  Mary 28
  Mary Ann 41
  Ruth 42
BENTHAM Elizabeth 32
  Henry 32
  John 32
  Richard 5, 32
  Thomas 32
BENTLEY Ann 2

BERRY Charles 58
  Elizabeth 58
  Mary 58
BESTON Elizabeth 27
  Sarah 27
  Susana 27
  William 27, 52
BIDDLE Miss 54
  Mrs. 56
  P. 56
  Peregrine 54
  Susan 56
BIGGS Araminta 46
  Benjamin 47
  Elizabeth 46
  Henry 47
  John 47
  Joseph 46
  Mary 46
  Rachel 47
  Richard 46, 47
  Sarah 46
  William 46
BING Jane 82
BIRD Empson 75, 76
  Isabella 32
  Isaiah 32
  John 32
  Mary 75, 76
  Susanna 75
  Thomas 32
  Thompson 76
  William 32
BISHOP Ephraim 57
  Prudence 57
  Susannah 57
BLAIDENBURGH Benjamin 6
  Margaret 6
  Sabina 6
BLAIR Margaret 75
BLAKE Margaret(t) 1, 57
  Rebecca 57
  Sarah 57
BLEW Sarah 66
BLUE Sarah 76
BOGS Elizabeth 75
  William 75
BOHANING Eleanor 38
  Ja 26
  James 38
  Margaret 26
  Nathaniel 8, 38
BOLDEN Elizabeth 14, 24, 49
  Mary 14
  Richard 14
  Thomason 14, 24. 49
  Thomaston 14
  William 14, 24, 49
BOND Margaret 57
  Richard 57
  Sarah 57
BOOTH William 71
BORDLEY Mary 41
  Sarah 41
  Stephen 25, 41, 49

Thomas 9, 13, 53
William 9, 13, 41, 53
BORDLY Stephen 1
BOSTON William 12
BOUCHELL Ann Mary 38
　Catherine 38
　Isabella 38
　Joseph 38
　Mary 38
　Peter 8, 38
　Sluyter 8, 38
　Susannah 38
BOUCHELLE Benjamin 29
　Mary 29
　Peter 5, 29
　Rachell 29
　Sluyter 29
BOULDEN Richard 24, 49
　Thomasen 24
　Thomason 49
　William 24, 49
BOULDIN Mary 22
　Richard 4, 22
BOULDING Alexander 18
　Augustina 38
　Elizabeth 3, 38
　James 18, 38
　John 29
　Margaret 29
　Mary 29, 30
　Nathan 38
　Rachel 30
　Richard 29, 30
　Samuel(1) 11, 18, 51
　Thomas 6, 18, 29
　Thomasin 11, 18, 29, 51
　William 11, 18, 51
BOULTING Ann 66
　Ellenor 66
　John 66
BOURN Patrick 73
BOUSHALL Mary 12, 52
　Peter 12, 52
　Thomas 12, 52
BOUSHEL Mary 31
BOUSHELL Catherine 5
　Peter 31
BOWEN Anne 22
　Charles 22
　Ezachariah 22
　Jane 22
　Rebeca 22
　Samuel 22
　Solomon 22
BOWERS Jacob 19
　James 1, 19
　Margaret 19
BOWIN Charles 19
　Elizabeth 19
　Jane 19
　Mary 19
　Richard 19
　Solamon 19
BOYAR Ann 68
　Esther 68
　Peter 68

BOYER Augustine 15
　Mary 9, 15
　Phillis 15, 24, 49
　William 1, 15, 24, 49
BRACE Elizabeth 11, 14, 51
　John 11, 14, 51
　Sarah 3, 14
BRACKENBURY Catherine 31
　John 31
BRADFORD Benjamin 38
　George 38
　Margery 38
　William 38
BRADY John 63
BRANKLIN Ann 24, 48
　Judah 14
　Mary 24, 48
　William 14, 24, 48
BRAY James 50
BRISCOE Amelia Ann Elizabeth 54
　John T. 54
　Laura Cornelia 54
BRISTOR Ann 61
　Elizabeth 61
　William 61
BRISTOW Abel 60
　Elizabeth 59, 60, 62
　George 11, 20, 51
　James 65
　John 20, 65, 79
　Meliscent 65
　Mildred 20, 51
　Milfred 11
　Rachel 62, 65, 66
　Rebecca 59
　Tabitha 66
　William 11, 20, 51, 59, 60, 62, 65, 66, 79
BROCK Barnet 19
　John 19
BROOKINGS Charles 66
　Elizabeth 66
　Margret 66
　Richard 66
　Susannah 66
BROOKINS Charles 81
BROOKS Elizabeth 79
　Thomas 3
BROOM Elizabeth 65
　Frances 65
　Robert 65
BROUCH Thomas 13
BROWN Ann 66
　Elizabeth 64
　Frances 66
　John 9, 64
　Jonas 77
　Mary 76
　Milicent 64
　Robert 66
　Samuel 64
　Thomas 64, 66
BROWNING Ann(e) 24, 48

Elizabeth 1, 7
Esther 15, 24, 48
George 1
Thomas 15, 24, 48
BROXON Ann(e) 11, 18, 51
　John 18
　Thomas 11, 18, 51
　William 20
BROXSON John 1
　William 1
BRUMFELD Sarah 81
BRUMFIELD Agness 67
　Ann 68
　Cathrine 67
　Ed. Francis 67
　Edward 67
　Elise 67
　Elizabeth 67
　Frances 67
　Francis 67
　John 67
　Margaret 57
　Mary 67, 68
　Nathan 68
　Philess 67
　Rachel 67
　Sarah 67, 81
　William 67
BRUNFIELD Margaret 57
BRYAN Edward 70, 81
　Emilia 70
　John 70
　Lydia 70
　William 13, 52, 70
BUCHANAN William 81
BUCKWORTH Charles 20
　Elizabeth 20
　Ruth 20
BULL Catharine 64
　Constantine 64
　Mary 64
BULLEY Elizabeth 36
　Matthew 36
　William 36
BUNKERD Mary 66
BURGIS Anne 21
　Francis 11, 21, 51
　John 11, 51
　Mary 11, 21, 51
　William 21
BURK Honor 20
　John 20
　Mary 20
　Patrick 20
BURKE Jean 68
　Margret 68
　William 68
BURKER Richard 77
BURNAM Henry 31
　Mary 31
　Thomas 31
BURHNAM Mary 4, 12, 20, 29, 52
　Rachel(1) 12, 29, 52
　Thomas 5, 12, 29, 52
BURNINHAM Cathrin 5
BURRAGE Mary 79

BUTCHER Eliener 6
BUTLER Alexander 81

CAMPBELL Charles 20
  Elinor 23
  Elisabeth
  (Elizabeth) 7, 13,
  20, 23, 26, 42,52
  Isabela 20
  James 26, 42, 74,
  76, 77
  Jane 74
  Jean 68
  John 13, 20, 23, 26,
  52, 74, 76
  John Currier 42
  Joseph 76
  Mary 23, 42, 76, 77,
  81
  Mathew 77
  Rachael (Rachel) 13,
  52
  Ruth 77
  Sarah 74
  William 42
CAN Eloner 44
  Robert 44
  Sarah 44
CANER Richard 68
CANN John 8, 38, 41
  Mary Ann 41
  Rachel 38
  Robert 41
  Sarah 38, 41
CARE Marack 1
  Mary 19
  Susana 19
  Thomas 19
CARMACK Adam 80
  Margaret 60
  Sarah 80
  William 80
CARMAN Caleb 59
CARNAN Charles 12, 52
  John 8, 12, 32, 38,
  52
  Margaret 12, 32, 52
  Rachel 38
  William 38
CARR Arimento 66
  Elisabeth
  (Elizabeth) 74
  John 66
  Mary 66, 75
  Walter 74
CARRIN John 6
CARROLL Dominick 6, 33
  Eleanor 33
  Julian 33
  Mary 33
  Susannah 33
CARTER Dinah 38
  James 38
  Mary 38
  Miss 79
  William 79
CARTMILL Edward 57
  Nathan 57

Thomas 57
CASHNER John 21
  Margery 21
  Mary 21
  Urina 21
CASINE Elizabeth 78
CASTEEVER Elizabeth 78

CAULK Elizabeth 23
  Isaac 24, 48
  Jacob 12, 23, 28, 52
  Mary 5, 23, 24, 28,
  48
  Oliver 24, 48
  William 28
CAULS Ann 34
  Barrentdolley 34
CAULT Jacob 5
CAZIER Abraham 31, 67
  Catherine 31
  Phillip 31
  Richard 67
  Susanna 67
CAZINE Amy 79
  Edward 79
  George 79
CHAIMBERLAIN John 37
  Rachel 37
CHAMBERLAIN Elizabeth
  42
  Haulwel 42
  William 42
CHAMBERLIN John 2
CHARTER Elizabeth 76
CHARTY Elizabeth 77
CHEW Ann 74
  Benjamin 67, 74
  Mary 7, 67
  Sarah 67, 74
CHICK Catherine 37, 39
  Christian 19, 21,
  37, 39
  Johannah 38
  John 19, 21, 39
  Joseph 38
  Margaret 19
  Mary 19, 38, 39
  Nathaniel 19
  Sarah 39
  Susannah 39
  Tabitha 21
  William 19, 37, 39
CHICKEN Anne 18
  Edward 18
  John 18
  Mary 18
CHILD Ann 40
  Benjamin 26
  Eleanor 15, 26
  Elizabeth 21, 26, 27
  Francis 18, 26
  George 21, 26, 27
  Helinere (Helinor)
  11, 18, 51
  John 40
  Nathaniel(1) 10, 11,
  15, 18, 21, 26, 40,
  50, 51

Sarah 40
Sophia 11, 15, 51
Susanna 18
CHILDS Benjamin 6, 35
  George 35
  Henry 5
  Martha 35
  Mary 36
  Nathaniel 7, 36, 43
  Rebecca 43, 81
  Tamma 43
CHISUPS Sarah 2
CHRISTIAN Andrew 19
  Mary 19
  Sarah 5
CLARK Ann 6
  Cateren 77
  Elizabeth 65, 76, 77
  Frances 18
  Francis 65, 76, 77
  Hannah 5, 18, 19
  John 18
  Joseph 65, 76, 77
  Keesy 65, 76, 77
  Mary 19, 65, 76, 77
  Rubbey 19
  Samuel 65, 76, 77
  Sarah 5, 19
CLEAVES Benjamin 58
  Nathan 58
CLEMENSON Abraham 15,
  24, 48
  Cornelius 15, 24, 48
  Junibar (Juniber)
  15, 24, 48
CLEMENTS Andrew 4, 14,
  34
  Ann (Anne) 7, 17, 34
  Cornelias
  (Cornelius, Curnelius)
  7, 10, 34, 50
  Elizabeth 14
  Gabril 34
  Henry 11, 17, 21, 51
  Isaac 34
  John 17
  Joseph 34
  Mary 2, 17, 34
  Michael 2
  Sarah 11, 17, 21,
  34, 51
CLEMENTSON Andrew 26
  Eleanor 26
  Matthias 26
CLENSON Abraham 24
CLERK Cathrine 62
  Elizabeth 62, 79
  Jane 79
  John 62, 79
  Mary 62
  Richard 79
  Samuel 62
  Sarah 79
  William 79
CLIFT Izabella 58
CLIFTON Ann 25, 49
  Tabitha 25, 49
  Thomas 25, 49

INDEX

CLOUD Mordecai 81
CLOW Annacart 5
COCK John 25, 49
  Katherine 14, 25, 49
  Margaret 1
  Thomas 14, 25, 49
COCKRELL John 4
COLE Eleanor 36
  Hannah 32
  James Collins 36
  John 6, 32
  Margaret 32
  Mary 32, 36
  Matthew 7, 36
COLLENS Mary 1
COLLINS Abigail 21
  Francis 23
  James 4, 7
  John 4, 12, 23, 27, 52
  Julian (Julion) 12, 27, 52
  Jullieanne 23
  Mary 7
  Robert 21
  Thomas 21
COMEGYS Alphonso 54
  Miss 55
  Mrs. 56
COMES John 3, 22
  Mary 22
  Sarah 22
CONDON Anne 6
  Diana 22
  Edward 22
  John 22
CONERY John 71
CONNOLLY Elizabeth 81
  Susannah 82
CONOLEY Henry 44
  John 44
  Rebecca 44
CONWA James Hunter 75
CONYER James 19
  Mary 19
  Patrick 19
  Thomas 19
COOK Ann 34, 36
  Bartholomew 34
  Cornelias (Cornelius) 6, 34, 36
  William 34
COOKE Robert 9
COOPER Edward 30
  Elizabeth 38, 73
  Joanes 73
  John 38, 73
  Jonas 81
  Mary 30
  Nathaniel 73
  Rebeccah 38
  Sarah 73
  Thomas 73
COPES Miss 55
  Mr. 55
COPPING Angelica 15, 26
  Atkey 26

Azarias 15
  John 1, 15, 26
CORBIT David 74
  Ester 74
  James 74
  Margret Cowdan 74
CORTE John 63
  Joseph 63
  Margret 63
  Rebecca 63
COSDEN Alethea 45
  Catherine 45
  Jerh. 45
COSDON Alifere 9
  Alphonsi 9
COULTER Alexander 67
  Andrew 67
  Elizabeth 67
  Hannah 67
  John 67
  Samuel 67
COULYER Deborah 54
  Miss 55
COWAN Elizabeth 38
  John 38
  Margrett 38
  Mary 38
  Rosannah 38
  Thomas 38
COWARDEN Ann 41
  James Coppen 41
  John Coppen 41
  Peter 41
  Peter Ambros 41
COX Abraham 7, 36
  Albord 31
  Ann(e) 23, 31, 36
  Benjamin 10, 15, 23, 42, 46, 50
  Bridgett 26
  Charles 31
  Edward 46, 47
  Elias 46
  Elizabeth 10, 15, 16, 26, 46, 50
  Henrietta 46
  Henry 23
  Hester 47
  John 3, 22, 23, 27, 29, 34, 37, 38, 40, 42, 46, 47
  Katherine 26
  Kathrin 10, 11, 16, 27, 51
  Marg(a)ret(t) 15, 39, 40, 42
  Mary 2, 5, 11, 15, 29, 31, 46, 51
  Rebecca (Rebecka) 36, 37, 46
  Rigg 15
  Rosaman (Rosamond, Rosemond) 22, 29, 34, 37
  Rose 23, 27
  Samuel 23
  Sarah 22, 37, 39
  Susannah 38, 47, 59,

63
  Thomas 7, 8, 10, 11, 16, 23, 26, 37, 39, 40, 46, 50, 51
  William 37, 46
COXELL John 28
  Rebecca 28
  Sarah 28
COZINE George 1
CRAGE Ann Eliza 54
  Levi 54
  Rebecca 54
CRAIGE Blanchey 43
  Henry 43
  John 43
  Mary 43
  Robert 43
CRAWFORD Dorothy 26
  Quinton 26
  Thomasin 26
CREW Catherine 61
  John 14
  Katherine 14
CRISP Ellinor 23
  Thomas 23
CROCKER Rachel 36
  Robert 36
  Thomas 36
  William 37
CROKER Andrew 35
  Rachael 35
  Robert 35
CRONAGAN Frances 63
  Jane 63
  Sarah 63
  William 63
CROOK Robert 1
CROOKE Robert 49
CROOKSHANKS Francis B. 55
  John Chandler 55
  Mary E. 55
CROUCH Edward 67
  Elizabeth 24, 48, 67
  Isaac 67
  James 64
  John 63, 67
  Johnson 67
  Mary 16, 24, 25, 48, 49, 67
  Nathan 67
  Rachall (Rachel) 16, 63
  Rebecca(h) 63, 64, 67
  Robert 67
  Susanna 16
  Thomas 16, 24, 25, 48, 49, 52, 63, 64, 67
CROW Charles 10, 14, 50
  Elizabeth 11, 30, 51
  Ephraim 30
  Jellian (Jillian) 10, 14, 50
  John 3, 11, 20, 22, 51

Martha 20, 22
Mary 22, 30, 36, 38
Rachel 38
Rebecka 30
Sarah 30
Walter 11, 20, 22, 51
William 4, 14, 36, 38
CROWLEY Alley 70
  Truman 70
CRUIKSHANKS John 55
CULVER Ann 61
  Benjamin 60, 61
  Mary 61
  William 60
CUMMENS John 77
  Remento 77
CUMMINGS Araminta 77
  Elizabeth 61, 72
  James 61
  John 77
  Mary 72
  Remento 77
  Robert 61, 72, 77
  Thomas 77
  William 77
CUMMINS Robert 80
CURRER Ann 61
  Benonee 67
  Elizabeth 75
  John 61, 62, 67
  Mary 60, 62
  Milicent 67
  Richard 68
  Sarah 60, 61, 62
  Thomas 62, 75
  William 60
CURRETHERS Mary 81
  William 81
CURREY Emme 16
  Marey 16
  Mary 3, 20
  Robert 20
  Thomas 10, 16, 20, 50
CURRIER Catharine 75
  Elizabeth 75
  John 75
  Katherine 80
  Mary 75, 76
  Michael 75
  Sarah 75, 76
  Thomas 75
  William 75, 76, 80
CURSINE Deborah 61
  George 61
  John 61
  Nicholas 61
CURYEUR Margret 61

DARE Margaret 2
  William 1
DARLING Hannah 5
DARLINGTON John 64
  Mary 64
  Sarah 64
DASON James 60

DAUGHERTY Ellenor 66
DAUGHTY Edward 66
DAVID Ann 42
  Catherine 42
  James 42
  Rachel 42
DAVIS Alice 6, 16
  Angell 16, 24, 26, 38
  Elizabeth 44, 45
  Emmeline Lavinia 55
  Fouch 13, 26, 36, 53
  Frances 44
  George 55
  James 51
  Jane 36
  Joanna 26
  John 44, 45
  Joseph Stockton 45
  Mary 2, 35
  Mauris (Morris) 10, 51
  Rachel(l) 13, 47, 52
  Rebecca(h) (Rebecka) 35, 36, 38, 44, 47
  Richard 45
  Rose 3
  S. 56
  Sarah 10, 24, 45, 48, 50, 51
  Thomas 5, 6, 9, 13, 26, 35, 36, 38, 47, 52
  William 11, 16, 24, 26, 38, 48, 51, 54
DAWS Benjamin 57
  William 57
DEAN Thomas 60
DEANE Margaret 3
DEATH George 60
  Honoria 60
  Honoure 63
  Jacob 63
  Martha 80
  Rachel 75
  Randal(l) 60, 63, 80
  Widow 81
DEGROATE Aron 1
DDGROTE Aron 10, 50
DEHOES Catherine 78
DEHOFF Elizabeth 5
DELAMOUNTAIN
  Charistian 24, 48
  Johannes 24, 48
  Nicholas 24, 48
DENBO Rachel 2
DENHOE Jane 3
DENLON Alicia 59
DENNE James 61
  Margret 61
  Simon 61
  William 61
DENTON Mary 59
DEORAN Elizabeth 57
  James 57
  Jean 57
  Mary 57
  William 57

DERMOTE Lucie 3
DERREL Sarah 7
DICKSON Sarah 76
DILLAFROE Andrew 20
  Jane 20
  Joseph 20
DILON Daniel 78
  Elinor 78
  Hannah 78
DIREKSON William 1
DONERGIN Ellener 67
  William 67
DORMATT Rachel 8
DORMETT Charles 8
DORRALL Mary 23
  Richard 23
DORRELL Elizabeth 30
  Margaret 2
  Mary 4, 30
  Nicholas 30
  Rachel 30
  Rebecka 30
  Sarah 30
  Shradrach 44
DORRLE Charisyan 24
  Christina 48
  Margaret 24, 48
  Nicholas 24, 48
DORSET James Henry 54
  Perry 54
  Sarah 54
DORSEY John 78
  Mary 78
  Silvia 78
DOUGLAS Anne 5
  Catherine 33
  Clear 33
  James 33
  John 33
  Mary 33
  Romaldus 33
  William 33
DOUGLASS Abraham 39
  Ann 39
DOWNEY Patrick 67
DRAKE Elizabeth 2, 24, 48, 60
  Margaret 24, 48
  William 24, 48
DRISCOLE Ann 42
  Casandra Susannah 42
  Catherine 42
  John 42
DUFFEY Charles 78, 79
  James 79
  Margaret 79
  Sarah 78
DUGALL Mary 7
DUGGING Alexander 64
  Ann 64
  Sarah 64
DUGIN Ann 76
  James 76
  Lady 76
  Mary 76
  Sarah 76
  Thomas 76
DUNIGAN Elener 67

Rodger 67
William 67
DUNOFIN Cornelius 58
Daniel 58
DUTTON Ann 60
DYER Cornelius 18
Margarett 18
Susana 18

EADES Elizabeth 1
Henry 1
EATHERINGTON Ann 37
Bartholomew 37
Benjamin 37
Thomas 37
EDEN Robert 82
EDERINGTON Thomas 5
EDTHRINGTON
Bartholomew 40
Elizabeth 40
John 40
Mary 40
ELIASON Cathrin(e) 5, 19
Cornelius 8, 19
Elias 19
Elizabeth 19
John 19
Rebecca 8
Susannah 19
ELLET Mary 57
ELLIOTT Elizabeth 67, 70
Mary 67
Thomas 67, 70
ELLIS Jane 1
Mary 55
ELLOT Joseph 81
ELLWOOD Mary 22
Richard 22
ELTHARP Thomas 6
EMMITT Susanna 82
ENGLISH Frances 21
Marey 21
Margaret 21
Richard 21
Robert 21
Thomas 21
William 21
ENSOR Augustine Herman 67
Joseph 67
Mary 67
EPTHORP Elizabeth 23
Ellinor 23
Francis 23
Thomas 23
ETHERINGTON
Bartholomew
(Barthow.) 26, 43
Elizabeth
(Elisabeth) 11, 15, 18, 26, 43
James 11, 18
Mary 15, 26
Nelly 54
Rebecca 43
Sarah 40

Thomas 11, 15, 18, 26
ETHERINTON Bartholomew
(Bartholemus, Bartholemew) 11, 21, 51
Elizabeth 4, 11, 21, 51
James 51
Mary 6
Thomas 11, 21, 51
ETHRINGTON Bartholomew 40
Elizabeth 40
EVANS Rachel 40
EVERDSON Catherine 32
Eleoner (Elionor) 12, 32, 52
Elizabeth 31
Everd 5, 12, 31, 32
Jacob 8, 31
EVERSON Catherine 5
Evard 5
EVETT John 22
Mary 22
EVINS Anne 2
EVITT John 16
Rachell 16
Walter 16
EWING John 58
Rachel 58

FANHAKE Thomas 6
FANN John 39
Rachel 39
William 39
FARIS Samuel 81
FARRIER Grace 77
FEDRY Mary 77
FELLOWS Honor 32
James 32
Mary 32
Mathias (Matthias) 5, 32
Rachel 32
FERGUESON Ann 67
Benjamin 67
Mary 67
FERRELL Margaret 21
FILINGAM John 38, 40
Margret(t) 38, 40
Martha 38
Richard 38
Samuel 40
FILINGHAM Benjamin 42
Jervis 42
John 42
Margrett 42
FILLENGAM John 6
John 35
Margarett 35
FILLINGHAM John 39
Margrett 39
Mary 39
FINLEY Jean 80
Robert 80
FINNEY Cathren 75
Elizabeth 75

Elonar 75
John 75
Mary 75
Susannah 75
FISHER Joseph 22
Mrs. 54
FITCHGARRELL Hyland 44
James Dorrell 44
FLIN/FFLIN Kathrin 22
Martha 22
FLINN Kathrin 3
FLINTON Frances 7
FOGG Amus 63
Elenor 63
Elizabeth 63
FORD/FFORD Charles 22
Edward 19
Elenor (Elinor) 19, 22
G. 56
George 22
Helinor 20
James 22
John 20, 22
Mary 37
Richard 19, 20, 22, 37
Sarah 37
FORESTER Catherine
Margaretta 68
George William 68
FORMAN General 54, 55
FORRESTER Frances 72
FORSTER/FFORSTER John 78
Margret 37
Mary 37
Richard 78
Sarah 37
Susannah 63
Thomas 37
William 78
FOSSETT Ann 25, 49
John 25
Js. 49
Mary 25, 49
FOSTER/FFOSTER Hester 34
Isabella 34
James 34
Mary 34
Richard 52
FOSTER/FFOSTER Ann 68
Anne 29
Elener 69
Elijah 67
Elizabeth 64
Ellener 67
Hester 34
Isaac 23
Isabella 34
James 16, 34, 67
Jesse 64
John 16, 64, 67
Margret 64, 67
Mary 29, 34
Nathan 64
Nicholas 64

Richard 3, 11, 12,
16, 23, 29, 51, 52,
67
  Sarah 11, 23, 51
  Susan 51
  Susana 11, 16, 29
  Thomas 11, 51
  William 4, 16, 29,
  67
  Zebulon 67
FOWLER Thomas 8
FRANKLIN Jane 22
  Kathrin 22
FFRAZZER Alexander 3
FREEMAN Mary 2, 6
FRIEND Mary 59
FRISBY/FFRISBY Ann 33,
37
  Arianna 20, 22
  Arianna Margarett 22
  Augustin 4
  Clear 33
  Elizabeth 33
  Ffrancina Augustina
  22
  Ffrancis 24, 48
  James 1, 2, 12, 20,
  22, 24, 33, 42, 48,
  52
  Mary (Marry) 6, 32
  Nicholas 33
  Peregrine 33, 37
  Peregrine Noxon 42
  Sarah 1, 20, 24, 42,
  48
  Susannah 33
  William 6, 32
FULTON David 45
  Elizabeth 45
  William Savin 45
FYFE Elizabeth 77
  Grace 77
  James 77
  William 77

GALEHER Margrett 68
GALLAWAY Francis 22
  James 4, 22
  John 22
  Margaret 22
  Mary 22
GANDY Constance 24, 48
  George 24, 48
  John 24, 48
GARRAT Jacob 3
GAZINE Edward 79
GEARS Benson 41
  Daniel 33, 41
  Elizabeth 33
  Jacob 41
  Rebecca 33, 41
  Sarah 33, 41
  William 41
GEERS Benjamin 24
  Benson 24
  Daniell 24
  Elizabeth 24

John 24
GENCE Mr. 55
GENEE Mr. 55
GEORGE Ann 79
  John 60, 79
  Mary 60, 63, 80
  Nicholas 60, 63, 68
  Rebecca(h) 64, 79
  Sampson 68, 79
GERRISH William 31
GIBBONS Elizabeth 12,
  15, 16, 51
  James 12, 15, 16, 51
  John 12, 15, 51
  Josias 15
  Mary 15
GIBBS Esther 41
  Joseph 41
  Mary 41
GIBSON Elizabeth 67
  Mary 47
GILDER Reuben 59
GILPIN Jane 61
  Rachel 61
  Samuel 61
GLANN James 3
GLASGOW John 80
GODMONT John 27
  Mary 27
  Miles 27
GOLAT John 41
  Peter 41
GOOD Jannet 69
  Jean 69
GOODING Margaretta 45
GORDON Anna Maria 44
  Charles 44
  Elizabeth 44
  Elizabeth Ann 44
  Hannah 44
  Jane 7
  John 44
  Joseph 44
  Margaret (Margret)
  66, 81
  Sarah Nicholson 44
GRACE Aaron 68
  Ann 68
  Elizabeth 64
  John 68
  Mary 64
  Peter Boyar 68
  Rebecca 68
  Will 64
GRADY Bryan 62
  James 61, 62
  John 61
  Mary 61, 62
  Susanah 61
GRAHAM Elizabeth 20
  George 20
  Henry 20
  Mary 20
GRAY Alexander 68
  James 1, 10, 68
  Margarett 68
  Mary 68
  Rebecca 68

Sarah 68
Susannah 80
Thomas 68
GREARY Jane 69
GREEDY Alice 68
  Hannah 68
  Richard 60
  Richard 68
GREELY James 78
GREEN Elizabeth 27
  John 57
  Thomas 27
  Timothy 27
GREENLAND Sarah 73
GREENWOOD Mrs. 54
GREGORY Rebecka 6
GREY James 1
GRIBBEN Henry 41
  Hugh 41
  Rachel 41
GRIFFETH Elizabeth 10,
  17, 50
  John 10, 17, 50
  Rebecca 10, 50
  Thomas 17
GRIFFIN Mary 2
GRIFFINS Abraham 54
  Delia 54
  Mary Ann 54
GRIFFITH Mary 7
GRIMES Elizabeth 76,
  77
  John 76, 77
  Joseph 76, 77
  Patrick 76, 77
GUILBERT Ann 78
GUILDER Elizabeth 57
  Emy 80
  Guilbert 78
  Hukill 80
GULLET John 20
  Sarah 20

HACK Anne 27
  Elizabeth 27
  John 27
HACKETT John 2
HACKNEY John 60
  Phebe 60
HADAWAY Mary 6
HADERICK Mary 71
HAGUE John 46
  Joseph 46
  Miss 55
  Priscella 46
HALL Abigal 78
  Ann(e) 41, 42, 69
  Francies Mary 42
  George 42
  Hannah 72
  Henrietta 42
  Jane 69
  Jeane 76
  John 41, 42, 54, 69,
  72, 76
  Mary 72
  Rachel 41, 42
  Robert 55

INDEX

Sarah 55, 69
Thomas 69
William 42
HALY Mary 9
HAM Abraham 36
  Elinor 30
  Ester 36
  Jacob 36
  John 30, 35
  Mary 30, 35
  Rebecka 35
HAMBLETON Elizabeth 61
  John 61
  Mary 61
HAMILTON Angel 68
  Ann Sophia 68
  Catherine Lettice 68
  Charles 68
  Jane 68
  John 64, 66, 68, 74, 81
  Lettice (Littice) 64, 68
  Margaretta 68
  Mary 68
  Mr. 73
  Patt 82
  William 64, 68
HAMM Abraham 16
  Araminta 69
  Elinor 20, 22
  Ephraim 16
  Helinor 16
  Isaac 16
  Jacob 20
  John 2, 16, 20, 22, 29, 35
  Mary 29, 35
  Thomas 22, 29
HAMMAN William 7
HAMN Eliza 8
  Ephraim 8
HAMONS Mary 58
HAMPTON George 6
  Mary 6
HANDERSON Jacob 68
  William 68
HARKIN Catherine 49
  Cornelius 49
HARNON Araminta 69
HARNONS Mary 58
HARPER Andrew 38
  Elizabeth 5, 21, 22
  Gartrey 38
  Jacob 21, 38
  John 7, 13, 22, 53
  Mary 13, 53
  Nicholas 21, 30
  Peter 30
  Susanah 30
  Thomas 21, 22
HARRIS Joseph 37
  Margaret 37
  Nicholas 37
  Patrick 37
HART Ann 34, 69
  James 69
  Jennet 69

John 34
Robert 69
HARTSHORN Joshua 59
  Samuel 59
HATREY Christian 19
  Henry 19
  James 19
HATTREY Mary 21
  Sarah 21
  Thomas 21
HAWKINS Rebecca 81
HAYATT Mary 5
HAYES Louisa 55
  Robert 54
HAYS Elizabeth 54
HAZELHURST Benjamin 16
  Diana 16
  Martha 16
HEATHCOAT Silvia 78
HEDRICK Margaret 70
HELLNAY An 55
HENDERSON Ann 43
  Anthoney 43
  Elisabeth 43
  Hannah 43
  Jacob 68
  James 68
  Jane 68
  John 68
  Mary 43
  Mr. 55
  Rebecca 43
  Robert 69
  William 68
HENDRICK Mary 57
HENDRICKSON Ann 46
  Augustine 46
  Bartholomew 40
  Catherine 31
  Christopher 18, 26
  Edith 46
  Elizabeth 22, 33, 36
  Henry 4, 8, 22, 36, 40
  Hester 18
  Hosea 46
  Margarett 8
  Mary 18, 26, 46
  Matthias 33, 40
  Noble 46
  Peregrine 46
  Peter 5, 31
  Rebecca 18
  Rozamond 46
  Samuel 31
  Sarah 18, 33, 40
  Sophia 54
  Susanah 31
HENNING Jediah 18
  Mary 18
  Sarah 18
  Susanna 18
HENRICKSON Christopher 25, 49
  Mary 25, 49
  Thomas 25, 49
HERMAN Augustina 14
  Casparus 12, 52

Casparus Augustine (Augt., Augustin) 1, 14, 25, 49
  Catherine 8, 14, 25, 49
  Cathrin(e) 5, 49
  Ephraim 14
  Ephraim Augt. 8, 12, 52
  Isabella (Isabella) 12, 52
HESSEY William S. 55
HEWES Gabriell 14
  Mary 14
  Owen 14
HEWS Mary 4, 14
  Morris 50
  Owen 14
  Samuel 50
HEWSTON Grace 40
  James 40
  Rachel 40
HILL Ann 9, 49, 74
  Elisabeth 1
  James 74
  Mary 2, 20
  Rachall 20
  Samuel 1, 74
  Sarah 1
  William 9, 10, 20, 49, 50
HINE Jonathan 5
HITCHCOCK Ann Moore 77
  Augusta 77
  John 77
  Nickles 77
  Rotch 77
  Samson 77
  Sarah 77
HITCHCOK Milicent 63, 64
  Richard 63
HODGSON John 79
  Rachel 79
  Robert 6
  Sarah 6, 79
HOLD George 9
  Jane 30
  Joseph 30
  Obadiah 30
HOLEOGER Philip 24
  Phillis 1
HOLLET Elizabeth 28
  Hannah 37
  John 28, 37
  Rebecca 37
  Sarah 37
  William 28
HOLLETT Hannah 39
  John 39
  Rachel 39
HOLLINGSWORTH Ann 61, 62
  David 64
  Elizabeth 61
  Henry 62
  Jacob 63
  Jesse 61

John 64
Levi 62
Mary 5, 63, 64, 68
Samuel 68
Steven 61, 62, 64
Thomas 63
Zebulon 61, 62, 63, 64, 68
HOLLINS Abigail (Abigall) 11, 18, 23, 51
Abraham 18
Elizabeth 18
Holinor 2
John 3, 11, 18, 23, 51
Mary 7, 11, 18, 23, 51
HOLLOGER Phillip 48
HOLT Cathrine 43, 44
George 43, 44
Jane 29, 43
Joseph 29
Lewis Price 44
Mary 43
Obadiah 29
Sarah 43
HOLTEN Elizabeth 29
George 29, 37
Jessey 37
Mary 29, 37
HOLTON George 5, 28, 34
James 35
Jessey 6, 35
Mary 28, 34
Robert 28
Sarah 35
HOLYDAY Hester 2, 18
Killon 18
Mary 18
Samuel 10, 18, 50
HOOD Alice 7
Elizabeth 8
William 7, 88
HOOPER Edward 21
Elizabeth 21
Sarah 21
HOOTEN Mary 6
HOPKINS Anne 22
Elexander 22
Sarah 22
HORNE Darby 14, 49
Sarah 14, 49
HORNE William 14, 49
HOTCHKISS Henry N. 54
HOUSTON Jane 8
HOWARD Alice 81
John 81
HOWDLE Elinor 60
John 60
HOWELL Benjamin 69
Catherine 72
Elisha 69
George 69
James 69
John 69
Levi 69

Mary 69
Sarah 72
William 69
HOWLAND Peregrine 9
Rebecca 9
HOWS Samuel 10
HOZER Elizabeth 21
Jacob 21
John 21
Rachell 21
Sarah 21
HUCHESON Alexander 39
Samuel 39
HUCHISON Alexander 52
John 22
Mary 22
Rachel 12, 52
HUCKEL Daniel 27
Eleanor 27
Henry 27
HUCKIL Henry 6
HUCKIN Bartholamew 19
Daniel(l) 11, 12, 19, 51
Elizabeth 11, 12, 19, 51
Gilder 11, 19, 51
Henry 19
John 19
Richard 19
William 19, 51
HUGG Mary 7
HUGHES Ailes 35
Alice 36, 39
Catherine 72
Deborah 72
Edward Forrester 72
Elizabeth Margaret 72
Hester 81
James 6, 35, 36, 39
Rebecca 35
Sarah 39
Thomas 72
HUGHS Ann 36
HUKILL John 6
HUKIN Carnelias 38
Daniel 38
Eleanor 39
Elizabeth 38
Henry 39
John 37, 39
Mary 37
Richard 38, 39
Susannah 39
Zebulon 37
HUNGARFORD Mary 7
HUNTER Andrew 75
Ann 74
James 74, 75
Mary 8
Sarah 74, 75
William 8
HUNTLY Margaret 2
HUSBAND Alice 22, 23, 27
Hanah 27
Herman 27

James 4, 22, 23, 27
John 13, 17, 27, 52
Kathrin 27
Marey (Mary) 17, 27
Sarah 13, 17, 23, 52
Thomas 13, 52
William 4, 17, 27
HUSBANDS John 19, 58
Mary 6, 58
Miss 58
Sarah 19
Thomas 19, 58
Williams 6
HUTCHESON Alexander 37
Mary 37
HUTCHINSON Elizabeth 40
Gavin 40, 42
Mary 40, 42
Sarah 42
HUTCHISON John 3
HYLAND Ann 64, 69
Araminta 69
Charles 62
Edward 64
Elizabeth 60, 63, 64, 68, 80
Isaac 60
Jacob 60, 65
Jaine 1
John 9, 47, 49, 62, 64, 65, 68, 69
Lambeart 62
Margery 69
Mary 65, 68
Michael 63
Milicent (Millicent, Milliscent) 62, 63, 80
Nicholas 60, 62, 63, 69, 80
Rachel 64
Rebecca 62, 69
Sampson George 68
Samson 63
Stephen 69
Steven 62
HYNES James 35
Jonathan 32, 35
Mary 32
Sarah 32, 35
HYNMAN Garrat 27
Hannah 27
Mary 27
Rachel 27
Rebecca 80
HYNSON Anne 25
Charles 34
Hannah 34
Jaine 24, 48
John 1, 24, 25, 26, 33, 48, 49
Mary 24, 25, 26, 33, 34, 48, 49
Nathaniell 25, 33, 49
Rachel(l) 25, 34
Thomas 25, 34, 49
William 34

INDEX

INGLE John 23
  Margaret 23
  Thomas 23
IRELAND Alethea
  Lavinia 55
  Hannah Wallace 55
  William Pope 55
IRWIN Rose 60

JACKSON Ann 33
  Betsey 73
  Edward 73, 75
  Elizabeth 81
  James 75
  John 75
  Margret 75
  Mary 66
  Sarah 67, 73
  William 33
JACOB An 62
  Frances 62
  Mary 63
  Susannah 62
  Thomas 62
JACOBS Ann 6, 60
  Barthw. 34
  Catherine 59
  Frances 65
  Grace 34, 60
  Hannah 60
  John 59
  Joseph 60
  Mary 34, 60
  Sarah 60
  Thomas 60
JAMES Evan 34
  Isaac 34
  Mrs. 54
  Persella 34
JAVYR Cornelia 74
  Ledia 74
  Philip 74
JEKSON Edward 75
  John 75
JENINS Frances 63
JOBSON Hester 18
  John 2
  John 18
JOHNS Ann 58
JOHNSON Andrew 60
  Ann 1, 59, 67, 69, 79
  Bartholomew 62
  Benjamin 69
  Catherine 63
  Daniel 80
  Edward 9, 49, 62, 69, 80
  Elenor 59, 60
  Elizabeth 60, 80
  Garrat 18
  George 69, 80
  Hester 18
  Isaac 76, 77
  Jacob 59, 60, 81
  Jane 80
  John 76

  Joseph 61, 62
  Josiah 76
  Kathrin 18
  Magdellin 61
  Margaret 59, 60, 78
  Mary 60, 62, 63, 69, 76, 79
  Mathias 61
  Mauldin 18
  Melecin 69
  Millicent (Milliscent) 62, 80
  Oliver 60
  Peter 60
  Phebe 59
  Rachel 59, 63, 77, 80
  Rebecca (Rebekah) 60, 62, 77
  Robert 76
  Sarah 62, 76, 79
  Simon 63, 76
  Susanna 18
  Thomas 60, 61, 69, 79, 80
  William 69
JOHNSTON Jacob 79
  John 79
  Magdalene 79
  Mathias 79
JONES Aliga 74
  Amey 74
  Benedict 54
  Catherine 62, 77
  Commodore 55
  Elizabeth 69, 77
  Hannah 61
  Hugh 5, 6, 7, 8, 13, 53
  Jacob 42, 55
  James 61
  John 1, 61, 74, 79
  John Currier 42
  Lewis 78
  Lieutenant 55
  Maly 74
  Margaret 45
  Mary 61, 62, 63, 77
  Mary Ann 53
  Miliscent (Millicent) 42, 45
  Mose 62
  Moses 74
  Mr. 8, 9
  Nancy 74
  Patience 61
  Rebakah 74
  Richard 74
  Samuel 63, 79
  Silvin 61
  Sylvia 81
  Teney 42
  Th. 35
  Thomas 45, 57, 63, 69, 74
  Will 61
  William 61, 62, 63
  William Ruten 74

JONSON Anne 21
  Bartholomew 21
  Charles 28
  Elizabeth 2
  Garrat 28
  Hannah 76
  Hester 28
  Hezekiah 76
  Jacob 28
  John 76
  Josiah 76
  Levi 76
  Margaret 21
  Mary 21, 28
  Peter 28
  Robert 76
JONSTON Hezekiah 76
JULIAN Mary 7
JUSTICE Catherine 61
  John 57
  Keady 65
  Mary 65
  Miriam 57
  Moses 57
  Peter 61
  Rebecca 61
  Sarah 57
  William 65

KANKEY Ann 61, 69
  David 69
  Elizabeth 69
  Harman 69
  John 61, 69
  Margery 69
  Mary 69
  Rebecca 69
KANNINGTON Hono 1
KARE Mary 3
  Sarah 3
  Thomas 11, 51
KASAY John 58
KEATLY Mary 64
KEEDLY John 80
KEITLY Catherine 74
  Henry 74
  Mary 74
KELLY Leiah 59
  Sarah 59
  Thomas 59
KELY Ann 66
KEMP Mathew 57
KENEDEY Margaret 6
KENNARD Mary 1
KENNERLY Sarah 70
KERSY Honour 80
KEY Ann 69
  Ann Arnold 69
  Elizabeth 12, 52, 69
  Francis 69
  John 81
  Philip Barton 69
KEYES John 81
KILLPATRICK Hannah 67, 69
  Jannet 69
  Jean 69
  John 70

Robert 69
Samuel 69, 70
KILPATRICK Elias 69
  Jane 59
  Samuel 69
KIMBALL Elizabeth 23
  John 4, 23
  Rebecca 23
KIMBER Catherine 39
  John 6, 7, 12, 27, 33, 39, 52
  Mary 12, 27, 33, 39, 52
  Rebecca (Rebeca, Rebecka) 12, 27, 52
KIMBLE Elizabeth 70
  Leeds 70
  Mary 70
  Sarah 70
  Titan Leeds 70
KING Isaac 15
  Jacobus 15
  Mrs. 10, 50
  Peter 10, 15, 50
  Susanna 15
KINKEY Mary 4
KINNARD Abraham 55
KIRKPATRICK Susannah 67
KIRTLY Elizabeth 30
  William 30
KITELY John 65
  Sarah 65
KNIGHT Frisby (Ffrisby) 10, 15, 22, 50
  John 8, 13, 22, 53
  John Leach 47
  Mary 6, 22
  Sarah 8, 10, 15, 18, 22, 50
  Stephen 2, 6, 8, 10, 13, 15, 18, 22, 50, 53
  William 18

LAKE Partiana 70
LANG Catherine 77
  Daniel 77
  John 77
  Mary 77
  Sarah 77
LANKASTER Henry 1
LAPAGE Edward 9, 14, 49
  Elizabeth 9, 49
  Joan 9, 14, 49
  Mary 14
LARAMORE Edward 10, 15, 50
  Margarett 15
  Rachel 15
  Roger 2, 15
LARKINS Jeremiah 5
LAROUN Anna 6
LARRAMOR Margaret(t) 11, 12
  Mary 11

Roger 11
Sarah 11
LARRAMORE Augustine 4, 23
  Margaret (Margrett) 16, 51, 52
  Mary 51
  Roger (Rogar) 4, 12, 16, 23, 51, 52
  Sarah 51
LASHELL William 81
LASSELL Ann 45
  William C. 45
  William Spencer 45
LASSELLS Ailes 36
  Joseph 36
  Mary 36
LATAMUS Anne 29
  Catherine 35
  Diana 35
  Elizabeth 29
  James 5, 29, 35
LATHAM Anne 11, 23, 51
  Aron (Arron) 23
  Esther 23
  Hanah 27
  John 23
  Joshua 3, 11, 23, 27, 51
  Mary 23, 27
LATHAN Joshua 3
LATTOMUS Diana 31
  James 31
  Jane 31
LATTYMUS Dianna 13, 53
  James 7, 13, 53
LAURANCE Anne 3
LAURUX Gerturett 6
LAWSON Anne 20
  David 20
  Elizabeth 20
  Peter 20
LEAK Jane 26
  John 26
LEDGWOOD Jane 59
LEE Jane 82
  Lewis 81
LEEPER Andrew 81
LEHITON Mr. 1, 24
LESHLY Ann 59
LESSLY Cornelius 58
LEWIS Amey 72
  Ann 72
  Elizabeth 39
  George 8, 39
  Izabella 57
  John 57, 70
  Mary 70
  Richard 72
  Sarah 70
LILISTON John 48
LINCKHORNE John 1
LINDSAY William 81
LINTON Elizabeth 81
  William 81
LITTELL Mary 66
  Nathaniel 66
LLOYD P. F. 54

Peregrine F. 54
Philip 54
LOATH Mary 78
LOFTIS Charles 47
  Francis 39
  Jean 47
  John 36, 39, 47
  Susannah 36, 39, 47
  Thelwell 36
LOFTY Hannah 58
  Izabella 58
  Miss 58
LOGAN Cathrine 44
  John 44
  Nancy 44
  Samuel 82
  William McCullough 81
LOGE Manaseh 7
LOW Margarett 54
LOWRY Ann 70
  Elijah 70
  James 70
  John 70
  Mary 70
  Robert 70
  Stephen 70
  William 70
LOYD Mrs. 54
LUM Ann 63
  Elizabeth 63
  Isaac 64
  Jacob 64
  Jonas 78
  Mary 64, 70
  Michael (Michel) 61, 64, 70
  Rachel 70
  Rebecca 64, 70
LUMM Anne 21
  Jonas 21
  Samuel 21
  Sarah 21
LUSBY Acel Cosden 45
  Ann 45
  Anne Maria 44
  Augustine Larimore 45
  Edward 45
  Edward Larrimore 45
  Elisabeth 44, 45, 46
  James 46
  John 35, 37, 39, 45, 46
  John H. 55
  John Henry 44
  Joseph 44, 45
  Margaret (Margret) 35, 37
  Margaretta 45
  Mary 35, 37
  Nicholas 45
  Pamelia 46
  Rebecca 44
  Robert Clothier 46
  Ruth 46
  Sally 56
  Samuel Cosden 45

INDEX

Sarah 45, 46
Sarah Veazey 44
Susannah 46
Thomas Veazey 44
William 45, 46
Zebulon 46
LYNCH Ailes 35
Anthony 35, 40
Elizabeth 35, 40
George 35
James 35, 40
William 35
LYNDSEY Ly--- 9
William 9
LYTNER Adam 22
Macklen 22

MACAHEE Alexander 15
Martha 15
Robert 24, 48
Susanna 15
MACARY Daniell 14
Ester 14
Mary 14
Richard 14
MACCANDRICK Kathrin 2
MACCARY Aron 32
Elizabeth 32
Francis 32
MACHAHAY Mary 1
MACHAKEY Alexander 24
Robert 24
MACHDOLWLE Ruth 6
MACKAHAY Alexander 48
Robert 48
MACKDOWELL Jacob 34
James 34
John 34
Ruth 34
William 34
MACKENY Alexander 57
Mary 57
MACKEVE Catherine 79
MACLAN Ann 7
MACLEGUN Mary 78
MACMANUS Elioner 36
Elizabeth 36
John 36
MAGEE James 55
Sylvester 54
MAGRUDER John 81
MAHANEY Charles 20
Denis 20
Margaret 20
Sarah 20
MAHEN Margret 66
MAINLY Ann 64
Elizabeth 64, 65
Jacob 65
Jesse 64
John 65
Mary 64
Rachel 65
Rebecca 64
Sarah 65
William 64, 65
MAKENNE Mary 61
MAKEY Alexander 11,
23, 51
Susan(n)a 11, 23, 51
MALDING Francis 6
Fransinah 6
MALONE Elizabeth 3
MALSTER Elizabeth 23
Godfrey 23
Mary 23
MANELY Sarah 78
MANHENY Elizabeth 58
Margaret 58
Thomas 58
MANICOZONS Anne 24
Mary 24, 48
Michaell 24
MANLY Elizabeth 70
Jacob 70
John 70
Mary 70
Rebecca 70
William 70
MANNERING Hannah 6
MANREAN Mary 35
Sarah 35
Thomas 35
MANYCOZONS Michaell 48
MANYPENY James 59
MARCER Ann 41, 47
James 47
John 41
Peregrine 41
Robert 47
Sarah 41
MARCUS Dina 24, 48
Hance 24, 48
Mary 24, 48
Thomas 24, 48
MARLEY Anne 26
Benjamin 26
Robert 26
MARQUES Elias 10, 50
MARTAIN Penellapey 33
MARTIN Nehemiah 33
Syna 33
MASH Cornelius 22
Esther 22
MASSY Mary 78
MATHEWS Patrick 53
MATHIASON John 29
Mary 28
Mathias 28
Sarah 28
MATTHEWS Catherine 42
Elizabeth 42
Hugh 42
James Egnatious 42
John 34
Mary 13, 34, 53
Patrick 6, 13, 34
Rebeccah 42
William 42
MATTHIASON Hugh
Richard 23
Mary 1, 23, 25, 49
Matthew 25, 49
Matthias 9, 23, 25, 49, 50
Mattoz Jonas 2

MAUGHAN Murty 59
William 59
MAUGHOR Ann 59
Anthony 59
Catherine 59
Edward 59
Mary 59
Patrick 59
MAULDIN Ann 61
Francis 60
MAYBURY Beriah 60
Francis 60
Rosannah 71
Sarah 58, 61
McCAULY Ann 65
Bryan 65
Samuel 65
McCAY Ann 27
Frances 81
Henry 6, 27
James 27
John 27, 81
Rebecca 27
Sarah 27
William 81
McCLEARY Bassett 39
Magdalen 39
Samuel 8, 39
McCLURE Ann 79
Catherine 79
Charles 79
Duffey 79
Elizabeth 79
James 70, 79
Margaret 70
Richard 79
Sarah 79
William 70, 79
McCULLAH Darnel 15
Kathrin 15
Thomas 19
William 15, 19
McCULLOGH George 77
Jesse 77
Levi 77
Mary 77
Rebecca 77
Sina 77
McCULLOUGH William 82
McDANIEL Randall 59
Sarah 59
McDOUGALL Charles 70
Jane 70
Mary 70
McDOWELL Sabina 81
McGUMERRY Margaret 5
McINTOSH Alexander 81
McKANDRICK John 12, 51
Kathrin 12, 51
Mr. 12
McKENTIRE Alexander 59
Ann 59
James 59
Jennet 59
Nicholas 59
McKEOWN Catherine
Abigail 70
John 70

95

McKEY Alexander 10
Anne 10
Susana 10
McKEYE Alexander 15, 50
Anne 50
Susana 15, 50
Thomas 15
McKNIGHT Sarah 4
McMANUS John 7, 13, 53
McMAUGHAN Agnes 60
McVINCHIE Edward 82
McVINISH Edward 82
MEAKINS Elizabeth 36
Joshua 7, 36
Richard 36
Sarah 36
MEDFORD Susan 55
MEEK Jean 75
Matew 80
Rebecca 80
MEKENEY Alexander 63, 64
Ann 64
Elizabeth 64
Garrit 61, 63, 64
Jesse (Jessey) 63, 64
Margret 63, 64
Mary 64
Sarah 63
Susannah 63, 64
William 64
MEKENNE Garret 62
Margaret 62
MEKINNE John 62
MELANE Charles 20
Elexander 20
Johnathan 20
Sarah 20
MEMULLEN Margret 75
MERCER Ann 30, 35, 47
Elizabeth 16, 25, 30, 31, 49
Jane 31
Jean 38, 47
John 16
Mary 4
Robert 5, 16, 25, 30, 35, 49
Sarah 9, 30, 45
Stephen 38
Thomas 5, 16, 25, 30, 31, 38, 47, 49
William 16
MERCHANT William 81
MERRALL Hannah 76
MERRET Elizabeth 13, 52
Mr. 13
Thomas 13, 52
MERRIT Benjamin 13, 31
Elizabeth 17, 21
George 17
Jane 17
John 17, 21
Martha 5, 31
Mary 17

Stephen 31
Thomas 5, 17, 21, 31
William 17
MERRUT Jane 4
MERSER Elizabeth 14
Robert 14
Thomas 14
MICHEL Mary 63
MIDFORD John 1
MILBURN Elinor 60
Robert 60
MILLEGAN Catherine 41
George 41
Margret 41
Mary 41
Robert 41
MILLER Adam 31
Agnass 78
Ann 64, 75
Chilion 31
Conrodde 31
Dorrity 31
Edward Veazey 44
Elenor 78
Elizabeth 44
Elizabeth Veazey 44
Henry 31, 75
Hester 60
Jane 61
John 31, 44, 75
Peter 31
Rachel 75
Sarah 75
Susanah 31
MILLIGAN Catherine 13, 41, 53
George 8, 13, 41, 53
MINAR Thomas 6
MOLL Christian 25
David 25
Elizabeth 25
John 25
MONEY Ann(e) 28, 43
Benjamin 42
Catherine 7
Elizabeth 42
Isaac 43
James 47
John 7, 13, 23, 36, 39, 40, 41, 43, 47, 53
Kathrin 23
Margaret(t) 6, 15, 17, 23, 28
Mary 5, 15, 40
Nicholas 28
Rachel 13, 36, 39, 40, 41, 43, 47, 53
Rebeccah 42
Robana 23
Robert 2, 6, 7, 15, 17, 23, 28, 35, 41
Ruth 35
Samuel 41
Thomas 28, 42
MOOR Briggett 1
David 81
MOORE Elizabeth 39

John 39
Rachel 39, 55
MORE Aron 21
Elias 19
Elizabeth 19
James 22
Joseph 61
Kisiah 61
Liddey (Lidey) 19, 21, 22
Ruth 61
Thomas 19, 21, 22
William 19
MORGAIN Deboraugh 37
Dorety (Dority) 7, 37
Elizabeth 40
James 40
John 7, 37, 40
John Roberts 37
MORGAN Ann 42, 78
Ann Catherine 77
Dority 31, 35
Edward 6, 17, 34, 36, 38
Elenor (Eleoner, Eleonor) 34, 36, 38
Elizabeth 10, 11, 15, 17, 31, 34, 42, 50, 51, 77
Henry 78
Hugh 77
James 9, 10, 11, 15, 17, 49, 50, 51
John 5, 15, 31, 35, 78
Margaret 78
Mary 9, 18, 49, 78
Rebecca 18
Richard 10, 15, 18, 50
Robert 11, 15, 51
Ruth 36
Sarah 5, 15, 35, 38, 42, 57
William 42, 54, 78
MORIS John 24
Margaret 24
Susanna 24
MORRICE Susanna 24, 48
MORRIS John 6, 48
Margrett 48
MORRISON Mary 17
Morris 17
Susanna 17
MORRISSE Jeans 75
MORSE Joseph 54
MOSS Elizabeth 24, 48
Mary 24, 48
Richard 24, 48
MOUNCE Ann 5
Anne 16
Casparus 10, 50
Charles 10
Christopher 10, 14, 16, 24, 49, 50
Martha 16
Mary 4, 16

INDEX

Sarah 14, 16, 24, 49
MULSTER John 41
  Martha 41
MURRAIN Daniel 49
  Daniell 23, 25
  Mary 23, 25, 37, 49
  Susanna 23, 25, 49
  Thomas 37
MURRAINE Daniell 27
  James 27
  Susana 27
MURROIN Thomas 6

NAGLEE Harriot Bonde 45
  James Caskey 45
  Rebecca 45
  Samuel 45
NELSON Benjamin 70
  John 78
NEVALL Joseph 78
  Sarah 78
NEVELL James 78
  Thomas 78
NEVIL Edward 63
  James 63
  John 63
  Mary 63
NEVILL Moses 75
NEWBANKS Dorothy 5
NEWGENT Andrew 71
  Campbell 71
  Daniel 71
  George 71
  John 71
  Mary 71
  Silvester 71
  William 71
NEWMAN Daniel(l) 17, 19, 23
  Elizabeth 20, 22
  John 3, 11, 20, 22, 51
  Jonathan 11, 20, 22, 51
  Kathrin 20
  Martha 3
  Mary (Marey) 3, 4, 11, 17, 19, 20, 22, 23, 51
  Peter 22
  Rebecca 4
  Samuel 20
  Sarah 3, 5, 17, 23
  Solomon 17, 23
  Walter 3, 11, 20, 22, 51
  William 19
NICHOLASON Abraham 33
  Ann 33
  Martin 33
  Peter 33
NICHOLSON Elizabeth 1
  Thomas 9, 49
NIDEY Abraham 31
  Ann 31
  Catherine 32
  Daniel 32

  Dorithy 31
  Joseph 31
  Mary 32
  Michel 31
  Susanah 32
NINDSON Henry 55
NITE Elizabeth 77
  John 77
NOBLE Rebecca 6
NOLAND Sarah 82
NORTHERMAN Ann 70
  Jacob 70
  John 70
  Margret 70
  Mary 70
NORTON Hannah 71
NOWELL Evan 21
  Hanah 21
NOWLAND Alfred C. 55
  Ann 31
  Benjamin 34
  Daniel(l) 2, 31, 34
  Denis 31
  Elizabeth 31, 45
  Hannah 34
  James 31, 54
  Maria 45
  Mary 34
  Peregrine 45
  Rachel 31
  Rebecca 45
  Stephen 31
  Thomas 34
  Thomas Savin 45
NOWLDHAM Sarah 82
NUMBERS Ann(e) 7, 15, 21, 23, 27
  Elizabeth 6, 16, 32
  James 7, 21, 27, 32
  John 16, 32
  Mary 15
  Peter 2, 13, 15, 21, 23, 27, 32, 53
  Rebecca 7
NUMERS Mary 5

OATS John 12, 52
OBRIANT Daniel 47
  Mary 47
  Richard 47
OGELVIE Jane 74
OGRISEY Jane 31
  Neal 31
  Thomas 31
OLDRON Ann 67
  Zeblon 67
OLIVER Ann(e) 5, 19
  Jane 5, 20
  John 19, 21
  Margery 19, 21
  Mary 19
  Thomas 20
OMULLEN Edward 78
ORRICK James 82
ORTON Alexander 62
  Ann 62
  Daniel 78
OTHOSON Garrat

(Garratt, Garriet, Garriot) 7, 13, 17, 27, 53
  Mary 7, 27
  Otho 28
  Robert 7, 17
  Sarah 17, 27
OTTERSON Samuel 54
OTTORSON Otho 1
OWEN Jane 26
  John 26
  Thomas 26
OWENS Blanchey 65
  David 65
  Elizabeth 61
  Glenn 65
  Lavender 65
  Mary 65
  Thomas 65
OWLFIELD Elinor 21
  Jerimiah 21
  John 21
  William 21
OYZER Rachell 5
OZEY El(l)inor 4, 19
  Francis 11, 19, 51
OZIER Elizabeth 7
  Ephraim 41
  Francis 7
  Jacob 41
  John 41
  Mary 41
  Rachel 41
  Sarah 41
OZMON Ann 80
  Phillis 80
  Rachel 80
  Sarah 80

PAINE Elizabeth 77
PALMER Ann Elizabeth 71
  Elizabeth 71
  Grace 71
  Hannah 71
  Joseph 71
  Mary 71
  Mary Elliott 71
  Rebekah 71
  Thomas 71
PARKER John 58
  Jonathan 58
PARR Alice 4
PARSLEY Ann 39
  Barrtholemew (Bartholamew, Bartholomew) 8, 17, 38
  Eleinor (Elienor) 6, 17
  Elizabeth 11, 17, 39, 51
  Israel 17
  Judith 38
  Mary 77
  Nathaniel 77
  Rebecca 39
  Richard 3, 77

Sarah 77
Thomas 11, 17, 38, 51
PARSLY Augustine 28
Elizabeth 28
Richard 28
PARSONS Catherine 7
Garterett 35
Gartrick 13, 53
Jehue 35
Kathrin 17
Margaret (Margret) 13, 53
Mary 13, 53
William 6, 7, 13, 35, 53
PARTRIDGE Elizabeth 2
PATTEN Samuel 59
PATTERSON John 58, 81
Mary 58
PATTIN Amelia 64
Rebecca 64
Richard 64
PATTON Rebecca 71
Richard 71
Thomas 71
PAUL John 81
PAULSON Rachel 75
PEARCE Andrew 30, 41
Anna 42, 56
Annastatia 42
Benjamin 6, 8, 9, 12, 13, 30, 35, 36, 38, 40, 41, 52, 53
Benjamin Francis 44
Benjamin Ward 13, 36, 53
Daniel 8, 30, 40, 41
Elizabeth 35
Henry 46
Henry W. 54
Henry Ward 35, 42, 44
Isabella 13
John 1
Joshua 46
M. 56
Margaret(t) (Margret) 13, 35, 36, 38, 41, 53
Mary 13, 30, 41, 42, 53
Mary Ann 46
Mr. 55
Rachel 30, 44
Sara(h) 9, 30, 40, 41
Susannah 41
Thomas 11, 51
W. 36
William 13, 30, 38, 41, 53
PEARSON Sarah 58
PECK Benjamin 68
Jane 68
PECOE Daniel 78
Hannah 78
Lady 78

Peter 78
Rebecca 78
PECOT Hannah 61
Mercy 61
Peter 61
PEDEN Henry C. 81
PEIRCE John 12, 52
Mary 12, 16, 52
Rebecca 2, 16
Thomas 12, 16, 52
Thomisson 16
William 16
PENINGTON Ailse 35
Alice 39
Ann 37, 38
Augustine Hyland 46
Benedict 28
Benjamin 28
Boyar 71
Cathrine 44
Ebenezer 37
Edith 46
Edward 36
Elizabeth 28, 38
Ephraim 37
Henny Ritty Mary 45
Henry 28, 36, 37, 38
Hesther 71
Hyland 36
Hyland B. 46
Hyland Biddle 46
Isaac 38
Jacob 38
James 8, 28, 38
John 6, 9, 13, 28, 35, 36, 37, 39, 40, 44, 53, 59
John Ward 39
Margaret (Margtt.) 6, 28, 36
Mary 9, 28, 37, 39, 40, 46, 59, 71
Phebe 46
Rachel 26, 37, 39, 40
Rebecca (Rebecka) 35, 37
Robert 26, 37, 39, 40, 46
Sal. 45
Sarah 13, 28, 35, 36, 39, 45, 53, 59, 72
Simon 37
Stephen 37
Susannah 39
Thomas 28, 35, 44
William 28, 37, 46
William Boyer 37
William Drake 37
PENINTON Alice 25
Anne 10, 26, 50
Elizabeth 16
Henry 2, 16, 24, 26
Isaac 25
John 3, 21, 23
Juliana 4
Mary 18, 19, 20

Matthias 14
Otho 18
Rachel(l) 23, 24
Rebecca 10, 50
Richard 2, 18, 19, 20
Robert 4, 10, 26, 50
Sarah 23
Thomas 14, 25
William 2, 16, 19, 20
PENNINGTON Ann(e) 2, 26, 32
Elisabeth 43
Henry 7, 32
Highland J. 54
John 7, 33
Joseph 32
Mary 30, 32
Mr. 55
Mrs. 54
Rachel 7, 30
Rebecka 30
Robert 30, 43
Samuel 33, 43
Sarah 33
William 43
PENNINTON Alce 49
Alie 14
Ann 24, 48
Henry 48
Isaac 14, 49
Rachel 48
Rebecca (Rebecka) 15, 24, 48
Robert 15, 24, 48
Thomas 14, 49
PENNOCK Mary 64
William 64
PERREY Anne 3
David 15
Elizabeth 4
Susana 5
Susana 15
PERYMAN Mary 60
Roger 60, 79
Samuel 60
PETERSON Adam 1
Haramonica 1
PEWE Phebe 60
PHELAND Margret 74
PHILLIPS Ann 62
Catherine 57
Elizabeth 6, 61, 79
Heston 57
Isaac 62
Jane 79
John 61
Mary 61
Nathan 79
Samuel 62, 79
Sarah 65, 79
PICOT Daniel 64
Hannah 61
Margret 61
Peter 61
PIERCE Mary 15
Rebecca 15

INDEX

Thomss 15
PIGGOT Abigal 58
  Benjamin 58
  Elizabeth 58
  Jeremiah 58
  John 58
  Robert 54, 55
  Samuel 58
  Susannah 58
  William 58
PIRKENS Mary 3
PLOW Annacart 5
POLSON Andrew 58
  John 34
  Margaret 34
  Mary 58
  Peter 34
  Sarah 77
POOLEY Nicholas 3, 11, 51
  Sarah 11, 51
  Susana 11, 51
POOLY Nicholas 20
  Sarah 20
  Susana 20
POPE Elizabeth 12, 15, 23, 52
  Jane 15
  John 23
  Mary 12, 52
  Thomas 2, 12, 15, 23, 52
PORTER Ann(e) 27, 44, 45
  Benjamin 44, 45
  Elizabeth 14, 26, 47
  Inibar 14
  James 6, 14, 26, 47, 53
  John 44
  Junibar (Juniber) 14, 26, 53
  Margaret 3, 5, 14
  Mary 14, 27
  Rebecca 47
  Robert 14, 26, 27, 45, 53
  Rosemond 14
  Sarah 6, 27, 44
  William 44
POTTER Ellenor 71
POULSON Elener 67
  Jecobas 62
  Magdalene 79
  Mary 63
  Peter 63
  Sarah 63
POWELL Elizabeth 21
  Richard 21
  Thomas 9, 48, 49
POWLSON John 57
  Jonas 63
  Mary 57
PRICE Alce 43
  Andrew 4, 17, 27, 28, 35, 36, 39, 42, 47, 55
  Ann(e) 28, 35, 43, 44, 54
  Anne Mariah 45
  Annica 9
  Augustin 28
  Bartholomew 39
  Benjamin 28
  Catherine (Cathrine) 9, 38, 45
  David 3, 22, 28
  Deborah 45
  Elizabeth 11, 27, 28, 35, 36, 39, 42, 43, 44, 45, 47, 51
  Fredus 55
  George 45
  Henry 22, 39
  Heszia 42
  Honner 5
  Hyland 17, 38, 55
  James 7, 27
  James Kimber 42
  Jane 45
  Jeremiah Cosden 55
  John 2, 9, 10, 11, 17, 21, 23, 39, 45, 46, 50, 51
  John H. 54
  John Hyland 39, 47
  Joseph 8
  Joseph 39
  Judith 39
  Julia Ann 45
  Kathrin 10, 12, 16, 22, 50, 51
  Kisiar 42
  Lewis 44, 45
  Margaret 17
  Martha 17
  Mary 2, 5, 7, 10, 11, 12, 17, 20, 21, 28, 36, 38, 39, 41, 42, 44, 45, 50, 51
  Mary Ann 48
  Morgan A. 54
  Nicholas 27, 42
  Noble 45
  Perrey 27
  Rachel 36
  Rebecca(h) 12, 20, 38, 39, 44, 51
  Richard 5, 17, 27, 35, 38, 48
  Robert 38
  Samuel Ruley 45
  Sarah 17, 23, 27, 28, 38, 41, 45, 48, 50
  Sarah Ann 38
  Terry 46
  Thomas 10, 11, 16, 17, 50, 51
  Thomas Browning 43
  Vachel Terry 46
  William 2, 3, 4, 7, 9, 10, 11, 12, 16, 17, 20, 21, 23, 28, 36, 35, 38, 41, 42, 43, 47, 50, 51
  William Roberts 45
PRISE Annice 49
  John 49
PRISLEY Andrew 29
  Anne 29
  Christain 29
  John Volintine 29
  Sarah 29
PRITCHARD Elizabeth 71, 74
  George 74
  Hannah 71
  James 74
  Mary 71
  Samuel 71
PROBAL Jacob 6
PROSLER Andrew 32
  Ann 32
  John Vollintine 32
PRYCE John 6
  Mary 6
PRYER Christian 64
  Jane 64
  Margarett 1
  Mary 72
  Thomas 1, 64
PRYOR Margarett 1
PURIFY Elizabeth 79
  Judith 79
  Nicholas 79

RAGON Charles 81
RAMSEY Margaret 5
RAWLEIGH John 55
REA Andrew 79
  Elenore 79
READUS James 8
REDICK Robert 5
REDMAN Benjamin 72
  James 61, 72
  Jane 72
  Thomas 61, 72
  William 61
REESE Ann 54
  George 54
REPOSE Anthoney (Anthony) 8, 37
  Eliza. 37
  Mary 37
REYLAND Fredus 31
  John 31
  Mary 31
  Stephen 31
  Thomas 31
REYNOLDS Edward 6, 34
  Francis 27
  John 27, 34
  Lucretia 34
  Margaret 27
  Mary 34
  Rachel 34
  Rebecca 27
  Richard 27
  Sarah 3
  Thomas 27
RIALY John 71
  Mathew 71
  Mathew 71

EARLY ANGLICAN CHURCH RECORDS OF CECIL COUNTY

RICE David 5, 31
  Elizabeth 31
  Ellinor 15
  Hugh 15
  Sarah 15, 31
RICKETS Ann 78
  John Thomas 7
  Sarah 7
RICKETTS Ann 72
  Catherine 72
  David 72
  Evan (Even) 8, 39, 40, 72
  Jane 72
  John 72
  John Thomas 72
  Margret 63
  Mary 72
  Paul 72
  Rachel 39, 40
  Rebecca 40, 47, 72
  Samuel 39, 47
  Sarah 72
  Tamar 40, 47
  Thomas 72
  William 40
RIDER Andrew 39
  James 39
  Joseph 39
  Mary 39
  Peter 39
  Rebeccah 39
RIDGE Anne 27
  Benjamin 27
  Curnelia 27
  James 27
  William 27
RILEY Mary 66
RIPPIN Augustine 27
  Henry 4, 27
  Mary 27
RIPPON Henry 5, 29
  Jane 29
  Mary 29
  William 29
ROACH Mary 78
ROADEN Margaret 18
  Prudence 18
  Robert 18
ROB James 7
ROBARDS Ann 63
  Elizabeth 61
  James 63
  Joseph 61
  Margret 61
ROBARTS Ann 62
  Francina 62
  James 62
ROBB James 35
  Jane 35
ROBERSON Elizabeth 39
  Frances 39
  Thomas 39
ROBERTS Ann 61
  Ann Rickets 71
  Anne 47
  Deboraugh 37
  Debra 16
  Elizabeth 47, 78
  Isaac Gooding 47
  Jacob 78
  James 47, 61, 71, 78
  John 7, 8, 16, 28, 47, 61
  Judith 8
  Jul--th 16
  Levina 71
  Lewis 47
  Lewis Clothier 47
  Lidia 78
  Mary 7, 61, 78
  Morgain John 37
  Rebecca 47
  Robert 5, 16, 28, 47
  Sarah 5, 16, 28
ROBINS Allen 80
  Jasper 80
  Martha 80
ROBINSON Ahip 1
  Ann 2
  Edward 11, 51
  James 11, 51
  Jean 25, 33, 49
  John 10, 50
  Margaret 25, 33, 49
  Michael(1) (Michall) 5, 25, 33, 49
  Sarah 2, 10, 50
  Thomas 1, 10, 50
ROCK Francis 72
  George 63, 73
  Joseph 71
  Marrabella 63
  Mary 63, 75
  Old 73
  Sarah 71
  Thomas 71
  William 63
RODGERS Martha 81
  Walter 81
RODICK Catherine 31
  Mary 31
  Robert 31
RODIN Frances 74
ROGERS Elizabeth 74
  Rowland 74
ROOKE Francis 71
  Rosannah 71
  William 71
ROOS Antony 61
ROSE Augusteny 71
  Ellenor 71
  Jean 38
  Mary 18
  Peregrine 38, 71
  Rebeccah 38
  Sarah 18
  Thomas 8, 18, 38
  William 18
ROSERTA Christian 48
ROSERTE Charistian 24
ROSS Allen 34
  Elizabeth 4
  George 73
  Margarett 34
  Susanna 73
ROSSER Jane 33
  John 33
  Rachel 33
ROTER Catran 65
  John 65
  Rebekah 65
ROTH Mrs. 54
ROWLAND William 81
RULEY Ann 35, 36, 43, 44
  Anthon(e)y 35, 43, 44
  Benjamin 43
  Elizabeth Ann 55
  James 55
  John 43, 55
  Julianna 55
  Michael 35, 36, 44
  Rachel 36, 43
  Rebecca 44
  Samuel 44, 55
  Thomas 43
  William 43
RULLY Anne 28, 29
  Mary 29
  Michael 28, 29
  Rebecca 28
RULY Michell 5
RUMSEY Benjamin 34, 72
  Catherine 6
  Charles 6, 7, 12, 30, 32, 35, 52
  Edward 5, 30
  Grace 1
  Hannah 72
  Margaret 6, 30, 32
  Mary 7, 72
  Sabina 12, 32, 34, 35, 52
  Sarah 7, 32
  Susanah 30
  William 6, 12, 32, 34, 35, 52
RUSSELL Ann 72
  Frances 72
  Mary 72
  Thomas 72
RUSTON Job 60
RUTEN Rebecca 74
RUTTER Ann 64, 71, 72, 78, 80
  Ann Rickets 71
  Catherine 62, 72
  Hannah 62, 78
  John 62, 72, 78
  Jon. 62
  Kenebah 78
  Kisiah 61
  Margaret 78
  Mary 62, 67, 71, 72, 80
  Moses 64, 71, 72, 78, 80, 81
  Rebecca 71
  Richard 71, 80
  Samuel 71
  Sarah 74
  Thomas 64, 71

INDEX

Whitton 78
William 71, 72
RYAN Edward 8, 39
  Elizabeth 81
  Isabella 39
  James 39
RYE John 2, 11, 17, 51
  Mary 17
  William 17
RYLAND Alice 15
  John 15, 23, 27, 41
  Mary 4, 15, 41
  Mary Ann 41
  Rebecca 23, 27, 41
  Thomas 15

SAPENTON Hartly 26
  James 26
  John 26
  Mary 26
  Nathaniel 26
  Thomas 26
  William 26
SAPINGTON James 10
  Mary 10
  Nathaniel(l) 2, 10
SAPINTON James 50
  Margaret 20
  Mary 50
  Nathaniel(l) 20, 50
  Sarah 4
SAPULDIN Sarah 33
SARTIL John 59
SATCHELL Anne 1
SAVIN Ann 27
  Elizabeth 27
  John 55
  Stephen 55
  Thomas 27
  William 1, 9, 27
SAYER Ann 13, 33, 52
  Stephen 13, 33, 52
SCHIELS Anna 23
  Ephraim 23
  John 23
SCHOTT Margaret 65
SCOTT Catherine 34, 36
  Charles 5, 15, 34, 35
  Eleanor 25
  Elizabeth 34, 35
  Esther 9, 25, 34, 50
  Ffrancis 3
  George 25
  Grace 15
  John 25, 28, 33
  Mary 28, 33, 34
  Sarah 36
  Walter 1, 5, 9, 15, 25, 34, 36, 50
  William 35
SCURREY James 48
  Mary 39, 48
  Thomas 39, 48
SCURRY Mary 81
  Thomas 81
SEALEY Joseph 12
  Joseph 52

SEDBERREY John 11, 51
SEENEY Denis 12, 52
SEFFERSON Jeffrey 17
  John 4
  Kathrin 4, 17
  Margaret 17
  Mary 17
  Peter 17
  Tabitha 17
  Thomas 17
SEGER Catherine 73
  Francis 73
  Jeremiah 73
  Joseph 73
  Mary 73
  Ruben 73
SEVERSON Ann 9, 34, 49
  Catherine 25, 49
  Diana 5
  Elizabeth 5, 14, 25, 36, 49
  Hans Marques 36
  James 38
  John 28, 34, 38, 47
  Katherine 9, 49
  Mary 15, 24, 28, 36, 40, 48
  Patience 34
  Peter 9, 15, 24, 48, 49
  Rachael 36
  Rebeccah 40
  Samuel 47
  Sarah 28, 34, 36, 38, 40, 47
  Simon 28
  Stephen 40
  Thomas 9, 14, 25, 36, 40, 45, 47, 49
  Zeckall 36
SEWALL Jacob 55
  John 39
  Mary 39
  Thomas 39
SEWELL Jane 25, 49
  Mary 5
  Mr. 3, 4, 5, 6
  R. 25
  Richard (Rich.) 1, 2, 10, 24, 25, 48, 49
  Thomas 25, 49
SHAW Jane 82
SHELLEY Rebecca 47
SHEPARD Ann 69
SHEPHERD Ann 79
  Mary 79
  Thomas 79
SHEPPERD Ann 66
  Mary 66
  Thomas 66
SHERWOOD Mary 15, 24, 48
  William 15, 48
SHORT Abraham 80
  Adam 75
  Araminta 73
  Catherine 73
  Charles 68

  Elizabeth 73
  Jane 73
  Jean 73
  John 73
  John Thomas 73
  Lettice 68
  Marty 73
  Mary 73
  Rachel 73
  Rebecca 73
  Sarah 73
  Thomas 73
  William 73
SHUTTEN Eleanor 2
SIMCOE Elizabeth 61
  George 61
  Jane 79
  Sarah 61
SIMMONDS John 26
  Mary 26
  Matthias 26
SIMMONS Elizabeth 34
  Rachel 34
  William 34
SIMONS Henry 17
  John 4, 17, 20, 21, 23
  Mary 17, 20, 21
  Rebecca 23
  Richard 21
  Robert 20
SIMPERS Ann 80
  Catherine 72
  Emy 80
  George 72
  Isaac 72
  Jacob 72
  Katherine 73
  Mary 72
  Richard 72
  Thomas 72, 80
  William 80
  William Howell 72
SIMPSON John 5, 80
  Margaret 80
SINCKLAR Rachel 5
SINCLAR Rachell 12, 23, 52
  Rebecca 12, 23, 52
  William 2, 12, 23, 52
SINGLE Elizabeth 3
SKURREY John 37
  Mary 37
  Thomas 7, 37
SKURRY Mary 81
SLUYTER Benjamin 13, 16, 29, 53
  Elizabeth 13, 17, 29, 53
  Henry 16, 29
  Isaac 16
  John 29
  Mary 29
  Peter 29
  Rachell 16
  Rebecca 29
SMART John 10, 50

Mary 26
Sarah 10, 26, 50
William 26
SMITH Ann(e) 15, 16
  Casparus 2, 15, 16
  Cath(e)rine 8, 30, 31
  Charles 30, 33
  Daniell 9, 15, 49
  David 81
  Elizabeth 4
  John 31
  Letticia 54
  Martha 81
  Mary 4, 15, 30, 31, 33
  Mr. 54
  Rebecca 4
  Richard 6, 10, 50
  Ruth 69
  Sarah 15, 31, 69
  William 5, 31, 33, 58, 69
SOMERSELL Mary 71
SOMERSILL Mary 71
SOMMERSILL Sheckaniah 71
SPAULDIN John 33
STALKUP Henry 64
  John 64
  Mary 64
STANLEY Jane 25
  John 25
  Katherine 25
  Luke 61
  Mary 61
  William 25, 61
STANLY Elizabeth 18
  Jane 11, 18, 51
  John 11, 18, 51
  Mary 11, 18, 51
  Rachell 18
  Sarah 18
STARKEY Catherine 63
  Elizabeth 63
  John 63
  Rachel 63
  Susannah 63, 64
  William (Will) 62, 63, 64
STARLING John 37
  Sarah 20, 37
  William 20
STEAK Matthew 37
STEAL James 37
  Margaret(l) 37, 48
  Matthew 48
  Robert 48
STEDAM Luliff 77
  Timothy 77
STEEL Andrew 37
  Margarett 37
  Matthew 37
  William B. 80
STEELE Francis 2, 10, 18, 50
  Mary 18
  Rachel 18

Rebecca 10, 18, 50
Thomas 10, 18, 50
STEPHENS Margaret 58
STERLING John 20
  Mary 20
STEVENS George 9, 49
  Jane 77
STEWARD Ann 37
  Hannah 37
  Miram 37
  Thomas 37
  William 37
STITSON Kathrin 20
  Yargin 20
STOCKTON Benjamin 63, 73
  Elisabeth 40, 63, 73
  Isabella 40
  John 40, 63, 73
  Joseph 63
STOKES John 6
STOO John 49
STOOP John 1, 15, 24, 28, 48
  Leonard 49
  Margaret 28
  Mary 1, 15, 24, 28, 48, 49
  Phillip 5, 15, 28
STOOPS Benjamin 18
  Edward 41
  Isabella 36
  James 44
  John 18, 25, 40, 42, 43, 44
  Jonas 44
  Leonard 25
  Margaret(t) (Margt.) 31, 34, 36, 40, 42
  Martha 31
  Mary 3, 18, 25, 40, 42, 43, 44
  Peregrine 44
  Phil(l)ip 31, 34, 36, 40
  Sarah 34, 41
  William 18, 36, 40, 41
STORY Marcey 63
  Mary 63
  Robert 63
  Thomas 63
STRATTON Thomas 6
STROUGH Mary 6
STUMP Henry 57
  John 57
SULLIVAN Elijah 46
  Henry 46
  John 46
  Mary 46
  Peregrine 46
SUTTON John 40
  Josiah 40
  Mary 40
SWANN Jane 63
SWELEY Milison 29
  Thomas 29
  William 29

SYMMONDS Susannah 8
SYMPERS Amey 72
  Ann 72
  Nathaniel 72
  Richard 72
  Thomas 72

TAYLOR Ann(e) 21, 22, 23, 27, 47
  Benjamin 62
  Catherine 37, 47
  Ealce 62
  Edward 60
  Elizabeth 27, 29, 32, 48
  Esther 27
  Hannah 60, 62
  James 8, 21, 27, 29, 32, 37, 47, 48
  Marey 22
  Mary 60
  Rebecca 37
  Richard 3, 21, 23, 27, 32, 35, 48
  Samuel 27
  Sarah 62
  Silas 48
  Susannah 35
  Thomas 54
  William 22, 32
TEAGUE Abraham 58
  Charity 58
  Elijah 58
  Susannah 58
  William 58
TERRY Alifere 40
  Alisha 30
  Anne 14, 25, 49
  Augustine 12, 30, 52
  Benjamin 9, 40
  Elizabeth 5, 30
  Hugh 5, 30
  John 30
  Rebecca 40
  Rosamond (Rosemond) 14, 24, 25, 48, 49
  Ruth 30
  Sarah 30, 40
  Thomas 14, 24, 25, 40, 48, 49
  William 30
THACKEY Hannah 75
THOMAS Ann 72
  Charles 71
  Edward 71
  Elizabeth 71
  Richard 73
  Sarah 70, 71
  William 70
THOMPSON Ephraim 9, 14, 24, 49
  George 10, 50, 59
  Hester 44
  James 28
  Jane 9
  John 7, 8, 9, 13, 14, 19, 24, 25, 35, 38, 43, 44, 47, 49,

INDEX

53
John Dockra 47
John Dockrey 44
Joshua 47
Judith 9, 19, 24, 25
Magdalen 19
Mary 8, 35, 38, 43, 47
Mrs. 14
Richard 7, 19, 38, 60
Robert 25, 28
Ruth 28
Samuel 35
Sarah 38
THOMSON Elizabeth 73
Gertrude 73
Jane Ramsey 74
John 49
Judith 49
Mary 73
Ross 73
Samuel 66, 73
Samuel Magaw 73
Sarah Howard 73
Susanna 74
Susanna Warrel 73
William 73, 74
William Biddle 74
TILDEN Martha 62
Rebecca 69
TILTON Elizabeth 35
John 35
TIPPIN Fredick 20
John 20
TOBIAS Cornelius 2, 18
Helinor 18
Thomas 18
TOUCHSTONE Andrew 57
Christian 57
Elizabeth 66
Henry 66
Jonas 58
Katherine 57
Richard 57, 66
Temperance 57, 66
William 66
TOULSON Andrew 24, 48
Mary 24, 48
TREADWAY Mary 64
TREW Ann 76
D. 76
Thomas 76
TULLEY Edward 47
John 47
Sarah 47
TURNBULL Ann 78
John 78
Miss 78
TURNER Francis 60
Mat(t)hew 58, 60, 61
Robert 59
Sarah 60
TYLAR Fredrick 7

UMBERSON Elizabeth 59
John 59
John 59

UMSTON John 4
UNGLE Augustin 21
Elizabeth 21
URINE John 60
URMSTON John 4, 6
Mr. 5
USHER Mary 14

VANBEBBER Anna 33
Arriamam 33
Catherine 33
Christian 25, 26
Christiana 10, 50
Elizabeth 26
Fronika 25
Haramantia 26
Haybartus 33
Hendrick 6
Henry 33
Hester 25
Isaac 25
Jacob 9, 10, 25, 26, 33, 50
James 6, 33
Matthias 1, 26, 33
Matts. 33
Peter 25
VANBIBBER Ann 74
Isaac 74
James 74
VANBURKELOO Abell 5, 12, 29, 52
Cathrine 12, 29, 52
Ephraim 12, 29, 52
Herman 29
Margaret 29
William 29
VANDEGRIFF Jacob 34
Nicholas 34
Rebecca 34
Susanah 34
VANDERBUSH Laurance (Laurence) 1, 24, 48
VANDERGRIFT Mary 27
Nicholas 5, 27
Susana 27
VANDERHYDEN Ariana 2
Matt. 3
Mr. 2
VANDEVEARE Catherine 63
VANDIKE Abraham 34
Agness 34
William 70
William 34
VANDYKE Agnuss 31
Elizabeth 31
William 31
VANGAGELY Gertruij 49
Jacob 49
Rynerius 49
VANGAZELY Gertruly 25
Gertruy 14
Jacob 14, 25
Rynerius 14, 25
VANHORN Barnett 7
Elizabeth 7
Hester 8

Nicholas 8
VANHORNE Jacob 31
Leticia 31
Mary 31
Nicholas 31
Rebecca 31
VANPOOL Jacob 79
John 80
Peter 80
VANSANDT Cornelias 42
Eleanor 8
Gararades 42
Garrict 8
Garriot(t) 37
Hester 42
Hitteybell 42
Nehemiah 37
Sarah 42
Susannah 37, 42
Zechariah 37
VANSANT Benjamin 30
Burenthia 30
Cornelius 30
Elin 30
Garriet 30
George 30
Rachel 30
Susanah 30
VEASEY George 1, 3
Robert 3
Susana 3
VEASY James 80
Mary 80
William 80
VEAZEY Alice 10, 16, 50
Ann 43, 47, 55
Arabella Ann 47
Edward (Ed.) 13, 17, 42, 43, 44, 53, 55
Edward Henry 43
Edward Thomas 55
Elisabeth (Elizabeth) 16, 26, 27, 42, 43, 55, 65, 75
George 10, 16, 50, 75
George Ross 47
Harriott 54
Hester 43
James 4, 12, 22, 27, 52, 65, 75
John 13, 17, 26, 27, 53, 54, 75
John Bauldin 43
John E. 9
John L. 47
John Thompson 44, 47
John Ward 43
Lucey (Lucie, Lucy) 22, 27
Martha 22
Mary 9, 12, 22, 26, 27, 44, 52, 75
Rebecca (Rebeka) 13, 42, 53, 54
Robert 22, 27

Sarah 43, 47
Susanna 17
Thomas 22
Thomas B. 9, 47, 55
Thomas Brocus 44, 47
Thomas Ward 44
William 12, 16, 52, 75
William Thomas 47
VEAZIE Edward 56
F. W. 56
J. T. 56
Miss 56
S. 56
T. B. 56
VEERES John 1
VESEY James 60
 Mary 60
 William 60
VEZEY Mary 70
VOICE Catherin 62

WAGGETT Jaine 24, 48
 James 24, 48
 John 24, 48
WALCH Sarah 74
WALLACE Cathrine 43
 James 4, 43
 John 7
 Margaret 6
 Mary 43
 Richard 43
WALLAS John 4
WALLEY Alice 81
WALLIS Sarah 3
WALMSLEY Alethea 45
 Ann(e) 15, 40
 Benjamin 38, 54
 Elisabeth 36, 40
 Eliza 45
 George 55
 Isaac 45
 James 40
 John 15, 36, 40, 45
 John Edward 55
 John Gording 45
 Katherine 15
 Kathrin 17, 27
 Margaretta 45, 46
 Mary 40, 55
 Nicholas 40
 Phillis 45
 Rebecca 45
 Richard 46
 Robert 17, 36, 40, 45, 55
 Sarah 38, 47
 Susanna 46
 Thomas 15, 17, 27, 36, 40, 46, 52
 Warner 46
 William 7, 38, 40, 45, 46, 47
WALMSLY Anne 5
WAMSLEY Robert 7
WAMSLY Thomas 12
WARD Alice 1, 7, 23
 Ann 9

Anna Chew 37
Anne 29, 45, 56
Catrin 60
Deborah 44
Ed 39
Eliza 56
Elizabeth (Elisabeth) 1, 9, 21, 23, 24, 43, 44, 45, 48, 49
Elizabeth Harrison 37
George 29, 44, 54
Hannah 38, 42
Henry 4, 13, 21, 29, 38, 42, 53
John 2, 3, 7, 8, 15, 23, 24, 28, 29, 30, 38, 43, 44, 48
Joseph 29
Joshua 43, 54
Julianna 56
Marg(a)rett 6, 21, 39
Mary 2, 15, 28, 35, 37, 39, 40
Nathaniel 12, 30, 52
Peregrine 7, 15, 37, 39, 40
Rachel 8, 28
Rebecca 9, 15, 43
Robert 43
Sarah 7, 9, 28
Susana 23, 28, 30, 43
Thomas 5, 15, 28, 35
W. 56
William 1, 5, 9, 12, 24, 28, 29, 43, 45, 48, 49, 52, 54
William Henry 45
WAREHAM James 81
WARIMER Edmund 82
WATKINS Ann(e) 15, 24, 48
 James 15, 24, 48
 Mary 15, 24, 48
WATSON Abram 57, 60, 61
 Elizabeth 57, 60
 Hugh 3
 Jacob 57
 Jane Daws 75
 John 59
 Mary 3
 Patience 59
 Sarah 59
 William 59, 60
WATTS Elizabeth 5, 11, 14, 24, 26, 49, 51
 Jacob 26, 28
 John 28
 Mary 11, 12, 26, 27, 28, 51, 52
 Peter 26
 Rebecca 12, 27, 52
 Susana 28
 Thomas 4, 9, 11, 12,

14, 24, 26, 27, 49, 50, 51, 52
 William 26
WATTSON Abram 60
 Catherine 31
 Charity 60
 Jeremiah 31
 John 31
 Margaret 31
 Peter 31
 Susannah 60
WEBSTER Ann 36
 Sarah 36
 William 36
WEITHERS Mary 7
 Robert 13, 53
WELDEN Edward 81
WELDING Catherine 33
 Charles 33
 John 33
 Sarah 33
WELLER G. 55
 H. C. 55
 James Birckhead 55
WELLINGER John 49, 50
WELLS Daniel(l) 11, 51
 Humphrey 6
 John 66
 Liddy 81
 Lydia 81
WELSH Ann 75
 Catherine 54
WEMS Eleaner 32
 Isabell 32
 John 32
 Thomas 32
WERREY Kathrin 2
WETHERS Lidey 32
 Mary 32
 Robert 5, 32
WHATSON Abraham 62
 Charity 62
 Isaac Deone 62
 Susannah 62
WHEELER Elizabeth 24, 48
 John 24, 48
 Mary 2, 24, 48
WHITAKAR Mary 62
 Rachel 62
 Ralf 62
 Robart 62
WHITE Ann 74
 Elizabeth 11, 18, 51, 81
 Hannah 79
 James 74
 John 2, 11, 18, 51, 74
 Mary 11, 18, 51
 Nathan 79
 Samuel(l) 11, 51, 79
 Sarah 74
 Thomas 74
 William 79
WHITEAKER Febey 63
 Mary 63
 Robert 63

INDEX

WHITELOCK Charles 82
WHITER Henry 5
WHITLE Elizabeth 23
  Kathrin 23
  Nicholas 23
WHITOR John 29
  Mr. 29
  Sarah 29
  Vinefrite 29
WHITTAKER Ann 74
  Elizabeth 74
  Mary 74
  Robert 74
  Samuel 74
  Thomas 74
WHITTAM Benjm. 28
  Elizabeth 28, 35
  Grace 35
  William 28, 35
WHITTIKER Mary 57
  Samuel 57
  Thomas 57
WICKES Alethea 55
  Widow 54
WIGHT Edward John 8
WILDS Ann 57
  Joshua 80
  Mary 80
  Ruth 80
WILEY John 41
WILKINSON Mr. 7
WILLHAM John 74
WILLIAMS Baruch 74
  Basil 74
  Baxter 74
  Cath(e)rine 64, 75
  Easter 75
  Frederick 16
  Jacob 2, 16
  Jean 75
  Margaret 6
  Mary Waugh 74
  Rachel 74
  Richard 64
  Robert 64, 75
  Thomas 64, 75
WILLIAMSON (Infant) 54
  Alexander 44
  Elizabeth 44
  James 44
  John 44
  Mary 44
  Meliscent
  (Millicent) 44
WILLSON Jane 36, 36
  William 36
WILMER Simon 6
WILSON Fanny 55
  James 79
  Jane 55
WINN Ann 1
WINTABURY Elizabeth 35
  George 35
  John 35
  Mary 35
  William 35
WINTER Laughlin 59
WINTERBURY Anne 5

WISECARVOR Margaret 3
WITTAM William 4
WOLESTAIN Catherine 34
  Cornelias 34
  Martha 34
  Richard 34
WOLLINGER John 10
WOLOSTEIN Cornelius 6
WOOD Alice 1
  Bennonia 75
  Catherine 7
  Elias 37
  Elizabeth 75
  Frances 36
  Jean 75
  John 7, 8, 21, 36, 37, 39, 75
  Joseph 6, 36
  Kathrin 21
  Mary 7, 37
  Nicholas 21
  Rachel 75
  Rebecca(h) 37, 39
  Robert 7, 21, 36
  Sarah 36
WOODBURY Catherine 9
  Jonathan 9, 43, 44
  Margaret 44
  Samuel 9, 43, 44
WOODLAND Alethea
  Lavinia 55
  Hannah Wallace 55
WOOLBARD Christopher 22
  Lydey 22
WOOLBARK Christopher 22
  Godfrit 22
  Lydey 22
WOOLESTINE Catherine 36
  Martha 36
WOOLESTONE Cornelias 36
WORGAN Joseph 9, 49
  Mary 9, 49
WORGIN John 19
  Joseph 19
  Mary 19
WRIGHT Ann 32
  Edward John 7
  Elizabeth 32
  George 32
  Hannah 32
  John 5, 30, 32
  Margaret 6, 32
  Martha 30
  Mary 32
  Sarah 30
  Susanah 32
WROTH Ann(e) 29, 36
  Benjamin 35
  George Wm. Fredk. 41
  Henry 36
  James 5, 29, 35, 36
  Julia 53
  Julian 13, 41
  Kinven (Kinvin) 35,

36
  Mary 13, 29, 41, 53
  Mary Ann 13, 41, 53
  Sarah 35, 36
  Tamar 41
  Thomas 9, 13, 29, 41, 53

YARDLEY Ann 44
  Joyce 60
  William 44
YARLEY Ann 43
  Elisabeth 43
  William 43
YORKMAN Nancy 55
YORKSON Catherine 25, 49
  Mary 25, 49
  York 25, 49
YOUNG Catherine 80
  David 3, 5
  Elenor (Elinor) 61, 80
  Jacob 2, 60
  James 13, 53
  Joseph 13, 53, 58, 80
  Mary 58, 61
  Rachel 55
  Samuel 55, 59, 61, 80
  Sarah 60
  Thomas 55
YUNG Elenor 63
YUNGE Elennor 61
  Prudence 61
  Samuel 61

ZILLAFROW Andrew 30
  Joseph 30
  Sarah 30
ZILLEPHRO Andrew 34, 35, 37
  Hester 37
  Jane 35
  Mary 34
  Sarah 34, 35, 37

Other books by the author:

A Closer Look at St. John's Parish Registers [Baltimore County, Maryland], 1701-1801

A Collection of Maryland Church Records

A Guide to Genealogical Research in Maryland: 5th Edition, Revised and Enlarged

Abstracts of the Ledgers and Accounts of the Bush Store and Rock Run Store, 1759-1771

Abstracts of the Orphans Court Proceedings of Harford County, 1778-1800

Abstracts of Wills, Harford County, Maryland, 1800-1805

Baltimore City [Maryland] Deaths and Burials, 1834-1840

Baltimore County, Maryland, Overseers of Roads, 1693-1793

Bastardy Cases in Baltimore County, Maryland, 1673-1783

Bastardy Cases in Harford County, Maryland, 1774-1844

Bible and Family Records of Harford County, Maryland Families: Volume V

Children of Harford County: Indentures and Guardianships, 1801-1830

Colonial Delaware Soldiers and Sailors, 1638-1776

*Colonial Families of the Eastern Shore of Maryland
Volumes 5, 6, 7, 8, 9, 11, 12, 13, 14, and 16*

Colonial Maryland Soldiers and Sailors, 1634-1734

Dr. John Archer's First Medical Ledger, 1767-1769, Annotated Abstracts

Early Anglican Records of Cecil County

*Early Harford Countians, Individuals Living in Harford County, Maryland in Its Formative Years
Volume 1: A to K, Volume 2: L to Z, and Volume 3: Supplement*

Harford County Taxpayers in 1870, 1872 and 1883

Harford County, Maryland Divorce Cases, 1827-1912: An Annotated Index

Heirs and Legatees of Harford County, Maryland, 1774-1802

Heirs and Legatees of Harford County, Maryland, 1802-1846

Inhabitants of Baltimore County, Maryland, 1763-1774

Inhabitants of Cecil County, Maryland, 1649-1774

Inhabitants of Harford County, Maryland, 1791-1800

Inhabitants of Kent County, Maryland, 1637-1787

*Joseph A. Pennington & Co., Havre De Grace, Maryland Funeral Home Records:
Volume II, 1877-1882, 1893-1900*

Maryland Bible Records, Volume 1: Baltimore and Harford Counties

Maryland Bible Records, Volume 2: Baltimore and Harford Counties

Maryland Bible Records, Volume 3: Carroll County

Maryland Bible Records, Volume 4: Eastern Shore

Maryland Deponents, 1634-1799

Maryland Deponents: Volume 3, 1634-1776

*Maryland Public Service Records, 1775-1783: A Compendium of Men and Women of
Maryland Who Rendered Aid in Support of the American Cause against
Great Britain during the Revolutionary War*

*Marylanders to Carolina: Migration of Marylanders to
North Carolina and South Carolina prior to 1800*

Marylanders to Kentucky, 1775-1825

Methodist Records of Baltimore City, Maryland: Volume 1, 1799-1829

Methodist Records of Baltimore City, Maryland: Volume 2, 1830-1839

Methodist Records of Baltimore City, Maryland: Volume 3, 1840-1850 (East City Station)

More Maryland Deponents, 1716-1799

More Marylanders to Carolina: Migration of Marylanders to North Carolina and South Carolina prior to 1800

More Marylanders to Kentucky, 1778-1828

Outpensioners of Harford County, Maryland, 1856-1896

Presbyterian Records of Baltimore City, Maryland, 1765-1840

Quaker Records of Baltimore and Harford Counties, Maryland, 1801-1825

Quaker Records of Northern Maryland, 1716-1800

Quaker Records of Southern Maryland, 1658-1800

Revolutionary Patriots of Anne Arundel County, Maryland

Revolutionary Patriots of Baltimore Town and Baltimore County, 1775-1783

Revolutionary Patriots of Calvert and St. Mary's Counties, Maryland, 1775-1783

Revolutionary Patriots of Caroline County, Maryland, 1775-1783

Revolutionary Patriots of Cecil County, Maryland

Revolutionary Patriots of Charles County, Maryland, 1775-1783

Revolutionary Patriots of Delaware, 1775-1783

Revolutionary Patriots of Dorchester County, Maryland, 1775-1783

Revolutionary Patriots of Frederick County, Maryland, 1775-1783

Revolutionary Patriots of Harford County, Maryland, 1775-1783

Revolutionary Patriots of Kent and Queen Anne's Counties

Revolutionary Patriots of Lancaster County, Pennsylvania

Revolutionary Patriots of Maryland, 1775-1783: A Supplement

Revolutionary Patriots of Maryland, 1775-1783: Second Supplement

Revolutionary Patriots of Montgomery County, Maryland, 1776-1783

Revolutionary Patriots of Prince George's County, Maryland, 1775-1783

Revolutionary Patriots of Talbot County, Maryland, 1775-1783

Revolutionary Patriots of Worcester and Somerset Counties, Maryland, 1775-1783

Revolutionary Patriots of Washington County, Maryland, 1776-1783

St. George's (Old Spesutia) Parish, Harford County, Maryland: Church and Cemetery Records, 1820-1920

St. John's and St. George's Parish Registers, 1696-1851

Survey Field Book of David and William Clark in Harford County, Maryland, 1770-1812

The Crenshaws of Kentucky, 1800-1995

The Delaware Militia in the War of 1812

Union Chapel United Methodist Church Cemetery Tombstone Inscriptions, Wilna, Harford County, Maryland

www.ingramcontent.com/pod-product-compliance
Lightning Source LLC
Chambersburg PA
CBHW070524100426
42743CB00010B/1943